PELICAN BOOKS

Pelican Library of Business and Management
Editor: T. Kempner

INTEGRATED MARKETING

B. G. S. James was born in 1922 and educated at Brunts School, Mansfield. He graduated in Economics at Durham University and has since lectured at schools of commerce. At the same time he has acted as marketing consultant to one of Europe's largest heavy engineering groups as well as to a leading proprietary brand of Scotch whisky. He is now Reader in Marketing at the University of Strathclyde where he supervises post-graduate courses. In his research he has studied the organizational situation of the professional buyer and weaknesses in the growth-point policy of regional development. His published work include articles in *Marketing World*, *Scientific Business*, *British Journal of Marketing* and *Journal of Industrial Economics*. His present concern is with the efficiency and future of marketing as currently conceived and practised.

INTEGRATED MARKETING

B. G. S. JAMES

Revised and abridged

PENGUIN BOOKS

Penguin Books Ltd, Harmondsworth, Middlesex, England
Penguin Books Australia Ltd, Ringwood, Victoria, Australia

—

First published by B. T. Batsford Ltd 1967
This revised and abridged edition published in Pelican Books 1972

—

Copyright © B. G. S. James, 1967, 1972

—

Made and printed in Great Britain by
C. Nicholls & Company Ltd,
The Philips Park Press, Manchester
Set in Monotype Times

Contents

CONTENTS

Preface

MARKETING must be seen to help enterprise succeed. In many cases a state of disillusionment has set in concerning the contribution which marketing can make to the wellbeing of a firm. This may simply result from bad marketing practice. Often, however, it is the consequence of extravagant expectation, in that it was too often believed that the function *per se* would perform some special alchemy converting an inadequate base managerial talent into glittering business success.

Marketing is only a special aspect of the entrepreneurial need to maintain a comparative advantage in order to perpetuate profit maximization. As the sources of comparative advantage change, so the content and practice of marketing will need to be adjusted if it is to assist in this prime element of successful business enterprise.

In the recent past, dissatisfaction with the effectiveness of marketing has often stemmed from an inhibiting restriction of the function: it has been allowed to analyse and prescribe within limited confines; appraisal and quality control of the total company activity have usually been denied to it. Yet such a wider function may often have allowed it to prescribe the source of comparative advantage or disadvantage and thus to perform its real purpose.

This book basically deals with the achievement and sustenance of a lead in competitive markets. Such a task is all-embracing in its implications – it may be called marketing. The function may vary in its detailed content; it may even vary conceptually; but its objective cannot be challenged. This book deals with the nature and position of marketing in modern business.

Such a treatment concerns itself mainly with concept and analysis rather than check-lists. Its main theme is the double task of integrating the activities of the firm into the socio-economic environment in which it operates and achieving optimum integration within the firm throughout all its activities. In this way the environmental opportunity for profit is exploited efficiently.

To succeed in business demands the ability to organize the factors at your command in such a way that consumer preferences are converted into optimum profits. Such an objective demands both the tools to uncover market opportunity and the ability to respond totally to the challenge presented.

Successful businesses are run by socio-economic dynamicists able to comprehend and manipulate the dynamic and interacting forces operating outside the firm, within it, and between the firm and its environment. Such people need to be masters of socio-economic tribology in a very complete sense in order to succeed in the intensity of today's market conditions. The practice of marketing is a vital element in such success, whether it is within the entrepreneur's own ability or is specially provided within the organization by functional specialists.

The need to identify the marketing function with the search for, and sustenance of, a comparative advantage was the thread going through the original version of this book. The revised edition has given the author a welcome opportunity to give even more emphasis to this theme, whilst at the same time retaining the basic approach that to succeed demands the total integration of all the business functions: that sales effort is greater than selling.

The revised edition has also given more prominence to the industrial market, reflecting not only the author's deep interest and wide experience in this field, but also the enhanced sophistication which is developing in this area of marketing.

Finally, a fuller treatment is given to the control of marketing, in keeping with the need for cost-effectiveness to replace mere effectiveness if maximization of profits is to accompany the achievement of comparative competitive advantage.

PART ONE

THE NATURE OF THE PROBLEM

1. The Nature and Intensity of the Marketing Problem

THE problem of marketing is truly one born of our time; it is a product of the standard of living enjoyed by advanced communities and the ways in which those communities organize their resources to meet that standard. The art of selling is as old as trade itself but the marketing problem, as it is understood today, has only really affected Western Europe in the last decade, and over large areas of the world the phenomenon of excess capacity and satiated appetites is still a dream.

In developed societies, the term 'selling' is considered inadequate to cover the job of getting people to buy: the persuasion of the customer has become the centre of a whole complex of activities ranging from the conception of the product through to a point beyond its sale where every endeavour is made to sustain the goodwill of the customer towards the product and its well identified producer. To cover this spectrum of activities, marketing can be defined as 'adjusting the whole activity of a business to the needs of the customer or potential customer'. This is really a definition of attitude within the firm which demands absolute customer-orientation; it covers every action by the firm and its employees which in any way might affect customers' attitudes towards the firm and the products or services it supplies. The allocation and use of resources to develop new products; the design of products; the efficiency of production; packaging; advertising; credit; branding; the method of personal selling; distribution; ability to deliver; after-sales service: these are some of the more obvious influences on the success of marketing today.

Marketing removes the distinction between making and selling; both affect customer attitudes; both are marketing. Whereas marketing is a comprehensive concept covering all activities and their relationship to the market, selling is specifically concerned with affecting customer attitudes so that they favour a particular product or service. Original investment decisions should be based on marketing, as should be the continuing profitability of such decisions; selling may be needed, as part of the marketing complex, to persuade customers that the products of investment and other decisions meet their needs and requirements. In this chapter we consider the factors which contribute to the nature and intensity of marketing and which have rendered the older and narrower 'selling' concept of marketing inadequate.

THE ECONOMIC SYSTEM

The organization of society is determined by political ideas and economic philosophies with some adherence to a code of ethics, all contained within a legal framework. Broadly speaking the 'free-enterprise' or mixed-economy countries give considerable economic freedom and, in the market place, support the concept of the sovereignty of the customer[1]: a man can spend his purchasing power as he wishes, within the legal framework, and, should he so decide, can refrain from spending it, or, in certain circumstances, decide not to earn it and opt for more leisure. On the supply or production side, the system allows goods to come to the market as a result of independent decisions by entrepreneurs who are trying to cater for an expected demand. Even an elementary analysis such as this shows the core of the marketing problem to be in the potential incompatibility of past investment decisions by producers and current needs of the market.

The possibility of excess capacity within an industry due to past investment decisions must always be present in an unplanned society. Decisions to increase production capacity may be, and often are, taken under buoyant market conditions with the consequence of excess capacity when the selling conditions deteriorate. Although this possibility of potential supply exceeding demand can occur in any industry, it is more dangerous in the consumer-durable, non-necessity industries, where the purchasing

1. It might be argued that this is mythical where the customer is subjected to sales-promotion devices which seduce him away from rational choice; or where the sovereignty of the customer can only be exercised by refusing to buy, e.g. where all prices move together for a generic group of products.

power which was directed towards an industry now finds its way to other, newer industries. The fact that the type of product to be sold is not a necessity and is often a postponable purchase, i.e. a replacement, adds to the risk and increases the possibility of excess capacity relative to demand. Such a marketing situation will then lead either to competition between the newer and older industries or, much more likely, to increased competition among the firms with potential excess capacity. This competition will cover the whole activity of marketing from the design of the product through to dealer relations and after-sales service, but it will be most pronounced in the pure selling activities, i.e. those more concerned with changing customer attitudes, rather than meeting them.

THE COST OF PRODUCING NOTHING

The most expensive quantity for a modern industrial enterprise to produce is nothing: this would result from being unable to sell the goods which the enterprise was created to produce; but this was not always so.

Under the domestic or merchant capitalist system, the capitalist organizer of the work to be done and the markets to be served risked little or no capital; he often owned no equipment and perhaps only rented a warehouse. In the event of a recession in the demand for his goods, he had little to lose except the profits he might have made; he had sunk nothing in fixed assets; the cost of producing and selling nothing was almost nothing.[2] Under these conditions the risks of business enterprise are small, and consequently the need to take precautions against investment risk, a basic function of all marketing, is correspondingly reduced. In contrast to this, ownership of a manufacturing business today carries with it quite fantastic risks in the form of investment

2. In fact, one of the reasons for the relatively slow acceptance of the factory system was the reluctance of entrepreneurs to give up this safe situation for the anxieties associated with heavy investment in plant, with the risk of heavy losses if demand slackened. They put off the 'age of anxiety' as long as possible.

in highly specialized equipment bought at considerable expense and only of economic use when the market for particular goods or services, or a narrow range of goods or services, is large enough to keep it profitably employed. Even in planned societies the problem of reconciling the investment of today and the demand of tomorrow will become more difficult as the society moves towards affluence and mass consumption, with its wider spectrum of goods and services, and the increasing sophistication of its members in the use of their discretionary purchasing power.

THE PROFIT MOTIVE

Behind any investment decision is the desire to utilize money as profitably as possible. The decision may result in a new enterprise, a new plant or an extension to an existing one; all are made to make money. This restlessness, which manifests itself in an endless search for fertile investment opportunity, is the result of funds and the possibility of using them which is deemed to exist somewhere; the money must not lie idle; it must work.

Once the investment has been made, then the need to make it profitable involves marketing. The greater the surplus looking for investment opportunity including reinvestment, the greater the production capacity, and the greater the need to sustain sales to keep that capacity profitably employed. In an unplanned society the decisions are autonomous and atomistic with no mechanism for reconciling production ability and demand except the marketing function in general and selling in particular.

BIOLOGICAL NEEDS AND MODERN MARKETING

In a society where wants are relatively simple and where basic biological needs are still not adequately met, the job of selling requires little sophistication; the customers must have the goods and, if these are consumable, the demand is perpetual (there may still be, however, competition among suppliers even at this stage). The contrast with present-day conditions is most marked.

6

Today, in the developed countries, the biological needs have long since been met; consumers no longer have real wants which they cannot cater for with ease; increasingly, man in these societies must be made to buy; he has become the focal point of a range of activities aimed at making him want goods and services in excess of his biological needs. Assuming a 'free' society, we are now faced with the problem of maintaining the maximum profitability of expensive capital equipment which can produce only a limited range of goods or services that may not be spontaneously wanted in sufficient quantities to satisfy the production capacity of the equipment. Modern marketing is a consequence of this situation. Once a society has achieved a certain standard of living in excess of biological needs[3] and has chosen a particular type of political and economic system, then marketing problems are introduced. The higher the standard of living and the more capital-intensive the means of production, the more intense the problem.

DISCRETIONARY PURCHASING POWER

As the standard of living rises beyond biological needs, individuals have an increasing amount of money which is not really required for any particular need; there develops a section of purchasing power over which they can exercise discretion in

3. The extent of biological needs is probably a function of the society in which a person lives. Thus transport by vehicle may be an adequate response to biological needs where no transport has previously been available, but satisfaction with elementary transport will be reduced as better types become possible. Thus the convenience of private means of transport as against public means may meet a biological need; similarly an automatic gearbox may meet a desire for less work, i.e. a biological need. The same sequence could occur whenever a real improvement was made to any mechanical or domestic appliance. Such improvements are genuine comparative advantages which should expedite sales; they are appealing to biological needs even in a society with an advanced standard of living. Nevertheless, these basic needs do reduce in urgency and, to that extent, products appealing to later needs require more positive selling. Where advanced biological needs and social motivation can be combined in a product, then there is a double drive acting on the customer, e.g. Rolls-Royce cars.

purchasing, perhaps to the extent of not using it at all. This is their discretionary purchasing power, sometimes called optional purchasing power. The essence of the concept is the degree of discretion and the lack of urgency to spend the money in any particular direction. For a period, the material standard of living might be reasonably maintained without using this purchasing power, as when we save; or a person could refrain from earning it by opting for leisure.

The advance of a society to a point where biological needs can be easily met results in the introduction of a new concept of needs which is related to the society itself, perhaps to a section of that society which is the term of reference for any individual. This does not alter the basic idea of discretionary purchasing power. The more a person moves through standards set by his social group, the greater the variety of goods and services from which he extracts a group to demonstrate his social achievements; he does not need to choose any particular selection of goods; extra clothing competes with this year's car model. To the extent that social pressures resulting in buying needs cannot usually be as strong as biological needs, there is, in any advanced society, a degree of discretion in purchasing.[4]

This discretion enjoyed by the customer as to how he should allocate his purchasing power between groups of goods and services, and within those groups, and the fact that he may not spend or earn the purchasing power at all, greatly increase the intensity of the marketing activity. To sell a drink to a thirsty man on a long, non-stop, railway journey requires little selling effort because he is meeting a biological need; to persuade a man with five suits that he needs a sixth when he does not possess a decent set of golf clubs requires all the techniques of modern marketing.

4. The composition of the group of products which gives social acceptance might be a direct result of marketing exploiting social instincts, e.g. car ownership.

THE IMPORTANCE OF DURABILITY AND POSTPONABILITY

Many of the articles making up the potential purchases by customers in an affluent society are durable; they are not consumed and replaced, they can last for a long period of time. Furniture may last for a lifetime; milk and bread are consumed and purchased daily. Broadly speaking, the more advanced the standard of living, the greater the proportion of goods in it which could be described as physically durable. Durability to the marketeer implies postponability; the good physical condition of the currently owned article directly affects the urgency of its replacement by another; the purchase can be postponed. Where the customer is under pressure to buy a wide range of competing groups of products and services, this degree of postponability may be the determining factor in switching the purchasing power to other channels and away from replacements for the durable goods already possessed.

Much of the intensity of modern marketing is due to this element of postponability, which applies to so many of the goods in affluent standards of living. Clearly, the marketeer, in order to perpetuate sales of durables, must shorten their life span; he must reduce their durability. This can be done by introducing a psychological or social life to a product which is not related to its physical rate of obsolescence; fashion, created by sales promotion, reduces the durability of goods in the mind of the owner. The whole of the marketing spectrum for durable goods, from product research to the act of selling, is geared to perpetuating sales by hastening the physical and psychological obsolescence of the articles already possessed by the customers. In societies just moving into the mass-consumption phase, this problem does not exist; it occurs when the phase has been in existence long enough for the members of the society to have obtained a stock of durable consumer goods.

THE IRREVOCABLE AND PERISHABLE NATURE
OF THE ACT OF BUYING

Supposing a customer has a given amount of purchasing power and he buys goods to the value x from manufacturers A, B, and C, then the outlay x to these producers is irrevocable; all other manufacturers have lost these sales for ever. Admittedly, at a later date, the customer may repeat the type of purchase and choose the products made by X, Y, and Z; but this in no way really compensates for the previous loss. Whenever competition for custom takes place, this irrevocable nature of the act of purchasing is a constant constituent of selling. Clearly, if all the suppliers of a type of product or service are brought under one control, the risk is reduced; but it is only eliminated if the article is a real necessity without a substitute. With the wide choice available today for the use of purchasing power, the multiplicity of competing brands within product groups, and the extensive nature of the competition between these groups, every effort must be made to prevent money being irrevocably spent on competing products.

MODERN PRODUCTION METHODS AND MARKETING

Much of the intensity of modern marketing can be directly attributed to the way in which goods are manufactured. In order to achieve the most efficient scale of output, it may be necessary to introduce a large piece of equipment which is completely and entirely indivisible; it is only of use if taken in one total piece. Giant presses and computer installations are obvious examples. To employ this equipment most profitably, however, requires a higher level of production, and consequently of sales, than would have sufficed under a simpler method of production. Thus the urgency of marketing is higher because of the need to achieve a scale of production which makes the use of these machines economic; it is also more urgent because the consequences of not achieving the necessary scale would clearly result in a more uneconomic average cost of production; the new large overhead cost would be spread over too few units of production.

The potential efficiency of modern production methods also creates a further problem for the marketeer in that the waste resulting from bad marketing decisions is increased the greater the rate of production of the manufacturing plant. Where goods are produced with great facility in enormous quantities, all of them alike, then the consequential loss, if the product is not acceptable to the market, could be very great indeed. When production was more difficult and laboured, the loss caused by a week's production of unwanted goods was negligible; now it could be disastrous. More attention must therefore be paid to assessing customer needs prior to production, moulding the product if possible to suit these needs, and to communicating changes in customers' attitudes quickly in order to prevent wasteful output. This is modern marketing.

Earlier systems of production were of a direct face-to-face type: products were either made to order, or the reaction of the customer to ready-made ones was instantly evident to the producer; in other words there was 'instant marketing research'. Today's production methods require the grouping together of large units of production, normally at some distance from the customers – this distance may be not merely geographical, but also in terms of communications through the many dealers who handle the products – thus consumer reaction is not so quickly noticeable to the manufacturer. The modern shoe factory, because of its production efficiency, could manufacture a mountain of articles which, unknown to the manufacturer, are no longer needed in the type and quantity being made. At a time when we most need the 'instant marketing research' produced in the face-to-face situation, we have the very reverse.

The modern marketeer must introduce research to reduce the gap between the market and the production decision; in addition, he must also take other precautions to reduce the risk of wasteful production. Marketing is concerned in the establishment of the standard product, and intensively occupied with the maintenance of a viable sales quantity to justify the method of production. Mass production results from marketing, and positive marketing is needed to sustain it.

The more complex manufacturing methods become, and the

greater the size of the manufacturing units, then the longer the period of time between the decision to build a plant to produce a specific type of goods and the supply of the goods to the market. The longer this period of gestation, the greater the responsibility thrust on those who advise on the eventual sales potential of the product and those who meet the challenge of selling that amount of goods which will make the original investment decision profitable.

Although emphasis has been laid on the instability inherent in the sale of consumer-durables and the use of discretionary purchasing power, excessive competition, and therefore marketing, also exist in the sale of consumable necessities. The economies of production engineering do not observe any product demarcation, as between luxuries and necessities; they are of universal application. It may be just as necessary to use indivisible expensive equipment to achieve the lowest unit cost in the bread industry as it is in the car industry. The period of gestation may be just as long. Additionally, there should be a tendency for more capital to be attracted to supply the more stable demand for necessities; this would result in possible over-capitalization or excess capacity, the demand being relatively inelastic, and consequently in excessive pressure on selling activities.

CREDIT AND THE EXTENT OF COMPETITION

The marketeer aiming at discretionary purchasing power should not limit his observations to those firms directly competing within his own product group; he should examine the likelihood and strength of competition from other sources for the discretionary purchasing power. The marketing of gas heating appliances does not merely compete with the coal, electricity and oil industries, but also with all the other industries which could absorb the potential customer's purchasing power. Even where affluence is very great, the customer is merely elevated to a higher plateau of decision: the choice will move from one television or a piano to an extra television, a holiday or a second car. The problems of decision, and therefore of persuasion, still exist.

Normally, the goods available to people wishing to spend their discretionary purchasing power would not vary greatly in value from the extent of the purchasing power immediately available. There could be an accumulation of such purchasing power, but this would be limited by the propensity or willingness to save; with only limited regular amounts of discretionary purchasing power, the amount which could be accumulated might be very small. Instalment buying creates a totally different selling situation.

When, to the range of goods competing for the discretionary purchasing power, we add goods available through the medium of regular credit payments or hire purchase, then the breadth of choice and the value of goods within this choice are enormously increased. The man can now choose between spending his weekly available discretionary purchasing power of £10; saving his available purchasing power to perhaps a total of £60; or a hire purchase contract valued at £1,040 (£10 per week for two years). The extra suit is now competing with the refrigerator, and both are fighting the attraction of a new car.

Credit or instalment buying is an accepted part of modern societies, and its attraction to the customer who is unable to save voluntarily before purchase is so great that many major industries, such as private cars, domestic equipment and furniture, are maintained in their present position by the market made available to them by this means of buying. The effects of instalment buying are not, however, limited to the extension of the range of choice available to the customer and the increased extent of competition; it also introduces a long-term commitment by the buyer which will distort his discretionary ability during the period of the credit contract: if our man does decide to purchase a new car, then he has no discretionary purchasing power available for other products during the course of his hire-purchase commitment.

PLATEAUX OF SIMILARITY

Sales practitioners prefer to sell a product which is really different, but unfortunately this is rarely possible, and, even when it occurs, its unique nature is normally short-lived. Many products are in themselves little different from their immediate competitors, particularly among basic necessities. When products are basically the same, then the whole range of marketing activities must be used to create distinctive features so that customer loyalty can be fostered.

Design, packaging, branding, advertising, price policy, and even the choice of dealers may all be used to create the image of a unique product where one does not really exist.

OTHER FACTORS CONTRIBUTING TO THE INTENSITY OF MARKETING, AND A LOOK AT THE FUTURE

As we have seen, the complexity and intensity of modern marketing are basically due to the need to maintain the maximum profitability of capital equipment in buyers' markets which are satiate, under conditions of extensive competition. Looking more deeply into the situation as it appears to the individual firm, we can see a more serious situation developing in that, whereas in the past its cost structure was such that it had some escapable direct costs associated with its output which could be stopped in the event of a reduced demand for its products, this may be denied it in the future.

The introduction of automation and the development of guaranteed annual salaries for all workers will leave only power, raw materials and maintenance as the main variables in the cost structure. Many new industries are highly capital-intensive by their nature, e.g. nuclear power stations; others will, perhaps, become so, as the cost of capital relative to labour (a feature of a mass-consumption society) becomes increasingly cheap. Some industries might develop this capital-intensiveness because of fiscal encouragement to modernize or reinvest profits; still others may fear the consequences of industrial unrest, higher social insurance contributions for employees, obligatory redundancy payments and training levies, etc.

Anything which results in an increase in the fixed cost of production increases the cost of producing and selling nothing: it increases the already great fear of idle capacity. Marketing, by identifying and/or creating the demand for the product, helps to reduce this anxiety. In the future, its role as an insurance or security factor will be increased.

QUALITY STANDARDS AND BRANDING

Paradoxically, the very technology which is often criticized because of its inability to maintain a regular supply of desirable innovations to sustain sales, has been so efficient in other directions that the maintenance of the perpetual sales needed to justify investment has become increasingly difficult: it has produced articles which are physically too durable. When a team of automobile engineers produces a new and better suspension, a more efficient lubricant, a better cellulose finish or a longer-life engine, then, although there may be a momentary upsurge in the particular company's sales, such developments could lead to a longer period of satisfaction by the customer with his car, and thus the worsening of the overall sales situation. These technical developments are usually highly transferable and, if the total market is not increased by the improvement, then the general situation becomes a more difficult one in which to perpetuate sales.

The introduction of branding into almost every type of industry has had a similar consequence in that quality standards are more important with branded goods; the brand owner accumulates any goodwill or ill-will associated with his product, and so has a bigger interest in maintaining quality standards.

Where it is necessary to perpetuate sales in order to achieve a reasonable spread of fixed costs, then any increase in the physical life of the product will make this more difficult. Obsolescence and customer-dissatisfaction will have to be the result of non-physical factors. Research which develops really worthwhile product changes is the method which is most favoured, but the rate of development may be too slow for the purpose of sustaining sales. It is then that we must turn to other devices such as social obsolescence and the cult of 'this year's model'; planned obsolescence; and the use of psychological extensions to the product or the social need to possess it.

THE FIXED COST OF SELLING

In certain markets where the production problems have long been solved and/or where brand susceptibility is great, there may develop an overhead or fixed cost associated with the selling activity itself. At the launching of a product a fixed amount of money will be invested to achieve a foothold in the market – a sort of 'key money'. Later, outlays will be needed merely to stay in the market – a kind of 'rent'. These costs can obviously assume the form of fixed costs which have to be met if the firm wishes to stay in the market. This situation is exacerbated in those markets where effective competition by price is ruled out, and resort must therefore be made to advertising and other forms of sales aid to attract custom. Unfortunately, such 'rents' only give the firm a place in the market; it must then so organize its marketing, from product development to after-sales service, that the 'rent' is worthwhile.

Much of the intense activity of modern marketing, as we have seen, can be traced to the heavy overhead cost of modern industry; but modern selling often has its own type of fixed-cost activity, a type of 'rent' to stay in a market; scientific marketing is needed to justify this 'rent'.[5]

The very intensity of the selling problem creates costs which are reciprocated by competitors and so, in turn, further intensifies the problem; reaction to intensity thus increases the intensity.

THE RECIPROCAL NATURE OF MARKETING – ITS ESCALATION POTENTIAL

The struggle for sales which follows investment is essentially a reciprocal one. Investment competes with investment for the same market; marketing is used by all to orientate the enterprise

5. In those industries with a low technical or production optimum, the cost of entry into a market may be so high that it offsets such an advantage. Thus in fields such as detergents, cosmetics, bread and domestic equipment, the optimum which causes the embarrassment is not always the technical one, but the one associated with selling which will require a large scale of sales promotion to be achieved in order that the return per unit of outlay is economic, e.g. on advertising or distribution.

towards the customer more perfectly than competitors; selling fights selling to win customer approval for goods. More sophisticated marketing and selling produces even more subtle counter-activities. None dares to relax.

THE TRANSFERABILITY OF ABILITY

Marketing is concerned with a perpetual struggle for the maintenance of a comparative advantage over competitors: this is possibly a better definition of the concept than any, if positive action is needed. Clearly, the maintenance of such an advantage is not governed solely by actions within the firm but by those of others seeking the same goal. There is a perpetual dynamic involved.

The ease with which any advantage can be maintained, assuming customer reaction to be given, may largely depend on the speed with which the constituent parts of the advantage can be adopted by competitors.

The source of the advantage may be within the product, and to the extent that this can be protected in some way, then it may represent a substantial basis for maintaining the necessary lead over competitors. Unfortunately, modern marketing techniques are themselves increasing the perishability of such product advantages and even creating situations where they may rarely even occur.

When product development and design were based on intuition then chance played a large part in the distribution of product advantages among competing firms. To the extent that market research eliminates chance and evolves standard transferable analytical techniques, so product equality will increase, and resort will have to be made to sources outside the product if a competitive lead is to be gained or maintained.

Perhaps the advantage may be only in the 'eye of the beholder': promoted imagery may give the needed lead in some markets. Unfortunately again, scientific marketing, in its contribution to sales promotion and its appraisal of techniques, may quickly identify image-building opportunities and so advantages may be

17

cancelled out. To the extent that sales promotion tends towards a science, even a social one, then the methodology becomes transferable among competitors. The result is again an intensification of the struggle for customers.

It could well be that a more permanent source of comparative advantage lies in those areas of activity within a firm which are not so transferable. Such areas give rise to company-patronage and have their bases in human activity, often applied to transferable techniques; e.g. one company may give better delivery or quality consistency than another, but both use the same basic methods: the difference is in the management of the methods. But even the identification of this better source of advantage inevitably leads to its transference, and again there is the intensification of the struggle on another periphery.

THE POLITICAL AND PHILOSOPHICAL FACTORS INFLUENCING THE INTENSITY OF MARKETING

Political parties today are judged more by their abilities to increase the individual wealth of the electors than their political philosophies. This emphasis on the material benefits which would accrue if a particular political party were elected has some important marketing consequences.

Full employment implies the ability of the manufacturing and service industries to sell profitably all the goods produced by the fully employed. There is more than a grain of truth in the contention that marketing, by maintaining full employment in free capitalist societies, helps to keep those societies viable and intact; and that without its stabilizing influence there could occur widespread unemployment and political discontent.

Productivity has recently been added to the list of desirable economic aims used by rival politicians. But this might only increase the strain on marketing in that the fully employed are now producing even more.

All might be well if the extra purchasing power obtained by full employment and increased productivity were required to buy articles which were really needed. Unfortunately, as we have seen, in a mass-consumption society many of the goods are highly durable and their purchase very postponable. People must be made to buy to maintain sales to keep them fully employed in increasingly productive activities.[6]

The chance of wellbeing[7] or welfare being accepted as desirable is perhaps influenced by an emotional attitude towards 'not working', rather than any rational evaluation of the expected satisfaction from more material goods as against the disutility of labour needed to get them. There appears to be an ethos, perhaps with ethnic or religious overtones, which would judge the moral rectitude of refusing to work when work is available. Where a miner in a dirty, dangerous job is criticized because he chooses leisure in preference to an additional amount of purchasing power which he does not really need, then the marketing men do appear to have society in general as one of their best allies.

THE GENERAL CONCLUSION

The fundamental reason for marketing is to be found in the type of society in which we live: where the decision-taking by producers is separated in distance and time from that of the consumers, and there is no overall attempt to reconcile the two sets of decisions, positive marketing will follow. The modern means of production, with their long periods of gestation, their size and expense, the composition of their costs, their speed of production, and the specialized nature of their output, intensify the need to identify a market for that output and to sustain that market.

The task is made more difficult, the more volatile the nature of consumer choice when the standard of living is beyond biological needs and contains a high proportion of consumer-durables, the

6. An interesting intellectual exercise, which cannot be pursued here, concerns the position of marketing in very capital-intensive economies where the return is on capital and not labour.

7. It is difficult to define exactly what is meant by 'wellbeing', and in fact the interpretation placed upon it has marketing implications. Thus, an improvement in a car or washing machine which reduced the physical strain of using these appliances might be said to increase 'wellbeing'; but such an improvement would also increase the desire to purchase the appliance, i.e. to increase the stock of material goods.

purchase of which is postponable. The cost structure of production and marketing exacerbates the problem in that the cost of producing nothing increases and the 'rent' of the market is fixed by outside reciprocating factors.

Political ideologies and the general ethos of a society may both increase and/or decrease the problems of the marketeer in that they influence the attitude towards material wealth and wellbeing.

The saturated nature of the markets and the durable nature of many goods lead to practices which are considered good by marketeers, but which are questioned by other observers.

It must never be forgotten that marketing is a type of insurance function against the possibility of unprofitable investment. It helps to reduce or relieve anxiety on the part of the owners of capital and those who, through their work, are associated with that capital. Marketing should be present at the conception of an enterprise with information about the possible vendibility of the product or service to be produced and assessments of its overall profitability. It is there throughout the life of an enterprise, modifying the product, finding new uses, opening up new market segments, introducing diversification or variety reduction, suggesting quality policies, helping to set credit and price policies, planning the actual sale of the product through advertising, branding, packaging, personal selling, and dealer relationships, appraising continuously the market and the compatibility of the product and its promotion with that market.

The need for positive marketing is an indication of the essential nature of the customer's power; his discretionary ability as between products and brands within product ranges creates a buyer's market throughout the majority of affluent free societies. Without this customer power relative to the producer, the very nature and intensity of marketing, as we know it, would not exist.

2. Marketing – Concept and Function

THE dichotomy of the entrepreneurial activity into making and selling has long been the established custom, even in allegedly successful firms. The priority given to the making function is in contrast to the prominence of the selling activity under the merchant capitalist system; it is a manifestation of the essential heavy investment needed in modern industry which created an obsessive desire to achieve that scale which will reduce the cost per unit of output to the minimum. The emphasis on mass-production advantages exaggerated the importance of the production function in the entrepreneurial activity to the detriment of those aspects which are concerned with customer relationships; the active selling function has become the consequence of production and the economies of scale. In fact, the marketing function is the prerequisite of worthwhile production, regardless of the scale of that production; the greater the scale, the more appropriate this principle.

Marketing aims at achieving the maximum compatibility between the assets of an enterprise and the attitudes of customers or potential customers; the profit motive exploits this. This compatibility should be present during the process of investment decision-taking before any commitment is made. It concerns those assets which are physical and fixed, such as machinery and plant; or 'committed', as when resources have been used to train a working force or management team, or money has been spent to gain entry into a market and establish a 'name' for the enterprise or its products. The assets may include a pool of ability and skill possessed by the firm, or special rights to manufacture certain products achieved by research or licensing. The liquid or readily available financial funds of the enterprise must be orientated towards meeting or changing customer attitudes, e.g. by developing new products, increasing capacity, extending credit or by advertising. Finally, and of special importance, is the goodwill already enjoyed by the business which

21

can be exploited in existing or potential markets to the advantage of the output of the physical, human and financial assets of the enterprise.

This approach to marketing recognizes the importance of selling, which may be needed to create a valuable customer attitude towards the products of the assets, either by drawing attention to their real comparative advantages or by helping to synthesize in the mind of the potential customer an apparent advantage over competing products. The liquid assets are used through selling to change customer attitudes and improve the desired compatibility. The established name, a form of asset, is used in the selling activity.

It will also be apparent that such a broad definition of marketing is not concerned solely with the present. Current assets may be used to sustain the goodwill of past customers as when after-sales service and customer-service departments are established, or even when a sales technique is used to dispel a past source of ill-feeling between the enterprise and its customers. The current assets will also be used in research to indicate the most profitable future relationship between the assets or company activities and customers.

Marketing is concerned with every aspect of a business which in any way affects the attitude of customers towards the present or future output of that business; it is that part of the entrepreneurial activity which makes production viable, and without it an enterprise has no value. It includes research and development and product policy to sustain the profitable life of the enterprise; production planning to meet customer needs; quality control of output; stockholding; credit extensions; price policy; after-sales service; sales organization; choice of distribution methods; dealer policies; manning the selling function; advertising; branding and packaging; and instructions to the switchboard operator and commissionaire on their marketing significance! It can even include location of plant where this is to gain a marketing advantage through tariff or currency avoidance. It is a comprehensive concept which includes within it the actual sales activity.

Selling is concerned with persuading the potential customers that the amalgam of qualities possessed by a product or a business is that which is best suited among competing products to the total wants, needs and purchasing ability of the customer.[1] This may extend into the realms of psychological adjustments between the subconscious desires and needs of the customer and the design of the product, its brand name or the content of the advertisement; but it still remains an attempt at reconciling two things, the customer's needs and means and the product's qualities or assumed qualities.

Clearly, marketing is at the same time bigger and more important than selling, which only forms a part of the whole. As a principle, it could be stated that the more marketing-orientated the entrepreneurial activity is, the less the need for selling. However, as stated earlier, the residual selling needed to maintain a comparative advantage may become even more vital as scientific marketing makes other things increasingly equal. Nevertheless, the hard selling which has become a feature of many modern businesses is often an indication of inadequate marketing. Marketing is not concerned with selling the output of a given input of capital equipment, labour, land and materials, but with so arranging the input that the output is geared to providing consumer satisfaction. Selling, itself, is really most successful when it is promoting the various elements of marketing which are within the capability of the enterprise and are compatible with customer motivation priorities.

The tendency is that the deficiency in the entrepreneurial make-up of a firm, lack of marketing in its true sense, will only become apparent when recessional conditions arise, or when there is a situation of over-capitalization and potential over-supply within the industry relative to those demands which even modern sales techniques can generate. The growing inadequacy of the selling activity in such situations will lead to a reappraisal of the relationship between the needs of the consumer and the output or potential output of the business, i.e. to marketing.

1. This is usually an offsetting activity in that it must demonstrate that where complete compatibility between the product and the customer does not exist, e.g. in price, this is balanced by some quality which more than offsets it, e.g. higher quality or better social rating. If quality is below desired standards, then this is more than offset by the price. It is the total appeal which matters.

Obviously we must not sell the sales activity 'short', because without its persuasive powers the techniques of modern production would not be possible. The decision-taking process in marketing assumes certain abilities and achievements on the part of the sales function to be possible. Spontaneous demand is not accepted as adequate; it must be stimulated. In the context of modern industrial methodology there must be an assumption that certain sales techniques will be available to a firm, and the decision to organize the factors of production to meet a consumer preference will take into consideration the active sales ability available in the form of the talent of the staff concerned and the funds at their disposal. This marketing decision-taking would also have to consider the likely selling reaction of competitors, not only to the conceived output, but also as reciprocal action to the positive selling of that output.

The principle remains, however, that the more marketing-minded the entrepreneurial activity, the greater the return per unit of outlay on selling. Thus, an investigation into consumer needs and motivation, availability of purchasing power, social factors likely to affect sales, quality requirements, reaction to price levels, followed by a policy to suit the findings, is more important than any detailed aspect of selling. Selling, even by using all the sophisticated aids possible, the wrong product to a man without money may give a masochistic pleasure to a successful salesman, but in terms of productivity per unit of input it is commercially disastrous. Again, we must guard against any under-estimate of the selling function in a competitive system.

Undoubtedly, where a number of companies in the same market have all researched correctly and have all understood the true meaning of marketing, then there still remains the act of selling which may be the marginal difference between the competitors. Also, where the combination of equipment, technical know-how, managerial and technical skill is already in existence and has only limited flexibility, with a consequent reduction in the product spectrum, then the selling activity becomes more important. In such a situation it could well be that the ability to continue profitably in business with the given assets and their nature will depend on the sales function's power in a market situation which has deteriorated.

Any discrepancy between the limited product range of a given investment and the current needs of customers will increase that function of marketing concerned with reconciling customer needs and the output of the enterprise, i.e. the selling function. The error might be in the capacity to produce as against the immediate and viable market potential for the products, and once again all the sophisticated persuasive means are needed to reconcile sales with the production optimum of the unit.

Another unknown dynamic factor is introduced into decision-taking. To the extent that modern industrial technology requires large indivisible investments in order to achieve the lowest unit cost of production and that this investment requires a long period of gestation, then the sales function will increase in importance, particularly where the decisions are taken in isolation from other producing units.

Neither should one overlook the possible need for selling to compensate for inadequacies at some other point earlier in the marketing sequence. The prior analysis of customer needs leading to product design and range may be faulty; price may be unrealistic; competitors may have researched better. In all these cases, the situation may be rectified by positive selling. This is the converse of the principle that good marketing prior to selling reduces the need for positive selling.

Good marketing should proceed through a sequence of activities covering investigation into the market environment and the customer; the conception of the products; the sales aspects of production, e.g. design, range and quality control; the act of selling; and the maintenance of after-sales customer satisfaction. Selling is the amalgam of activities which bring pressure to bear on potential customers and include personal selling, advertising, branding, packaging etc., the practice of which is based on a scientific analysis of customer motivation and the actions of competitors. The design of the product, price policy, method of distribution and credit policy are fundamental to the selling activity, but by their nature are part of other activities. Marketing research should be considered a continuous, investigating, creative, appraisal and control function applying to the whole of marketing, the efficiency of each element, and the relationship of elements one to another.

Earlier, it was stated that the better a company tackled the other aspects of marketing, the less the need for the active selling function. This is becoming increasingly apparent when motivational research is used at the design stage of the product. If it is possible to incorporate into a product features which make for compatibility of product qualities and customer attitudes and needs, then the need for persuasion through advertising and personal selling to bring this about is reduced; selling then communicates the desirable features. If the motivational research has extended to the subconscious and has suggested ways of reconciling the personality of the product with that of the potential purchaser, then the job of selling is made so much easier. This is the essence of marketing, in that it is concerned with identifying and meeting consumer attitudes and needs both physical and psychological; whereas selling is occupied with solving the problems created by the existence of production capacity and any other assets of the entrepreneur. Marketing is based on customer needs; selling is producer-orientated. Nevertheless, selling as a communication function is still needed even when marketing has been well done; potential customers are not automatically aware of the new orientation of your product and/ or supporting services. Old ones may have to be converted to the idea that you have mended your ways; selling then communicates the facts of the new situation.

As a motive for purchasing, price may be dominant, and yet there are situations where the price decision is taken from those actively engaged in selling and becomes exclusively a sales-policy decision; it is a dominant part of the marketing function in that it affects customer attitudes, but it is divorced from selling. In so far as the price of a product is inconsistent with customer needs relative to the potential output of the assets committed to it, then the sales activity must make up for this inconsistency between demand at a given price and the optimum output for the production unit concerned.

Companies faced with a price policy decision always have the fundamental choice as to how much they are going to use price as an incentive to purchase and to what extent they are going to fix a price on the assumption that a given investment in sales promotion will maximize net profits. Company A might choose to sell a product at a gross profit margin of 200 per cent above cost of production and give such good commission to salesmen that a certain sales figure is achieved; salesmen's salaries, expenses and commission together with any other sales aids may take up 50 per cent of the gross margin, giving a true profit of 100 per cent per product. Company B may decide to reduce price and decrease the gross profit by 25 per cent (of 200 per cent) and limit its expenditure on selling to $33\frac{1}{3}$ per cent of the gross margin. The final sales and net revenue figures for both companies might be the same, but the sales function is more important in A than in B. Such a situation occurs in brand-minded and socially conscious markets where the difference between cost of production and price is very great, but where net profits are limited because of the intense selling effort needed. Motivation research may suggest that the promotion of brand images rather than price manoeuvring is the correct policy, and in such cases the selling function is of increased importance.

Observation of the selling function in action suggests that its intensity is not always directly proportionate to the need to achieve a given scale of manufacturing operations, but is conditioned by selling itself – selling creates selling. Certain industries, where sales promotion is at a very high pitch, are based on methods of production which require relatively low production optima, long since achieved; the current expenditure on selling must have its causes in some non-production aspect. What are these causes?

In the development of a market for a product, a certain expenditure on sales promotion may be budgeted, and this may help to establish a brand name for the product. This move has two possible consequences; it will result in additional expenditure to the company which may be considered a once-and-for-all or overhead type of expenditure; it will also very likely result in retaliatory action by others in the same market. These two consequences when projected into the future may result in increasing amounts of money being used to achieve or maintain the sales of the product and the increasing belief that to reduce this expenditure, relative to others, will reduce market share. The outcome is that selling creates further reciprocal selling and a fear of contracting out of selling in competitive markets.

Successful marketing depends on the possession of a comparative advantage over competing firms, and it is worthwhile to trace the place of selling in this process. If competitors are equally proficient at supplying goods to the needs of the customers, then patronage arising out of the product cannot occur because none has a comparative advantage. If price is also the same, then again the situation is one of stalemate. Differences in service to the customer, in the form of consistent quality and prompt delivery, may now attract patronage, i.e. company patronage. However, if these are also similar, then the total non-selling activity is equal between competitors. Comparative advantage must then be created in the mind of the customer by selling. This may be a simple, face-to-face, selling matter or it could contain the whole complex of selling, including branding, packaging and advertising.

A similar situation can occur where dealer margins are fixed by convention or agreement making all products equally profitable to the dealer; selling must then persuade the dealer that certain products are a better means to his economic objective.

It is not necessary to have all goods, prices and services equal as between suppliers; if the several amalgams are equal, a higher price being equated with an obviously better product, then the resulting dependence on the persuasion function will be modified, but will still remain. It will now be concentrated on creating distinction and comparative advantages out of different amalgams.

If an industrial product is specified by a customer and price is fixed, perhaps by agreement, recommendation or pure economics in a largely rational market, then comparative advantage must be sought elsewhere. However, before the contract has been placed, these two aspects of the supplier, product and price, are the only forms of comparative advantage which could have been obvious; the company patronage motives of service and co-operation have to be proven by experience. How then is the choice made between the unproven comparative services of suppliers? Is there no room here for selling by public relations, advertising, exhibitions and face-to-face activitities?

If the industrial buyer employs a vendor-rating system, how does an unproven supplier break into the field of the rated suppliers? If the buyer only alters his source of supply when he is dissatisfied with his current one, how does he choose the new one?

Finally, in industrial marketing, how does the current supplier maintain his position in the face of competition if he has been guilty of 'unselling' activities in the past? How are inconsistencies in quality and late delivery cancelled in the mind of the offended customer? Selling may be needed in such cases merely to re-establish a company so that it is not considered to have a comparative *dis*advantage.

Although selling is normally associated with the emotional content in persuasion, it can also be used to inform, in a producer-orientated way, on economic or rational content. This can obviously occur in the industrial market, but we can see it in the consumer market too. Selling may be used here to instruct on the features of a new product and may contribute to the buying knowledge of the customer, as when special tyres are sold for motorway driving; the ignorant potential buyer probably was unaware of such a need.[2]

This informative or communication function of selling is needed regardless of the comparative advantage of the product or company; without it the product's features would not be known. Selling here draws attention to good customer-orientation. To the extent that the product has been correctly created, or the service exactly suited to customer needs, then selling will be more effective or productive.

We thus move all the way from selling as a means of creating comparative advantages where few or none exist, to selling to inform on real differences between competing products. Similarly

2. Some selling can be considered completely socially beneficial in that it is informative in a manner which does improve the life of a customer. Consider the sale of life assurance and its contribution to the family security, labour-saving devices, safer cars, vitaminized foods etc.

selling can draw attention to economic as well as emotional advantages, according to the nature of the product and the customer; correct customer-orientation, the hallmark of good marketing, must be highlighted – by selling. When goods are equal, we have selling to create differentials and loyalty; when goods have comparative advantages, we use selling to inform on these advantages; when prices are equal, we again use selling to show that values are not; when prices are unequal, selling is used to justify the inequalities on the one hand and exploit them on the other. Throughout all these activities selling is seen, in its true nature, as a positive communication and persuasion function which is product- and producer-orientated. Implied in all its operations is the assumption that the necessary demand is not given but must be generated. Even before a spontaneous, non-stimulated demand can be generated, the potential buyers must be informed of the product – an act of selling.

MARKETING AND SELLING – THE INSURANCE OR SECURITY FUNCTION

Although marketing is normally associated with the positive function of converting production and other assets into cash through good customer valuation of the products or services produced by these assets, it also has a more basic purpose – that of insurance.

The heavy investment risks associated with most modern industries require some form of insurance aimed at reducing them. Marketing provides the cover, but without the certainty of indemnity found in other branches of insurance. Judgement will still be needed; the better this judgement, the greater the cover.

Production capacity and, where they exist, facilities to distribute products should result from marketing, in that they are a response to an existing or latent customer demand; the more correct the foundation of the capacity, the less the anxiety of its owners. Once committed, the assets will maintain their economic worth by the application of marketing. Product policy will provide it with goods of value, in that they are needed. All other functions will become customer-orientated in order to sustain goodwill on the part of the buyer, the only source of value for the capacity; product development, design, inspection, production control and distribution will be seen as consumer-centred. Sales promotion will be used to attract attention to the qualities of the enterprise and its output. Processors may be taken over and retail outlets controlled to guarantee a market for the capacity. Marketing in this way, like all insurance, reduces anxiety.

Selling may have a special part to play in sustaining demand when spontaneous demand is inadequate to meet the capacity needs of the enterprise. It assists design in generating a gap between pride in the possession of an existing model and a new one, which is wide enough to create a preference for a replacement. It compensates for deficiencies in any of the non-selling activities of the enterprise which could affect the viability of the committed assets; this can cover all such eventualities, from over-commitment in specialized capacity with only a limited product spectrum to explaining a late delivery. It creates comparative advantages where none exist.

Conventional insurance does not cover the risk of idle capacity, the business possibility of producing nothing, the devaluation of capacity because its potential is unwanted. Marketing does this and sometimes requires a special effort from one constituent part – selling. Conventional insurance cover requires finance to meet the premiums demanded; marketing, although needing some funds, requires an attitude of mind which accepts customer orientation and a scientific approach to the only source of value – the buyer.

3. Scientific Marketing

BOTH marketing and general management represent an amalgam of disciplines and activities brought to bear on a given problem. Some of these may border on true science, e.g. statistics and econometrics. Others, like the behavioural sciences – economics, sociology, psychology – are looking for universal principles, but cannot achieve the universality of the true science. Still others are essentially intuitive and are concerned with innate ability, personality, temperament and volition; these are associated with the commercial artist, the inspired copywriter, the 'born' salesman, the real entrepreneur, the creative package designer, the instinctive sales manager, and the author of brand names.

Like all management, marketing is not really a separate study, but represents an ability to recognize the need for, and to call on, all the relevant disciplines to supplement intuition and innate ability. In fact, one of the real problems of modern marketing is to find means of bringing together all the relevant information needed for decision-taking; there is a danger that the communication system will become overloaded and unable to handle the many types of information; specialist advice from each field must be appraised individually and weighed in relation to other fields.

Although dispute may continue on the true description of marketing, there can be no argument that to be successful it must be scientific. Facts must, wherever they are obtainable, be the basis of marketing decisions and plans. Factual appraisal of plans in action must always be the foundation of control and changes in plans. Even the effectiveness of any intuitive or 'arty' element should be factually assessed wherever possible; advertising should be measured as to the degree of awareness created, regardless of the alleged brilliance of the copywriter or the whole agency; packs should be pretested for customer and dealer acceptance, etc.

In any activity concerned with the social sciences, mechanical calculation is impossible, and to assume that it is credible may be dangerous and misleading, but this does not rule out scientific methodology in these fields.

Scientific marketing is concerned with the method of operation and does not imply any belief in the possibility of mechanical calculation; it requires the willingness to adopt an attitude of mind towards marketing problems and to operate along a sequence of research, forecast, plan, control, co-ordinate, and motivate – a sequence familiar to all associated with scientific management. But does this sequence represent the total marketing activity?

For the really successful marketeer there would appear to be the need for a prior element, 'foresight-tinged-with-flair'. Many firms could have made excellent garden equipment, but only one saw the marketing consequences of wartime building restrictions, bombing, slum clearance, the resulting surge in housebuilding, the increased purchasing power likely to be available, and the likelihood of shorter working weeks. This ability to bring together the relevant facts and to see their commercial viability represents the essence of entrepreneurial activity. The decision to proceed to exploit the situation should have been preceded by a complete scientific appraisal of all the relevant facts. The proper performance of marketing requires an ability to come to a conclusion ahead of proof; the scientific content can then be used to verify as far as possible the logic of the conclusion.

THE 'GIVEN' FACTORS

There is one aspect of marketing which very closely resembles the physical sciences and that is the need to accept that certain factors are 'given' in a situation or problem. Just as the engineer must accept gravity, so the marketeer must accept the existence of a given amount of purchasing power. Further, as with the physical sciences, the market investigator or analyst has no effect over these 'given' factors, regardless of the importance or size of the firm for which he is working: gravity is the same for the British Aircraft Corporation as it is for a window cleaner; the taxation policy of a country is the same for a multiple store as it is for a village general dealer.

Whereas the physical scientist is concerned with both static and dynamic influences on the problem, the marketeer is rarely, if ever, allowed the luxury of static factors; influences on marketing, like those in other branches of social science, tend to be dynamic, subject to multiple correlation, less predictable, and more non-linear than in the physical sciences. Twice the cause only rarely has twice the effect in marketing. It may have more or less today, and vary tomorrow or the next day. Marketing, as an amalgam of social sciences, cannot escape from this, but it can attempt to discover the nature of relationships with which it has to deal. It can study past and present relationships and use the information to help in future decision-taking; this is scientific marketing, but only if such historical data are used correctly. The tendency to make a positive inference from an uncertain assumption is always attractive in social sciences, perhaps particularly in management studies, but it is the antithesis of scientific method.[1]

Unlike the physical scientist, the marketeer is unable to create laboratory conditions to observe and test hypotheses. The only really valid test must be in the market place itself when the interactions of human beings in large numbers on each other is an integral part of the activity, as in marketing.

This does not rule out attempts at limited experiments, but it does preclude the automatic projection or extrapolation of the results obtained. Products can be tested in specially selected pilot areas before national launching, and this will reduce the risk of complete failure, but it cannot guarantee the success of a national campaign. Panels can be used to test brand names and packs, but the results, although of great value, cannot be automatically translated into bigger terms. Scientific marketing implies the maximum amount of pretesting, but it also demands a complete awareness of the limitations of such tests. Without this attitude,

1. There may also be a danger of over-valuing the importance of one identifiable and easily quantified factor affecting a marketing situation to the detriment of a proper valuation of other relevant factors, particularly if these are more difficult to handle; e.g. an obvious and positive correlation between incomes and sales may mask other influences which are ignored until the correlation ceases.

we might again have positive inferences based on uncertain assumptions.

The marketeer then must accept certain factors as 'given' and he must recognize, in addition, the dynamic nature of these factors. He uses scientific method to identify all the influences which might affect his market and then tries to establish the dynamics of these influences, and their interaction upon each other. He can then create a model of the factors influencing his marketing situation.

Once a plan has been made and has been put into action, the marketeer must continually track the movements of the various factors in order to reorientate his plan should a new situation arise. In so far as this new situation has been foreseen as a consequence of a change in factor strength, then it can be planned for, and action can be taken immediately to meet it. This is scientific marketing.

The successful firm is the one which most efficiently identifies factor changes and most adequately reacts to the new situation. Sometimes, successful firms are called growth firms, implying that they are in industries with a built-in ability to grow; rather is it perhaps a built-in ability on the part of the firm to react to new situations by scientific marketing. In uncertain conditions, such as those found in marketing, reaction must be planned on a basis of probability – the degree of probability requires scientific assessment.

4. Decision-Taking in Marketing

So far the emphasis has been on an understanding of the environment in which marketing decisions take place and the elements and the dynamics of that environment. There is, however, another consideration which must be taken before a decision is made; an estimate of the strength of competitors within a market. So far the analysis has centred on demand, but even if an adequate demand has been located it is still necessary to estimate the actions of others who are already doing so or might try to meet the same demand.

This need to quantify the expected competition for a market or segment of a market can be encountered in many ways, but never without presenting one of the most difficult problems in the whole of marketing. The decision to enter a market immediately throws up this question; a further decision to apply the resources of the firm to supplying a particular segment begs the same issue; the problem of price policy for a new product is partly based on the estimate of the speed with which competitors might enter; advertising appropriations can be influenced greatly by forecasts of reciprocal action. Even fundamental aspects of marketing, such as research and development of new products and product design, are carried on in the shadow of an unknown power, the ability of your competitor to out-do you.

Quantifying in all marketing tends to be difficult, and to expect mechanical calculations to be applied when dealing with the future ability and actions of competing suppliers is unrealistic; even attempts at quantification as to future activities *within* the firm are fraught with problems. Nevertheless, although mechanical calculations are impossible, a scientific appraisal of competitors is a necessary part of any decision-taking in marketing.

This scientific assessment is more difficult in the markets for postponable consumer-durables when unexpected design idiosyncrasies can be introduced, unlike the situation with consumable necessities such as food. Additional complications for any market model would also arise from the extensive nature of the competition which is present in many fields; to make more carpets may appear a good decision when only considering the demand for them and the current state of supply, but this situation could be upset if the current consideration was also extended to all types of floor covering, and then to all other ways of spending the discretionary purchasing power of the potential customer.

Estimates must also be made of the relative effectiveness of the sales-promotion plans of the competing supplier, the amount of money likely to be devoted to such plans, and the skill of the respective sales executives.

Decision-taking in marketing is carried on in a situation of extreme dynamism, in the state of both demand and supply. Quantification of the strength of those dynamic forces in the future, in exact terms, is impossible, and determination of the exact correlation of all the interconnected causes and effects virtually so. The most practical solution is to allow for the difficulty, rather than ignore it. Marketing decisions and plans are based on probabilities and not certainties, and to the extent that certain events occur, so the plans may be valid; but if unforeseen developments take place, then alternative courses are already planned to meet the new situation.

The degree of probability of certain events will lead to the decision to follow a plan, but other degrees of probability for other events to happen will produce alternatives. The final success throughout a period of time will depend upon the speed with which changed circumstances are met. Scientific marketing implies planning to meet changes in conditions should these occur, together with an estimate of the probability of their occurrence.

A marketing decision and plan may be the result of a detailed inquiry into the socio-economic conditions in the market, the potential suppliers, and the ability of the firm itself to compete; but such an analysis should also indicate the possibility of other situations occurring, and their degree of probability. The complexity of the forces acting on marketing is so great that plans based on probability with their assumptions of alternatives and flexibility are the correct approach to this uncertain situation. The computer can be a great aid in its ability to identify correlations and to simulate marketing situations into which information can be fed; but it is difficult to imagine that it will ever cope with future socio-economic developments or the decisions of competitors with any degree of certainty. Once the socio-economic change has taken place, or the competitor has shown his hand, then the computer will more rapidly supply information about the possible consequences, leading to a new plan based on the new situation more speedily analysed than before. It is even possible to develop future marketing programmes on the assumption of certain socio-economic changes if the necessary correlations have been identified beforehand; the computer could be of assistance in determining these complex correlations. To demand specific forecasts is to be too expectant.

Quantification is of course the basic problem when trying to achieve the certainty of mechanical calculations in a social science such as marketing. Quantification would be necessary of the following factors at least before a certain solution could be assured:

1. The possible alternative objectives of the marketing or selling plans and their relationships to maximum profits, e.g. the importance of building up goodwill, mass coverage or segmentation, long- or short-term profits, etc.

2. All the socio-economic forces within a market; within this complex of factors, the action of the state in modern societies is often the least certain and most difficult to predict, e.g. changes in direct and indirect taxation, international trade policies, etc.

3. The general future trend for the products of the industry concerned.

4. The effectiveness of each aspect of marketing and selling undertaken by the firm itself, e.g. product development, design, price policy, advertising, branding, packaging, dealer relationships, personal selling, credit extensions, customer services, the method of distribution, and production efficiency (meeting delivery dates and quality standards).

5. The effectiveness of the overall marketing and selling strategies of the company.

6. The possible policies of competitors in all aspects listed under 1, 4 and 5 above and their effectiveness.

Clearly, such a task is beyond current capabilities; it contains too many uncertainties for completely positive quantification. So we must return to a scientific rather than a mechanical approach to decision-taking in marketing; this demands an identification of the correct objective and of all the forces influencing its achievement, a scientific estimate of their strength and future movement, and a plan based on probabilities with its assumption of alternative plans to meet lesser probabilities. To proceed along a more optimistic sequence would incur the danger of making certain and positive inferences based on uncertain assumptions.

PART TWO

THE FRAMEWORK OF MARKETING

Introduction

THE great successes in business have normally been due to the recognition and exploitation of a favourable opportunity. The ability to recognize a business opportunity must begin with the recognition of a market, and proceed through identification of all the factors likely to affect the market and an analysis of these factors; the marriage of finance and production ability to this market is a second stage.

The great success of Marks & Spencer Ltd in the United Kingdom has not been due primarily to selling, but to changes in basic policy which resulted in a reorientation of the business to meet a different market situation. This was due to identification of the main framework forces acting on the consumer-goods markets, the ability to analyse these forces, and to draw the correct conclusions from this analysis. Had this company applied the most sophisticated selling techniques within its old policy framework, it could not have approached the success it has achieved by moderate selling based on a good policy which foresaw and responded to changes in the distribution of purchasing power. Its pre-war product, quality and price ranges were not compatible with the post-war marketing forces.

The British co-operative movement demonstrates the consequences of inability to identify the socio-economic factors or, if these were identified, then an apathy in responding to them. This movement, as a whole, made little attempt to reorientate itself in the light of changes in the pattern of family budgets with a smaller percentage going on food and more to durables and services[1]; was unwilling to come to terms with a new class

1. This over-dependence on foodstuffs is not the sole cause of the stagnation of the British co-operative movement in the mid-twentieth century, but, in so far as a larger share of family budgets is going to non-food products and these have a higher profit margin, then the movement was acting incorrectly in not diversifying its range. Nevertheless, there are large multiples with a bigger bias towards food than the co-operatives, and these have not attracted attention by their inability to prosper; in fact the reverse is the

structure based on the new distribution of income and education; ignored the impact of national branding promotions on an affluent society seeking personal satisfaction through brands catering for idiosyncrasies; and refused to appreciate the reduced attraction of delayed discounts, the dividend, in a well-to-do welfare-state economy. Although other factors, related purely to selling, have helped to retard this once-great consumer movement, basically its stagnation has been owing to incorrect framework identification and analysis.

British motor-cycle sales were threatened as soon as they reached the price, and approached the fuel consumption, of the smaller car, at a time when the members of their old market were better placed financially. The marketeer ignored the fact that the motor-cycle was not loved for itself by the bulk of its old market, but only as a substitute for, or a stepping-stone to, a car. The product policy of the manufacturers should have accepted this as given and then searched for a new product suitable for their assets and capable of being distributed through their established names and channels. This might well have led to the conclusion that the need was for a cheap and convenient form of transport for that segment of the market which could not afford to buy or run a car, but which also could not afford the type of motor-cycle which was being produced. The scooter is a logical outcome of this analysis of manufacturing assets and the socio-economic forces in the market.

In all these cases, it would be fair to say that the most able selling would have failed in the face of the strong forces acting against the companies and industries concerned. Correct analysis of the framework of marketing coupled with only average selling ability is in most cases better than the application of good sales plans to an inadequate analysis and a badly identified objective. Growth firms and industries are those which recognize the forces at work within a market and respond quickly, sympathetically and scientifically to them.

case, e.g. Allied Suppliers, Sainsbury's. The current desire of food stores to move into non-food items, and for established non-food multiples and departmental stores to set up food departments, tends to demonstrate that inadequate product range is rarely the sole cause of decline in retailing.

1. The 'Given' Factors – Ethical

ETHICS AND PROFITS

IN marketing, the test of what ought to be done is a conflicting one. On the one hand there is the economic necessity for maximizing profit or for sheer economic survival; on the other hand there is the code of behaviour which is held to be correct by society at large. The individual concerned in marketing decisions may have some difficulty in reconciling the two aspects of his problem.

The package consultant who so designs a pack as to give a deceptive idea of size; the artist or copywriter who exploits basic human weaknesses rather than informs; the sales manager whose recommendations on price and quantity relationships encourage impulse purchasing; all could be considered unethical. The battle between the ultimate buyer and the seller in the consumer market is between a professional and an amateur.[1] At the same time, where the aim of the business is long-term profitability rather than short-term maximization of profits, then any unethical activity which became apparent to the customer would defeat the aim or objective. The speed with which it became apparent would vary with the knowledge of the customers, the speed of communications between them, and the degree of dissatisfaction created by the difference between the expected satisfaction created by sales-promotion methods and realized satisfaction after purchase.

If we define unethical marketing as the use of any methods which utilize emotions not directly associated with the product, then the bulk of modern consumer marketing techniques might have to fall into this category. However, in so far as social drives receive fulfilment in the possession of certain goods, these

1. At this point, it should be remembered that in marginally profitable markets only a small proportion of alert customers can remove the profitability of the enterprise; ethical policies and alertness of customers are clearly related.

emotions, it could be argued, are directly associated with the product or its possession. When the range of articles offered for sale contains many which are close substitutes one for another, then merely making factual descriptive statements would lead to stalemate. Faced with this situation of similarity, the marketeer must find something unique about his product or create a distinctive feature by sales promotion.

Factual and informative advertising of many goods would be a useless selling exercise and so resort has to be made to potentially associated emotions or synthesized psychological extensions to the product; motivation research into the subconscious of the consumer provides the necessary information on emotions which can be exploited. Alcoholic drinks are not sold on their intrinsic intoxicating potential, but by showing that they are a social necessity or an indication of masculinity. Cigarette marketeers use the herd instinct, emulation and sex to persuade people to buy a product which would be difficult to sell by factual description.

Should a manufacturer find himself in a 'gullible' market, could he be expected to follow an ethical packaging policy in contrast to the policy of his competitors? In a self-service market, would the smaller-looking, less attractive pack gain custom? If sex is used to attract by competitors, dare one firm stick to factual presentation? Clearly, in many cases the unethical is potentially the more profitable. However, we shall examine the dynamics of this later.

PLANNED OBSOLESCENCE, MOTIVATION RESEARCH AND ETHICS

The practice of sustaining sales by means of planned obsolescence is commercially a valid exercise. The slightly defective component or finish; the use of peripheral design changes; the lowering of the general durability of a product; all can be justified by reference to the need to maintain a market which is sufficient to make an enterprise with fixed assets profitable.

Motivation research at some levels has always been and must

continue to be the basic tool of all good marketeers. The fact that it is now more systematized does not in itself make it more unethical; rather is it the new lower level on which it is conducted which makes it suspect.

Branding, with its word connotations and associated images, is a vital part of selling in an affluent society but, in so far as the connotation given to a product by its name is not related to the real intrinsic value of that product, then questions of ethics will arise; the customer is being sold an illusion of a product rather than a reality. However, in affluent societies the extra increment of satisfaction which is obtained from a branded product which gives distinction, social standing, or caters for idiosyncrasies, must be considered before coming to any dogmatic conclusion on ethics.

Packaging must take the place of product design in the marketing plans of many goods which do not lend themselves to design, e.g. cornflakes, sugar, etc. Package design must appeal, like product design, to the motivation of the customer. Where this motivation tends to be emotional, then the way is open for unethical practices. Shapes, colours and sizes may be chosen to appeal to subconscious drives which have been uncovered by motivation research. If competitors are using packs which exploit these basic emotions, then the package designer would be unwise in many markets to act otherwise. Packaging which is aimed at encouraging impulse purchasing by using a combination of price, quantity and size of pack can be considered as unethical almost by definition, but it is often commercially the correct answer to a marketing problem.[2]

Any act of selling involves the modification of the potential customer's spontaneous needs to suit the product or service being offered; without this activity the provision of goods and services in the quantities, at the cost and at the time that we want them would be impossible. The claims made by an advertisement or a

2. This was and still is the situation in certain markets such as breakfast cereals, detergents, bar chocolate, biscuits and confectionery. These are also good examples of a weakness in legislation protecting consumers, which makes an indication of weight obligatory in many cases but these weights are not 'standard' ones, such as 4 oz., 8 oz., 1 lb., etc.

salesman may be true, but they are intended to highlight only those parts of the product which will persuade the customer to buy. The claims made are rarely comprehensive; they do not cover the total amalgam of qualities which the article possesses. This fundamental characteristic of selling is perhaps the most open to the charge of being 'unethical'; it implies a biased description to the favour of the seller.

As goods become more complex, the problem of complete appraisal at the point of sale becomes more difficult for the average customer in the consumer market. In so far as the customer cannot adequately assess the products available for purchase, then the need for preselling is apparent; an image of the product must be in his mind and, if possible, a predisposition to buy a certain brand before he reaches the point of sale. Articles which are technical may have to be sold on non-technical appeals; scientific brand names or model numbers are used to give a good connotation; semi-technical jargon may be used in advertising copy. All these are devices to promote a product because of the lack of technical know-how of the potential customer. It would be difficult to think of any alternative methods of sales promotion, given the nature of the product and the ignorance of the average customer.

It might be contended that the national standards enjoyed by certain societies would not be possible without the scale of production used, but that this scale is only viable because it is supported by positive marketing – some of which might be unethical.

ETHICAL POLICIES IN PRACTICE

Good marketeers assume that some degree of mental alertness exists on the part of their customers or potential customers, a level of awareness which covers not only a knowledge of the product being sold but also the methods used in selling it. If this awareness is high, then the code of selling behaviour must be high to be successful; this is the situation in the industrial market and in some segments of the consumer market. If the level of customer awareness is low, then the development of unethical activities to exploit this can be expected.

The degree of awareness in the market can vary from time to time, within a country, and even within a product market. Increased awareness of selling techniques can result from the spread of education and the content of that education; the development of consumer associations and the publicity given to their activities[3]; trends in newspaper readership and the editorial policies of newspapers; the attitude of those responsible for radio and television towards consumer enlightenment; and the public utterances of people in the public eye, such as Ministers of the Crown, Members of Parliament, churchmen, etc. The publicity surrounding legislation to protect consumers and cases brought under existing legislation will both tend to affect the alertness of the customers within a market. Awareness can also result from communication between customers.

Sometimes the level of awareness within a market and the incipient demand for more ethical treatment may result from the actions of individual firms who, by trading with an ethical policy, draw attention to the less ethical activities of others. If one manufacturer of biscuits says that 'weight matters', he draws attention to the impulse pack policies of less ethical firms; if one retail store achieves a more ethical image, it highlights the others.[4]

3. In all matters of consumer education the effectiveness is dependent on the segment of the market under treatment. Thus, if the more alert belong to consumer associations and read those newspapers which carry product tests, then the net effect of this education will be less than would be the case if the less alert segment of a market were exposed to these influences. One of the weaknesses of consumer associations in the United Kingdom is that they have tended to be patronized by the already more alert segment of the market.

4. The impact of the multiple-store order on the power of the manufacturer may have had considerable effect in those markets which were imperfect, whether with regard to competition between producers or weakness and ignorance on the part of customers. To the extent that the multiples compete with each other and are of equal strength to the producers, the lack of competition previously found among the producers and possibly retailers will be replaced by competition among the multiples. The atomistic ignorant consumer market will be replaced by a few influential and knowledgeable buyers to the probable benefit of the ultimate consumer. The

The onset of more stringent economic pressures on any purchaser will tend to reduce the emotional content of the purchasing activity. In the industrial field, economics almost always rules, and in less affluent societies the unethical appeal to emotions will probably be less effective than it would be after biological needs have been easily met. Even in affluent societies, the desire to buy more material goods and services than can be easily accommodated by a person's purchasing power may lead to an increasing awareness of the economic content of the buying activity, with a consequent greater awareness of the emotional and perhaps less ethical aspect: the desire to buy cars can lead to a more economic and rational approach to foodstuffs and clothes.

Policy decisions on ethical content will be determined jointly by a study of the degree of awareness within a market and the policies of competitors. The ethical content or standard should be the one which, in the existing conditions, maximizes profits either in the short or long period, whichever is of interest to the enterprise. Generally, the shorter the period under consideration, and the less the need for repeat patronage, the lower the standard of ethics required.

In a period of increased customer awareness and, at the same time, some degree of unethical behaviour on the part of competitors, the better policy might be a contrasting ethical one; the very existence of unethical practices would enhance the comparative ethical standing of the non-conformist. The profitability of ethical trading would depend on the potential demand for it, relative to the profits to be gained by maintaining the present standard.

In the industrial field the knowledge of the customer rules out unethical selling except in the sense that false claims might be made, e.g. on quality or delivery dates, to gain an order. The outcome of such behaviour in this market would be disastrous because of the nature of the customer and of communications between customers. Even in this market a distinction or comparative selling advantage can be gained by a reputation of

multiple is acting as a powerful intermediary between the strong producer and the individually weak customer. Thus multiples can completely reverse the previous buying-selling situation.

complete dependability and honesty in all that is said by the servants of the business.

Once an ethical standard has been decided on by the policy-makers of a business, then it must be communicated to all those who influence consumer attitudes towards the business or its product. In this way consistency of action throughout the organization will be achieved. Recruitment, induction, training, method of payment, and sales-promotion policies will all be geared to the ethical standard set for the enterprise. All those concerned with selling require special attention, both those within the firm and the agencies and advisers from outside. Everyone employed in the persuasion of people to buy the product or service of the enterprise must know their ethical terms of reference, good or bad.

CONCLUSION

This chapter is not intended as an indictment of the methods used in modern marketing to exploit the gullibility and ignorance of customers. Rather is it an attempt to show that some breaking of the ethical code of our private lives is widely accepted in sustaining the sales needed to make industry viable. The situation is dynamic and varies between different classes of goods and even within single markets. The marketeer assesses the awareness of his market and constructs a marketing policy, within the law, to maximize profits assuming this awareness. In a dynamic situation he may identify a more alert segment or potentially alert segment which he may find profitable to exploit by using a different method with perhaps a higher standard of ethics. The awareness of the market and the trading standards of his competitors are parts of the marketing framework which are 'given'.

2. The 'Given' Factors – Economic

ALL economic activity, of which buying and selling is a part, takes place in, and is part of, the grand state of the national or international economy. Many buying decisions are influenced directly by the actual state of the economy at the time of the decision-taking; this occurs when the amount of purchasing power itself has been affected by the economy, either for or against certain types of purchase. All marketing requires the availability of purchasing power, but the extent of this availability, both in total and its distribution, is a given factor beyond the control of even the largest commercial undertaking.

THE GREAT STAGES OF
ECONOMIC DEVELOPMENT AND MARKETING

The great stages of economic development are of special interest to policy decision-takers in marketing, because one of the distinguishing features of each stage is an emphasis on a particular form of development or outlay of the national income. In the second or transitional stage (from the traditional non-trading society) there is an emphasis on agriculture, but some attention is also paid to the accumulation of social capital in the form of education, transport facilities, power supplies and health services. In the third or take-off stage there is increasing industrialization and consequently a greater proportion of the national income is spent on capital goods. The fourth stage, which takes the society up to technological maturity, will see a further increase in the allocation of income to capital goods, probably over a wider range of industries. The stage following technological maturity is that of high mass consumption and it is this which is mostly at the heart of modern marketing. This stage is indicated by a large increase in income per head, reaching a point where a fund of discretionary purchasing power is available because of income being in excess of the basic needs. Consumer-durables begin to figure more prominently in outlays. This fund of wealth beyond real needs may give rise to increased social outlays on education, health services and the welfare state, overseas aid to developing countries, and military commitments, basically generated by the desire to preserve the high standard of living. Service industries begin to assume importance.

Beyond mass-consumption societies there is the possibility and consequence of reduced marginal satisfaction from material goods as society becomes satiate. This type of situation can perhaps be seen where the first wave of mass-consumption durables have been purchased, thus making sustained marketing dependent on the net utility gain of the replacement article and the disutility of the labour needed to obtain the means to purchase it.

In addition to these grand economic stages and their product or outlay idiosyncrasies, there are trends in the relative costs of the factors of production and distribution which also interest the marketeer and to which reference will be frequently made. Thus, the high cost of labour and land relative to capital of mass-consumption societies is of great importance in the distribution of goods; labour costs are important in the sale of labour-saving devices; land values affect the demand for building types, ventilation equipment, etc.

CYCLICAL TRENDS AND MARKETING

Certain types of buying are wholly affected by the current state of a national economy: inflation, deflation, reflation, recession, boom, 'stop', 'go', credit restriction, credit derestriction, credit expansion – all affect buying. Investment decisions on the purchasing of industrial equipment are not wholly affected by the current situation, but an amalgam of estimates of the future and the circumstances at the time of the decision-taking.

Enlightened governments exercise some control over the amount and direction of the nation's purchasing power, either through taxation, monetary policy or physical planning. Scientific marketeers must be aware of cyclical tendencies and their effects on the market for particular classes of goods and services. Similarly, they must also be acutely alive to the possibility and nature of government influence to affect these markets.

The various theories of the trade cycle are concerned primarily with saving and the propensity to purchase consumer and industrial goods; government policies and intervention are often intended to affect these propensities. The significance of these purchasing patterns is very important to the marketeer.

All these marketing decisions revolve around the fact that booms and slumps are 'given' and that these conditions affect luxuries and necessities in opposite ways; booms favour luxuries, slumps turn customers towards the necessities of life. The fact that an economy has reached the mass-consumption stage makes recessional swings more obviously a major factor in marketing durable postponable goods; a stock of these is already possessed, and replacement can more easily be delayed. Certain industries may be adversely affected by affluence: bread and certain types of fish may be recognized as unsatisfactory foods which will only be consumed with enthusiasm when economic circumstances dictate. Action is needed to change customers' attitudes, to alter price–quality relationship to elevate the image of the product, or broaden the product range.

Upgrading or downgrading of goods and the broadening of product ranges are the more obvious reactions to reconcile marketing policies with the 'given' economic circumstances, but in some cases the individual firm may go beyond this. The decision to move into another quality or price range,[1] or to diversify products, may result in the taking-over of existing firms with

1. 'Trading up' is the name given to product policies which, by increasing the value (price) of each unit sold, endeavour to participate in the increasing affluence of their customers. Such policies are apparent in the food industry with its more sophisticated products; consumer-durables such as furniture, domestic equipment, cars, etc.; clothes of all types; holidays and travel, etc. etc. These policies have much to recommend them in that they utilize the current assets, i.e. goodwill of the enterprise, to the full in terms of profitability; the better-off customer will continue to patronize the familiar brand or shop but, in keeping with a new state of affluence and the motivation based on this, will make more expensive purchases.

established markets in the areas or segments desired. This diversification by take-over broadens the basis of the company's activities so that it is more able to meet different socio-economic conditions. However, should a company be producing a product which is a low-price necessity and this has involved heavy outlay in equipment, this outlay and its marketing consequences are not reduced by the taking-over of another company which is selling a product more in keeping with affluence. The better policy in terms of real risk-reduction is to reorientate the current production asset to a product compatible with the new conditions.

Dynamic marketing to maintain maximum profitability regardless of the state of the economy is always needed in all fields. Industrial marketeers must respond to price-consciousness created out of these conditions. Retailers must vary the price-quality image of their stores to suit the currently most profitable segment of the trade.

We now turn our attention to more specific economic factors, some of which can change rapidly; the grand phase may show a need to cater for more leisure; the cyclical trend may reinforce this; but the decision to tax leisure pursuits would demand a quick reaction to adjust policy and execution to a new and perhaps unexpected situation.

IMMEDIATE ECONOMIC INFLUENCES ON MARKETING

Although the size and rate of growth of the national income, and so of purchasing power, are of first-rate importance to market planners, the distribution of this purchasing power is perhaps even more so.

We have seen how in certain phases of economic growth the proportions allocated to the purchases of capital goods will tend to increase; there are also trends even within the grand stages where the amount of national income devoted to industrial and consumer goods will vary. If an economy chooses, either by state planning or private decision, or a combination of both, to increase its stock of capital goods by modernizing equipment, constructing more roads and railways, increasing research, building hospitals and schools, developing military might or promoting national prestige projects, then the producers of consumer goods can only benefit indirectly from such means of using the national income; producers of industrial goods will have a direct interest in such developments.

If the central government took positive action to redistribute purchasing power so that the ability to buy consumer goods was reduced in direct proportion to the increasing production of capital goods, then the consequences to the marketeer of consumer goods could be considerable. This type of government action can result in increased taxation on consumer goods to 'mop up' purchasing power; increased taxation of incomes; direct control over the supply of consumer goods and the consequent increase in savings, due to inability to buy; or 'controlled' rises in prices which again 'mop up' consumer income.

Any business which has assets which are capable of producing a flexible range of end-products must reorientate its product policy to meet the current and future allocation of national purchasing power. This may involve a switch from the consumer to the industrial market; or from private buying to government departments and local authorities. The building industry and its component suppliers can switch from private to public, from houses to schools, offices, factories, shops, etc., as the purchasing-power trend manifests itself.

Where national planning has become an accepted part of the tools of government, then the scientific marketeer is aided in any assessment of future developments in that it can be assumed that fiscal and other methods will be used to achieve the objectives set out in the plan.

National economies dependent on international trade, if subject to planning, will endeavour to sustain the investment in up-to-date methods of production either to foster exports or replace imports; where balance of payments problems are serious, the need to plan in this direction is increased. Similar plans would emerge from underdeveloped countries making a positive effort to build up their economies. Companies selling overseas will watch, not only the national plans of the countries to which they are marketing, but also the development of international economic plans and rehabilitation schemes.[2]

Basically, the successful company must change direction to fit the dynamics of the national allocation of resources; such a change could affect the whole structure and philosophy of a firm. Research and development may need to be reappraised; quality policy adjusted; price may become more or less related to production costs depending on whether the change is towards or away from industrial goods; design will be similarly influenced as to its real purpose, functional or emotional. Sales-promotion plans may be even more seriously disturbed. Assuming a switch from consumer goods and private buying, a new type of sales force with greater technical knowledge may be needed; the sales organization may be changed to deal with a more clearly demarcated and numerically smaller market; advertising and branding might be greatly reduced and changed in content; in some cases personal selling, in the conventional sense, may disappear and be replaced by contract work open to tender. Similar types of movement within design, quality, price and sales-promotion policies will also be needed when purchasing power is redistributed among groups within the private consumer section.

In mass-consumption societies the rate of growth of non-durable goods markets is directly related to the rate of growth of population. Specific goods may also be related to particular sections of that population – ethnic groups, male or female, young or old, married and unmarried, etc. The distribution of the population throughout a country is also clearly important to sales planners. The growth rate of durable consumer goods markets in these circumstances is more closely related to changes in national income and in the distribution of that income. Equal distribution will favour markets for necessities and lower-price durables; unequal distribution will favour higher-price luxury goods at the expense of lower-priced goods and necessities.

Wage trends are an obvious influence on purchasing power,

2. It must not be overlooked that this information contained in public plans is known to all who look for it. To that extent the degree of competition for the realigned purchasing power may still be great and call for top-class sales policies.

showing the sales planner the relative affluence of each section of the community. This can be regarded in terms of industry, region, age groups, sex groups, etc., whichever is relevant to the marketeer; if wages to teenagers go up in general, this is information which can be exploited; if a region is adversely affected by wage trends or unemployment, this also is relevant to sales plans. Although the total amount of money available for spending is of significance to all marketeers, many show a special interest in that part of income which is available for discretionary spending. Wage drift, in so far as it shows available purchasing power in excess of the conventional needs of a section of a community, is of prime importance to marketeers.

Progressive direct taxation and subsidized social services, houses, children's allowances, etc. have the effect of reducing the number of people at the two extremes of the income spectrum. There will be fewer excessively rich and fewer really poor, and the bulk of the income will fall into the middle income category, although this may cover a wide range.

Manufacturers must cater for the existing distribution of the national income and, if this distribution changes, so should their sales policies. Any improvement in the position of the surtax payer should draw a response from those manufacturers who are able to upgrade their products and services. Subsidized housing, where rents are not related to income, has the effect of transferring purchasing power from the non-discretionary segment, i.e. housing or shelter, to the discretionary one. Subsidies will have the same effect on discretionary purchasing power as a reduction in the higher rates of income tax, although probably at different levels of price and quality – both would increase the amount available for luxury and consumer-durable spending.

Any form of subsidy affects the pattern of purchasing by reducing the price charged to the customer, but not the revenue received by the producer. Both producer and consumer are therefore the recipients of additional discretionary purchasing power. The marketeer must find this purchasing power and exploit it.

Double incomes could also be powerful determinants in the availability of discretionary purchasing power and be of special interest to marketeers of goods and services purchased by house-holds, e.g. furniture, cars, holidays. The entrance of another in-come into the household may not materially affect the basic 'cost of living' of the household unit, in which case all the second in-come would be added to the fund of discretionary purchasing power of the family. The consequence could be a general up-grading of the heights of the purchaser.

Although it may no longer be realistic to regard class stratifica-tion as a universally reliable term of reference in marketing, income being more important than class, the extent of discretion-ary purchasing power may have a class basis in some cases. Thus, if a particular section of a community had an aversion to local authority housing or public education, then this attitude would require the use of purchasing power for its satisfaction which would otherwise have been available for discretionary purchases. Consequently, although we talk of 'middle-cost' goods rather than middle-class ones, class consciousness should not be ignored.

The types of influence on purchasing power so far discussed are not likely to be over-night revolutionary changes in national policy, but rather evolutionary changes. There are, however, other governmental actions which can be more sudden.

INDIRECT TAXATION

One of the most obvious, and most direct, forms of interference by governments in marketing is the imposition of a tax on goods. Although the size of the tax may often be completely unknown, the good marketeer should normally have some prior knowledge of the intention of imposing such taxes. Every sales plan must have built-in qualifications concerning the possible effect of taxation, so that sales can be measured against a realistic stand-ard; increases and decreases in tax render most sales estimates out of date.

A decision must be taken on the division of the incidence of the tax between manufacturer, distributor and customer. This would depend upon the elasticity of demand for the end-product and the importance of the distributor in the scheme of selling; where the elasticity is great and the dealer is assisted by massive brand advertising, the manufacturer might feel justified in sharing the bulk of the tax with the dealer rather than shedding it on to the customer. Other lines of response to tax change might include a change in the price and quality of the product, particularly in price-conscious markets; any reduction in basic price resulting in an even greater reduction where an *ad valorem* tax is applied.

The potential selling aid of an *ad valorem* tax must not be overlooked – it can be said to be a sales aid to the more efficient; any cost saving incurred in any section of manufacturing, selling and distribution, prior to the point at which an *ad valorem* tax is applied to the product, is enhanced to the extent of that tax.

As such taxes apply to all firms making a specified product, then it is really a tax on inefficiency; the more efficient firm can actually benefit from its imposition in that any price differential over competitors is increased by the tax. This whole argument does not imply that the total market will not be affected by the imposition of a tax; clearly to the extent that the demand is elastic, it will be reduced. However, by the same reckoning, this elasticity will transfer customers to those firms able to show a greater price-advantage differential after the tax imposition.

Taxes on goods are frequently imposed on goods entering from outside a market. This might result in restricted imports by total ban, licences and quotas, or by the imposition of increased import duties where the national balance has become negative; liberalization of trade will perhaps follow when the country's indebtedness has improved. Every marketeer must be able to project or extrapolate the possible consequences of an overseas balance to the market for his own goods. If a company is currently protected from overseas competition by a restriction on the import of goods, it should constantly study the relative positions of its own and competing products if there were no such restrictions. This type of analysis might then show certain strengths and weaknesses of both the home-produced and the foreign products which could be developed to the advantage of the home company. A company making fertilizers for British farmers behind a protective duty might, on seeing the possible entry of the United

Kingdom into a larger European market, begin to develop sales to domestic gardeners; the smaller units of sale found in this market would not be so susceptible to transport economies as the bulk supplies needed by farmers, and so the home producer would retain an economic advantage in the new situation.

GOVERNMENTAL MONETARY POLICY

The struggle in marketing is for purchasing power, and, to the extent that governmental policy restricts or changes the distribution of that purchasing power, so it affects marketing. Sales estimates made prior to a restriction on personal loans and overdrafts, more severe restrictions on hire-purchase dealings, or an increase in the cost of borrowing money are unrealistic after these changes.

Credit restrictions or increases in bank rate will affect the inventories held by manufacturing units, as these are affected by a reduction in the end-market which results in a lower scale of production. Lower inventories at production and distribution points, e.g. those held by retailers, to bring the stocks down to the new or expected level of sales are best achieved by not buying until the new level has been reached; but this implies not selling. Consequently, there might be a temporary severe drop in sales until a new level of stocks has been reached which is more compatible with the new level of buying; then the sales will increase, but not to the old level, as they are replacement sales in a deliberately reduced market.

Where a governmental credit policy has grander economic implications, e.g. the encouragement of export trade and the reduction of consumer-durable sales, then it may be possible for a company to reorientate its marketing towards the favoured sector.

PRICES AND INCOMES POLICIES AND MARKETING

Where a government is faced with a need to contain prices and incomes in order to ward off inflation, then certain consequences to marketing may follow.

Firstly, the income policy may be less favourable to the distribution side, particularly if emphasis is laid on relating increases in income to productivity.

Secondly, the necessity may arise for accommodating an increasing amount of costs,[3] such as material, selling and even distribution costs, into a more rigid end-price. If the ultimate production efficiency has been achieved, then any increase in material prices will have to be accommodated within the 'controlled' price by a reduction in selling and distribution costs or an increase in their efficiency.

In practice, this could result in a reduction in the importance of expensive sales-promotion activities. If reciprocal and costly advertising were used in an inelastic market, then the salutary nature of a prices and incomes policy might even create a new lower level of inter-brand sales promotion as the price becomes incapable of holding all the increased costs involved.

Should the central government introduce taxation priorities which favour manufacturing as against distribution and at the same time practise control of prices, then the continuing inefficiencies of transport and distribution would have to be offset by an even greater effort in those elements of sales policy which affect post-production costs. Packaging and the organization of depots would become more important.

The overall impact of a price 'freeze' or containment could be that greater emphasis will have to be placed on product and range policy to keep down costs and sell on product-patronage motives. Value analysis may be increasingly practised to reduce material costs, and regular and more intensive audits carried out into overall managerial and production efficiency. But the most serious consequence is likely to be felt in the non-manufacturing activities in that, whereas labour, materials and similar costs are easily identifiable and justified as a cause for an increase in price,

3. The inflationary reason for the policy in the first place.

any other costs, e.g. advertising, personal selling, dealer margins and distribution, may be more difficult to introduce to support a socially acceptable increase in price. The outcome would be that the firm would need to contain all its non-manufacturing costs within the smaller margin resulting from the new higher level of production costs and the 'frozen' price.[4]

INDUSTRIAL GOODS AND GOVERNMENTAL POLICY

Financial influences on the markets for the final consumer goods will be projected backwards to affect directly the market for raw materials, supplies and components, and to affect indirectly the decision to purchase new equipment for expansion or replacement. Any forecasting of the demand for tinplate or nylon would have to consider all the above-mentioned influences on the end consumer market.

In addition to these indirect influences, there are certain more specific ones which would affect the decision to buy capital equipment of all types; these are the taxation incentives given to those installing equipment, undertaking research, developing training, etc. The good industrial marketeer appreciates the effect of investment grants and depreciation allowances on the net cost of the equipment he is trying to market; financial inducements to encourage industry to settle in particular areas should be fully utilized; special grants to aid research and training etc. are helpful aids to selling. Taxation policies which distinguish between distributed and undistributed profits can distort the direction of capital investment; industrial marketeers follow the distorted purchasing power.

4. In many ways, this external analysis of total activities and costs could be the greatest incentive to efficiency – both in the production and post-production functions. Firms which cannot meet the conditions needed to remain profitable within a restricted price would be eliminated. It could be one method of rewarding efficiency and really penalizing inefficient management. The consequences would be felt on the level of the individual enterprise which could go out of business if it were inefficient; but it would also operate on a functional level as certain activities were condemned as being inefficient and/or not in the public interest.

CONCLUSION

Economic forces play a dominant part in influencing the extent and distribution of purchasing power, and therefore are of prime importance to the marketeer who must identify or locate purchasing power as a prerequisite to any other marketing or selling activity. These forces may be associated with the grand phases of economic development which tend to stimulate demands for certain classes of goods and services. The free play of economic forces may create periods of varying economic activity and so of purchasing power. Governments may step in to control economic swings, to redistribute the national income, to divert money to particular ends, or to encourage and discourage the consumption of certain goods and services. All these activities affect purchasing power and its location. Good marketing demands an understanding of these forces and their effect on the purchasing power of groups, without which marketing is impossible. All these factors are 'given'; the marketing plan must work within them. Economic escalators must be found – if possible going upwards.

3. The 'Given' Factors – Social

MARKETING is really a behaviour: it is a study of men persuading men through themselves and through the goods and services they are marketing; it requires a study of men being persuaded. The social environment of the customer must be investigated to discover the forces which influence him in the market; although purchasing is a private, esoteric activity, its terms of reference are increasingly social. Briefly we examine here the 'given' social factors which affect the market.

The terms of reference for an individual customer may come from within himself, as for example when he wishes to emulate others by the accumulation of goods and services which will show his position. In modern societies where the craft content of work has been reduced by modern production methods, where even the extent of his productive effort is beyond his control, and where physical combat and achievement is socially out and is replaced by organized displays, the individual might provide for his instinctive emulative needs by accumulating a stock of material goods and services. Modern society by frustrating an instinctive desire has created an ideal vehicle for stimulating sales of material goods.

When society has passed the biological-needs stage, the terms of reference will change to more sophisticated needs associated with the society in which a consumer is living.

Conceivably, the principle of diminishing marginal utility may be applicable to a society's stock of material goods so that society will look increasingly to non-material means to achieve increases in satisfaction. This might result in increased families, or a greater awareness of the needs of others, both at home and overseas. Where the innovators have failed to create the necessary flow of desirable and therefore satisfying goods, the only outlays

65

available to the consumer will be on additional versions or replacements of the goods already possessed. The rate at which consumers will become dissatisfied with their present stock of material goods clearly depends on the additional satisfaction expected from the replacements as compared with that obtained from those already possessed.

Where a society exerts pressures which create social satisfaction out of the possession of goods, then the rate of diminishing marginal utility may be delayed, despite the inability of innovators to produce a stream of new types of products; the source of satisfaction in the newly launched product or model is now governed by the dissatisfaction associated with the continuing possession of the existing one which it replaces – the cult of 'this year's model'. Consumers may use the socio-economic group in which they are living as the terms of reference for purchasing, or they could refer to standards of an assumed higher socio-economic group to which they aspire. Where the terms of reference are fundamentally material, then the marketeer is aided by this social ethos; but need they be material?

The peripheral or discretionary purchases of this generation may appear to be the conventional necessities of the next, but this assumes the existence of a stratum of goods and services above those possessed by each new generation and made desirable either by their intrinsic value or by reference to the purchasing and social ethos of society.

The inclusion of wellbeing rather than wealth as an element in a consumer's living standard could result from a personal psychophysical assessment[1] of the relative satisfaction expected from the goods and the dissatisfaction of labour; but it could, perhaps, assume a smaller increase of satisfaction from the goods than would be the case where possession of goods was the main criterion of social standing. To the extent that society moves towards wellbeing as a desirable condition, then the individual's social terms of reference will also move in this direction. This could greatly prejudice marketing.

In addition to the grand sociological terms of reference con-

1. Such an assessment would also consider the guilt complex of 'not working'; this is basically a product of the society's attitude towards leisure.

cerning the desire to possess goods and services, there are others which influence the types of goods and service. Where the desire for wellbeing results in a demand for more leisure this could lead to a realignment of consumer purchasing; leisure itself need not be a lost marketing opportunity but it may require a new orientation of product or service.[2]

Any form of class consciousness based on the possession of goods and services is an advantage to the marketeer; the design of products, packaging, brand names, advertising, price policy and even the choice of retail outlets are used as instruments to exploit the desire of customers to show that they belong to one social group rather than another. The 'Jonesmanship' of the 1950s and 1960s in the United Kingdom was a product of the confluence of two forces; the class basis of the society, and the input into the economic system of an unprecedented flow of goods and services, many of them new, which allowed this class consciousness to manifest itself.

What the marketing problems of the post-maturity or post-mass-consumption stage of economic development will be is not yet known, but there is reason to assume that if the hallmark of wellbeing and social position moves away from the possession of a stock of material goods, then marketing will be faced with difficulties not previously encountered.

OTHER SOCIAL FACTORS

There is not an automatic or universal acceptance of women, and more specifically married ones, being gainfully employed in industry, commerce and the professions. The attitude towards this may vary from one country to another, or even within a country. Class influence may also play a part. Again, some types of work may be socially acceptable but others not. The impact of war,

2. The possession of an automatic washing machine could be a source of leisure in that it reduces the burden of work and gives greater time and energy for leisure pursuits. Washing machines are not sold by appealing to laziness, but by showing that the time and energy saved by their use can be devoted to leisure, preferably within the family circle.

universal suffrage, education, emancipation of women, and the nature of work will all affect attitudes towards women being at work. Even the desire to acquire a stock of goods and services in class-conscious, affluent societies may not be enough to offset the social opprobrium of a wife working. To the marketeer these social influences are of vital significance, because they help to determine the availability of double incomes in a household unit, and so the amount of discretionary purchasing power in that unit.

The acceptance of credit could also depend on social terms of reference. Religious training could be allied to a class attitude towards buying goods on credit terms. It may even tend to distinguish between different types of credit; bank overdrafts and personal loans are 'in', hire purchase is 'out'. Credit can even be said to become respectable. If credit is ruled out, then the range of competing goods will be much smaller in affluent societies.

One of the major influences on most of the social forces is, of course, education. The method and content of education might lead to a new approach to the concept of wellbeing, greater acceptance of women working, and a more intelligent appraisal of credit buying. In addition, education could contribute to-towards 'public taste'; the emphasis on free expression in art education could, perhaps, lead to a more flexible attitude on the part of customers towards changes in the design of goods. Taste, itself, could also be affected by the general aesthetic environment of the customer: school fitments; street furniture; the interior and exterior of public buildings; shops and offices; the design of public transport vehicles; the standards projected by mass-communication media; and the general advisory and mandatory government activities, such as the Council of Industrial Design and the powers of planning authorities in the United Kingdom. Clearly, the more the design of a product is in sympathy with the general trend, the more likely it is to be accepted by the market at large.

Sometimes, design trends are discernible even to the layman; the tendency towards functionalism in architecture and then throughout all industrial design has been a feature of the last three decades in the United Kingdom. Functionalism and hygiene have often been projected jointly when people have become increasingly health- or dirt-conscious. Functionalism and cost-consciousness are also fortunately coincidental in contemporary design.

Education must be considered a major influence on the consumer by affecting his knowledge at the point of purchase. Educational curricula might deal directly with marketing practices and household economics, but just as effective might be the influence of education in general on the degree of awareness of the customer. A demand may be created for a 'better' type of newspaper which tends to be more critical. Education is a dominant contributor to customer awareness.

The exploitation of sexual instincts in marketing is frequently considered an ethical matter which is influenced by the general attitude of society. The liberalization of entrenched positions towards sex could perhaps lead to a reduced use of it for selling purposes as the 'novelty' aspect began to recede.

Social influences might be better observed when they are rudely interrupted. It has been suggested that the attitude of the United States towards profligacy changed when the nation was jolted by the first Russian sputnik; the purchase of more, bigger and shinier cars became suspect.

Other influences of importance to marketing are the dominance of various groups within a national ethos; this could involve paedocentric philosophies, a highly exploitable phenomenon; woman worship, equally commercially useful; or the liberalization of teenagers, with well observed marketing consequences.

As with the economic factors dealt with previously, the social factors are 'given' to the marketeer; he takes them and exploits them to the best of his ability. There is, however, a difference in that the very activity of marketing may help to generate or increase the strength of social factors; marketing, which exploits class-consciousness, could increase it; the availability of goods on credit might increasingly help to overcome any emotions working against this form of buying; the promotion of certain designs might advance or retard the standard of aesthetics. Nevertheless, such influences would be slow-moving and would not affect the immediate problem of the marketeer, that of identifying, quantifying and exploiting the social influences on his market.

4. Other 'Given' Factors

THE three previous chapters dealt with some of the more dominant 'given' factors, but there are others which, although not such powerful influences, are still important for decision-taking in marketing.

THE LAW AND CUSTOMS OF THE TRADE

In most societies there is a body of statutory or common law to protect the customer against unscrupulous selling methods. In sophisticated democracies, where complex selling methods are used, the political atmosphere might make consumer protection obligatory.

Marketing must stay within the law of the land. However, there are other terms of reference which, though not legally binding, can greatly circumscribe the freedom of action of the marketeers.

The power to enforce a common price or condition of sale may or may not be permitted by law, but this does not rule out common prices or conditions. The strength of an association might be such that it merely advises its members, and this brings about the necessary results. Where trade associations can enforce conditions of sale, then the consequences to a manufacturer or retailer of defying the conditions prescribed could be disastrous; the strength of the sanctions is equal to the value of the business.

Sometimes, formal association is not needed to create a term of reference for the conduct of those within a trade or market; the maintenance of the *status quo* is often a strong enough incentive in established markets to restrict marketing conduct to certain well defined 'rules' governing the extension of credit, dealer profit margins, the conditions of after-sales service and, of course, price.

Inertia in trading policies can also result from price leadership, which implies that competition will be restricted to non-price fields; price may be 'fixed,' but advertising therefore becomes more active. Wherever there is pressure, formal or informal, to restrict the freedom in one section of competitive marketing, then an additional burden is thrown on to other sections. Retailers who are not allowed to cut prices will improve the amenities of their shops; petrol companies with common price policies will try to influence customers by high-pressure advertising and control of filling stations; durable consumer goods manufacturers, faced with 'fixed' common dealer profit margins, will have to use methods outside the dealer to promote their products.

DEPENDENT DEMAND

In markets where an intimate joint-demand relationship exists, one of the main influences on total market potential is under the control of other marketeers. Records depend on radiograms; garden equipment on gardens; kitchen equipment on houses with space for it.

This type of relationship can be a guide to various policy decisions for the dependent product. Sales forecasts can be more accurately given by mere reference to the trend of sales of the other product; price policy may be influenced directly by the value relationship, e.g. the cost of buying a motor-car tyre is negligible when considered against the price of the car which it makes useful.

The dependent-demand product can be said to be at a disadvantage because of its lack of freedom to develop markets even where there is some lack of good marketing on the part of the main-product promoters. But, by definition, the converse is true.

The industrial market is pre-eminently one dominated by dependent demand. The total market for material and components is directly related to the demand for the end-products to which these contribute. The same situation exists in the sale of equipment which tends to be dependent on the state of a final market. In all these cases the marketeer can do little, if anything, to affect the total market for his product; it is 'given'.

THE EFFICIENCY OF OTHERS

All firms depend on others to a lesser or greater extent, either as contributors to production or as a means of distribution. A distinguishing feature of the modern manufacturing unit is that it is virtually an assembly plant at the hub of a huge complex of suppliers. This horizontal disintegration is likely to result in production economies, for it is possible that the suppliers, although inefficient, are relatively more efficient than the assembly firm could be; where this occurs, the effect of this inefficiency on the part of the supplier is felt by the main assembly unit. In the shipbuilding industry more than 70 per cent of the cost is bought out; any increase in efficiency in the yard itself would only have a small effect on the total price. Inadequate suppliers might also affect quality standards or the ability to maintain delivery dates – two vital aspects of competitive marketing.

When a manufacturer distributes and actively sells his products, as with most industrial goods, then the only external non-production factor which can affect him is the cost and efficiency of the transport available to him. Manufacturers of consumer goods selling direct to their customers, either by mail or through their own outlets, are in a similar situation. However, where it is necessary, for good commercial reasons, to use independent distributors, then clearly one of the most vital factors affecting the sale of goods is beyond the immediate control of the producer. The organization and efficiency of the distribution system at a given time is something which must be accepted. We must now examine the main characteristics of the distribution system, excluding transport, in order to have a better understanding of the decisions which have to be taken in this field by the manufacturers.

DISTRIBUTION – WHOLESALERS AND RETAILERS

Behind all problems of distribution, as with production, lies the consideration of costs – in particular, fixed costs. The retailer and wholesaler in their attempts to reduce costs per unit of throughput will try to achieve the most economical mixture of land, labour and capital. In mass-consumption societies, where land and labour tend to be costly relative to capital, there will be a tendency to increase the use of equipment and to replace labour; additionally, every effort must be made to make the maximum use of land. This is the economic justification for the replacement of traditional counter-service stores with self-service or self-selection stores.

The manufacturer must arrange for his whole policy to accommodate this reorientation of resources by the retailer, because the forces behind it are the product of deep-seated economic change. If self-service conversion requires large-scale initial capital outlay, even though in the long run this is justified, then this could result in increased domination of retailing by those companies able to finance the necessary conversions – joint-stock multiples.

Similarly, as land becomes more valuable, then this tendency to concentrate ownership into fewer, larger units will be sustained; these units being more able to afford the increased site values or, by take-overs facilitated by joint-stock organizations, to secure control of retail outlets already occupying good and valuable sites. Manufacturers must accept this as a 'given' factor in their distribution policies; to support independent retailers would be acting against basic economic factors.[1]

The cost of labour tends to be a fixed cost in retailing and, if this cost is increased because of the scarcity of the type of labour required, then the self-service store is an automatic solution; it replaces skilled labour by unskilled, and labour in general by capital.[2] The manufacturer using this type of outlet must design and pack his product in order to reduce to a minimum the amount of skilled labour needed at the retail point.

The multiple store could also well reinforce its strong market-

1. In countries where restrictions are placed on land use, the pressure on existing land is even greater; with a consequent increase in site values and so of the fixed costs of retailing, e.g. restrictions on 'ribbon' development in the United Kingdom.

2. The multiple type of retail organization (with or without wholesaler participation) is also better placed to employ the necessary specialists to advise on the most efficient use of expensive labour, capital and space.

ing position *vis-à-vis* manufacturers by utilizing the appeal of its bulk orders to the practitioners of modern production planning.

The attitude of manufacturers towards middle-men is a result of an analysis of trends in shopping habits and retailing. The more the larger retailer dominates a particular market to the detriment of the small unit store, the less the need to use wholesalers in distribution.

In most markets there are conventional gross profit margins in distribution. The manufacturer must recognize these or, if he decides on margins which do not conform, then he may have to adopt a positive promotion and distribution policy. Should he alienate dealer support, then it may be necessary to increase advertising to counter this.

The restricting effect of the price, which is involved if conventional margins are maintained, may be so great that it is detrimental to the marketing policy of the enterprise, e.g. it may possess modern and efficient idle capacity in a market which is saturated at the currently inflated level of prices. If such a firm can reduce market prices by cutting down the profit margins of dealers, then the demand may benefit in a price-conscious, elastic market, particularly if it can benefit from the continuing conformity to margins of its competitors.

The scientific marketeer when planning distribution policies will identify the basic socio-economic factors which can influence the pattern of retailing and distribution. On to the fundamental economic bases are superimposed economic and social influences peculiar to a region or even a town; the control of development; the counter-attraction of non-retailing employment; attitudes towards shops themselves; laws on hours of business, etc.

Decisions are taken within a 'given' framework. If shop assistants who can really sell are not employed at retail level because of the inability for social reasons to recruit them or because they would be too expensive relative to other forms of selling, then the manufacturer must sell his product 'in spite of' the assistant not 'because' of him. If multiples are dominating a trade, then it may be madness to deal exclusively through wholesalers, as multiples tend to by-pass them.

CONCLUSION

Good marketing must be conscious of the framework in which it operates, otherwise it may well be wasted. An attempt has been made in this section to show some of the main ethical, economic, fiscal, social, trade and other indicators which should be watched by the scientific marketeer. He must discover the most fertile areas in which to practise his ability; more barren fields he must avoid if he wishes to maximize his returns per unit of input of skill and money. He must exploit the good opportunity, since time is highly perishable in his trade. Upward trends must be found, preferably before they are on the move. Sometimes the indicators are clear and obvious to all, as with the distribution of purchasing power; at other times a deep investigation may be needed into possible political and social influences.

This section could have been continued until it resembled a series of minor textbooks on economic analysis, applied economics, the state and business, international trade, public finance, sociology, sources of information, etc., etc. This might even have been valid and correct in that marketing requires the focusing of all these social sciences on particular problems.

We must now turn our attention to the creation of the marketing policies which will be executed in the framework we have discussed.

PART THREE

THE BASES OF MARKETING STRATEGY

1. Marketing Research

SCIENTIFIC marketing is based on facts and not intuition. If intuition is present, it is subjected to objective assessment wherever possible. Research, forecast, plan and control is the sequential path of scientific marketing; sales research precedes the plan and is an essential part of the control.

The older term 'market research' is, perhaps, too narrow in connotation for the spectrum of activities required in contemporary conditions and practised by enlightened enterprises. It was too closely associated with the counting of heads and the attitudes of mind in those heads to given products or buying situations.

Marketing research contains within it product research, market research, sales policy research and sales promotion planning research. It is a continuous activity of investigation, recommendation and appraisal.

A well briefed sales force can convey a continuous stream of timely information on consumer reactions to product, range, price and after-sales service. The pace of modern production is such that information on consumer reactions must be provided with the utmost speed.

Analysis of the present sales will also provide information which can influence sales planning. Trends in sales to various types of customers and outlets can be discovered, and these may show tendencies which are not apparent in the grand total of sales.

Trends in sales can also show the development of potential and the segments of decline; published statistics from the trade or other sources can confirm or reject. Steps can then be taken to exploit the new potential, by greater attention to this segment, perhaps a new quality market or a developing industrial buyer. Movement of sales of the product from small-unit retailers to multiples might require a new policy towards wholesalers.

To be really effective, marketing research must be comprehensive, and this presents the problem of dealing with all the influences which affect marketing decision-taking. The small-scale entrepreneur can identify and track without difficulty the factors which affect his enterprise, because of the intimacy between him and the market. The larger unit with wide markets may have to employ all the latest analytical techniques of the social sciences and mathematics to provide a similar standard of intelligence for decision-taking. Studies of the market are not, as formerly, based on intimacy, but on the use of psychology, sociology, economics and applied mathematics in the form of econometrics and statistics.

Decision-taking, without the necessary range of information, may be faulty to the extent that it is deficient, but even with all the intelligence available, there remains the need for analysis and judgement of the relative importance of each part. The decision-taking process has always involved this analysis and synthesis in the deliberation of the senior executive, but there is an assumption that such executives have the generalist knowledge which is needed; there is the implication that they can identify, track and weigh each influence on a decision; and are also familiar with the latest methods and findings of social sciences and mathematics.

THE NEED FOR MARKETING RESEARCH

It is the scale, costs and methodology of modern industry which have emphasized the need for research into all influences on markets. This research, by heightening the calibre of marketing programmes from product development and design to sales promotion, has further increased the possible commercial consequences for those firms which do not undertake such studies. Research, through better marketing, creates the need for research by competitors. Marketing research itself becomes deeper and more sophisticated in competition with other marketing researching.

The cost consequences of failure are mainly dependent on the fixed or committed assets of an enterprise. Means must be found for confirming the wisdom of the initial investment decision to purchase plant and equipment and employ talent and skill to produce a specific product or selected group. The narrower the spectrum of end-products, the greater the need for research before investment takes place.[1] Where extensions to capacity are under consideration, the likely return on this investment relative to other uses must be discovered by research.

Once the outlays have been committed, then marketing research will keep them as profitable as possible, as it is a partner, perhaps a dominant one, in the evolution of new products without which profits cannot be sustained.

Marketing research will provide information on which the design of the product will be based, its price, and the most suitable method of promotion. It will appraise its own recommendation in practice in the field, and make new ones if these are needed. It will be the basis of the marketing 'mix' and the constituent selling 'mix'.

The period of time between the decision to invest and the production of goods has increased with the scale and sophistication of modern industry; the longer this period, the greater the need for marketing research.

The centralization of production to obtain optimum production returns has widened the gulf between maker and consumer. The face-to-face situation no longer exists; it must be created: marketing research is really face-to-face 'by proxy'.

The speed of modern production makes quick transmission of consumer reaction to the product vital, if waste is to be prevented. Goods which are no longer wanted by the consumer are doubly wasteful in that, in addition to the lost outlays on the unwanted goods, there is the profit on the wanted goods which has been forgone because of slow communication of consumer reactions. Methods of sales promotion have become increasingly sophisticated. The promotion of the brand has become, in many cases, more important than the product. The greater the intensity of sales promotion, the greater the need for research as a basis for selling plans and appraisal.

1. Throughout all such decision-taking the opportunity-cost of a line of action must always be assessed, particularly in the light of the extreme perishability of market opportunity.

Marketing research should be as total in its application as marketing itself; it is the basis of all scientific marketing. It is not a separate scientific discipline, but the application of social and mathematical disciplines to a specific business problem. It is concerned with the probabilities which are the basis of decision-taking in uncertain situations.

THE CONSTITUENTS OF MARKETING RESEARCH – PRODUCT RESEARCH

This aspect of marketing research is of greatest significance to firms aiming at patronage through the product rather than through the company; it maintains the market value of research and development by keeping it customer-orientated.

Product research, unlike market research, is concerned with the nature of the product and consumer reaction to it, with a view to maintaining complete compatibility of the two in the dynamic conditions of modern marketing.

New Products

Product policy should have its basis in the only source of value for the product – the market; new products are intended to utilize the assets of an enterprise as profitably as possible.

The product should be in keeping with the motivation 'mix' of the market for which it is intended. This will determine the combination of quality, price, value and associated image potential. The detailed shape, colour and size of the product will be linked with both conscious and subconscious purchasing drives.

Product research in the industrial market may be concerned with the provision of a service rather than a product, the latter being specified. Patronage will then arise from the company which so arranges its services as to appeal most successfully to the customer. In all markets, a decision may be needed on that combination of product and service which will most profitably utilize assets in the light of researched customer motivation.

Estimates should be made of the net consequences of introducing a new product. To what extent, if any, will it encroach on the sales of existing lines? If so, is it likely to be more profitable than the one it might replace? Does it make the range more comprehensive and attractive? To what extent does the present or impending product policy of competitors compel action on new products, regardless of their encroachment on existing sales?

Marketing is concerned with comparative advantages, but this demands a knowledge of competing products; their advantages and weaknesses and the reaction of the market to them. Discovery of a weakness in the product of a competitor may suggest a new product, but without this drawback to selling. Any comparative advantages possessed by other products may lead to product plagiarism (within the law); or a decision may be taken that the comparative advantage enjoyed by the competing product is unassailable. An imported product with a cost advantage would represent such a situation to a domestic manufacturer, who might then institute a new product involving a real or imaginary quality advantage over the imported product to offset his own price disadvantage.

The 'natural' value placed on a new product by potential customers would have to be established along with the evolution of the product itself. Too low a 'natural' valuation may preclude certain features or quality standards in the product, in that to provide them would be uneconomic as they could not be contained within the 'natural' evaluation. At the same time the potential increase in value which could be achieved by sales promotion would also require investigation; where the product could carry a social connotation, then it may be possible to create a consumer valuation in excess of the normal, and such an excess in value could accommodate and reflect additional qualities and characteristics.

Research and development is naturally a speculative activity; product research[2] in the market will increase the productivity of internal research by reducing the risk of worthless scientific success.

2. See later sections on Product Policy and Industrial Marketing for further treatment of this subject.

Improvements to Products

The borderline between new products and improvements to existing products is obviously not a distinct one. Improvements, from a selling viewpoint, will always occur when a change is made in the product or service which keeps it in harmony with any changes in the emotional or rational motivation of the customers.

An intimate knowledge of the reaction of the consumer to the product, either at point of sale or during use, is vital for effective product research. Changes in colour and even size do not necessarily affect the intrinsic worth of a product, but they could favourably influence the attitude of the consumer. Improvements can be genuine in that the product fulfils its function better. The size of packs and their suggestion of value may be incorrect, to the detriment of sales through self-service stores. The use of a gearbox by an ordinary driver may refute the findings of the professional test teams and so gear ratios may have to be changed; after-sales service may deteriorate because the design of the product does not accommodate the calibre of worker available to perform this service. New markets, which involved more handling and transport could lead to the need for redesigning the product and its container to reduce transport costs and the possibility of breakage.

Where an enterprise is supplying a product which is exactly available from a number of competing sources, then improvements in the service provided will replace improvements in the product in its sales policy. In the industrial market, this may involve extra attention to quality, tolerances, reliability, credit and overall dependability. In the supply of goods to retailers, competition through service will require special attention to the cost and stockholding problems of the retailer, which might necessitate a revision of distribution and credit policy.

A product which is not currently a reflection of consumer motivation is, in marketing terms, an inefficient product. Similarly, where product patronage is difficult to achieve, then companies must provide a service which is comparatively more in harmony with consumer requirements than that of their competitors. Product research is the activity which maintains maximum sales efficiency of product and service and so increases the productivity of all selling outlays.

Product Range Policy

Just as product policy should be scientifically based, so should the range which is to be sold. Variety reduction could entail the introduction of substitute models, fewer in number, which involves the risk of losing customers; to carry out such a policy without careful prior investigation of the reaction of customers to the new range increases the risk. The investigation could cover the extent to which the needs of the customers could be met by the new range, the extent of the price differential required to retain their patronage with a 'standard' model, and the possibility of attracting customers who, at the moment, purchase elsewhere, if the price reflects the probable cost structure of a reduced range.

From a business security and profitability viewpoint, diversification and segmentation are two means of reducing overdependence on one market or a section of it. Identifying and assessing the potential profitability of a segment can be based on a socio-economic trend which might show itself in the desire for a higher-quality product; this might lead to an adaptation of the present product to make it suitable for the motivation mix of the developing segment. If heavy outlays are needed to develop a new segment, e.g. expensive advertising, then research is doubly necessary to indicate that the outlay is justified.

Segmentation, unlike diversification, may lead to cannibalism between products and ranges. Wherever a range is extended, then research is needed to find out the overall consequences of the extension on sales; if a new product or a range encroaches on an existing one, then it is necessary to estimate the net effects of the policy.

Analysis of existing sales may show that items within the range are becoming more difficult to sell or that the whole range is declining. Research is needed to identify the decline in the demand for the existing range, the potential markets for the suggested new products, the compatibility of these with the existing production, sales and distribution assets, and the supply situation in the new market.

Range research may require deep investigation into the activities of competitors and the existence of production capacity within a market. A highly competitive and over-capitalized supply situation might prevent the introduction of a simplified range of goods because of the availability of alternative suppliers willing to meet the special needs of customers.

Periodic stocktaking should be undertaken of the relative profitability of products within a range. Where holding stocks of products or spare parts is expensive, then the need to eliminate those lines which are unprofitable is increased in order to divert funds to maintain better stocks of those products which are currently more desirable to the customer.

Research would be needed to estimate the importance to the customer of the whole range together; an apparently unprofitable product may be making a selling contribution which increases the vendibility of the other products in the range. Further research might be needed to assess the opportunity-cost of all forms of sales promotion on marginal or unprofitable products in terms of the possible returns which could be obtained by diverting these outlays on to other products or developing new ones.

The existence of heavy fixed costs in production may stimulate the need to widen the market through range policy. Underlying socio-economic trends in advancing societies might show the validity or otherwise of such a policy. Extending the spectrum upwards to higher-value products is a convenient method of increasing profits where the market for the existing quality range of products is saturated.

New Uses for Products

This is really synonymous from a marketing viewpoint with extensions to the range, and in some markets this branch of product policy is more realistic as a means of increasing sales than the evolution of new products. Moreover, from a manufacturing-cost viewpoint no changes will be needed in the product itself, only in its application.

In the industrial market there is a tendency to assume that the market is strictly defined and is less flexible in extent than the consumer market. This is largely true in that sales pressure cannot increase the total sale of an industrial product, the demand for which is determined by economic rather than emotional influences. Nevertheless, the market for an industrial product can be greatly increased if new uses can be found for it; the extension of the market for fibreglass is an indication of such possibilities. The steel industry, the tube industry and the cement manufacturers are perpetually seeking new uses for these products, often in common fields. Wood is attempting to replace bricks in house building; concrete and prefabricated sections to replace bricks in all building. Paper appears to have beaten wood in the packaging industry, but plastics are now competing with paper for use in the same market. Nylon replaces cotton in tyres. On another level, housewives are recommended to use whisky and breakfast cereals for baking. Ice-cream is now an accepted form of dessert; the weather need not be warm.

All these cases represent increased marketing opportunities as a result of investigation into alternative or additional uses for the basic products.

Examination of Competing Products

To fight efficiently, it is better to obtain some knowledge of the opposition. This is eminently true in marketing. Knowledge of the strength and weakness of competitors should extend into the past in order to discover the attitude of consumers towards them and their products. Analysis should be made of the present situation in order that the advantages and disadvantages of competing products and services, both real and imaginary, can be estimated. A competitor may well have developed a connotation in the mind of the customer which might offset the qualities, good or bad, of his current product or service. An examination of future trends should be carried out to assess the possible relative strengths of known or expected competing products.

Advantages claimed for a competing product, which are attractive to the consumer and also substantially true, will have to be met by positive action. It may be possible to incorporate the advantage into a product. Where this is not possible, for legal or other reasons, then the relative amalgams of qualities of the two competing products will have to be re-created, either in reality or in the mind of the consumer. A change in price may be needed to re-establish a comparatively attractive product. Sales promotion will be used to inflate alternative comparative advantages in order to counteract attractions of competing goods.

Planned sales techniques used by representatives must have their bases, not only in a realistic appraisal of the article to be sold, but also in its comparative position alongside competing articles. The sales representative must be briefed to meet the expected comparisons made between his product and others. The methods he employs will be intended to offset any alleged defects in his own products relative to others, and also to deflate the attraction of the advantages possessed by competing goods. To be really effective, such techniques must be founded on the true reactions of consumers to the competing products.

Advertising must also be based on objectively assessed comparative advantages between products. Attention can then be drawn to comparative advantages which exist, or it can be used to create new ones if the product is at a comparative disadvantage. The practice of 'knocking' competing products is clearly based on a knowledge of those products.

Examination of competing products may in some cases lead to a radical change in product policy. Thus, imported textiles may possess price attractions with which a home producer cannot compete. The answer could well be to realign the present price and quality standards and move into a higher segment where a comparative advantage over the imported textiles might be sustained.

Motivation

The reasons for buying a product may remain the same, but the importance which the customer attaches to each reason may vary. Sometimes even the reasons themselves may change. The strategies of the marketing and selling 'mixes' are based on current motivation priorities which must be discovered by investigation. The possibility of stimulating latent or potential buying motives must also be considered relatively to the cost of stimulation. All aspects of sales policy and sales-promotion planning are dependent on current motivation knowledge in order to be efficient.

Changed motivation will show itself in product policy through variations in design and quality. It will play a dominant part in price policy and in all means of persuasion. It is obviously inefficient to design a product and promote it by appealing to 'Jonesmanship' if the potential customers are troubled by economic pressures on their standard of living. To sell to industrialists on quality only may be inadequate if their end market has recently become more price-conscious.

Packaging Policy

In many cases the design of the pack replaces product design in the marketing spectrum. In other cases package design cannot be divorced, in selling, from the articles contained within the packs. The efficiency of the pack should be under constant observation.

Changed consumer attitudes may dictate the need for more convenient dispensers. Bigger families, the frequency and attraction of shopping and economic pressures could all affect the ideal size of pack.

At retail point, a new quantity-price relationship might be needed to maximize impulse purchasing. Increased use of self-service is an obvious influence on pack design. Instructions on packaged goods may have to be more precise and complete if traditional service at retail point declines. Any increases in distribution costs should set in motion an inquiry into the contribution that the pack can make to offset such increases to the company, and also exploit them by appealing to the cost-benefit motivation of the dealer.

The efficiency with which the surface area of the pack is used in the current situation must always be maximized. It should make the greatest contribution to selling by conveying the brand name and any other sales devices. It should also increase the efficiency of distribution by facilitating selection, e.g. by using a colour code.

THE CONSTITUENTS OF MARKETING RESEARCH –
MARKET RESEARCH

Market research investigations are concerned with quantifying information rather than the creative function which is attached to product research. This quantification is normally concerned with two distinct but related concepts: the forecast of sales, and the potential sales.

Sales forecasts are estimates of the sales likely to be achieved in a period at a given price and using a stated method of sales promotion costing a stipulated amount of money. The optimum sales forecast, in terms of revenue and cost, is included in the sales budget, which is concerned with reconciling this optimum with the optima of other aspects of the business. Sales forecasts form the basis of quotas which are used as control devices for sales effort and also possibly as a basis for payment to the sales force and for incentive inducements.

Sales potential is that part of market potential which is considered within the possible reach of a particular enterprise. Both market and sales potential are concerned with estimates of the buying strength within a market which can be converted to potential revenue. Obviously, the strength of the potential will be infinitely variable, particularly for articles and services which are above biological needs. The potential market for bread is more consistently strong overall than that for specially vitaminized varieties which cater for affluent idiosyncrasies. Postponable durable goods will have potentials which vary in their strength with the availability of discretionary purchasing power, competition from other goods for that purchasing power, and the existence or otherwise of a current stock of similar goods. The greater the strength of any potential, the easier and more profitable its exploitation.

The dynamism of the market potential is associated with cost-effectiveness – the response in revenue to inputs into selling. Every person is a potential consumer of beer, but the cost of converting this potential into revenue will vary from the inveterate imbiber to the president of a temperance society.

Working sales potential resembles the farmer who tilled the most fertile field first before moving to those fields where greater effort was needed to get the same results. In much the same way, the potential buying drives within a market may be so strong that the revenue returned per unit of outlay on providing and promoting the product is very great; the product may represent poor value, the price may be kept deliberately high, and sales-promotion costs kept to a minimum. Where potential is strong and profits from it are above average, then this will attract other enterprises able to provide the desired product. The result will be a reduced profit relative to the potential because of the cost of staying in the market under more competitive conditions; the new situation might show itself in a reduction in price, a better product, or more costly sales promotion to meet the competition. These increased outlays and economic sacrifices (lower prices and better products) represent the cost of occupying a position in a more fertile market; they resemble a rent paid for the privilege of exploiting the greater potential which exists there.[3] Where the product is a consumer-durable, then an easy market could become more difficult to exploit when the first wave of sales had been completed and had exploited most of the potential. The need would arise for additional expenditure to sell replacements, for which the potential is normally much lower; the additional fertilizer required to maintain the crops may make the field less profitable than moving to inherently less fertile areas.

When working the potential, the point will be reached where previously sub-marginal potential segments become attractive relative to the profitability of the first segment. So the product, price, and sales promotion will be geared to these other segments. Price may be lowered to cater for the intrinsically lower potential

3. The increased competition in the segments of greater potential does assume that no barrier exists to the entry of competitors. Barriers could be legal, as when the article is patented; fiscal, when the product is protected; technical and financial, when large scale is needed; or commercial, when heavy outlays are necessary to break into a market, e.g. on advertising.

in these segments, and sales promotion will be more intensive than it was initially in the first segment, but lower than is currently required in that segment. Provided profit can still be made, movement will continue into other segments where initially potential was considered too weak. In an inflationary period, the price may remain stationary in order to tap lower strata of the potential.

Technical and cost factors can also influence the speed of exploitation of potential. New production processes or innovations to the product may enable a lower price to be charged, or it could result in a bigger margin being available for the additional sales promotion required to persuade weaker potential segments. The economies of scale and production could have a similar expansionist effect on the potential as lower unit cost enabled price to be reduced or offset selling diseconomies in segments where there was more consumer resistance.

Potential sales are basically the long-term possibility rather than probability of marketing. However, the period of time for exploiting potential may not be under the control of the enterprise. The expectation or arrival of competition may accelerate the utilization of potential and prevent its steady exploitation at low cost over a longer period of time. Such a situation will be more likely if the potential is obviously and easily profitable and entry into the market is unrestricted.

The concept of potential sales is particularly useful when considering the viability of marketing decisions. The basic decision on investment to produce is founded jointly on an estimate of the total market potential and of the potential likely to be available to support the production capacity which will be created by the investment decision, i.e. the sales potential.[4] Decisions on new products are similarly based on the strength of sales potential relative to the cost of developing and tooling-up for the products. Advertising outlays for new brands or products, or new markets, must be justified by potential profitability which is

4. Estimates of sales potential must incorporate an inquiry into the supply aspect of a market. This would cover the strength of competing products in terms of the products themselves, the capacity behind them and any sales promotion ability.

based on sales potential. Break-even points must assume that a given potential is available for exploitation.

Any initial cost of entry, whether in production, product development, distribution (depots, vehicles, etc.), after-sales service installations, or advertising, must be considered along with the sales and profit potential before reliable decisions can be taken.

Research into the Infrastructure

This aspect of market research can be so comprehensive that it will provide information for the grander decision-taking and could resemble business forecasting.

Socio-economic investigations would cover all the social, economic, fiscal, political and legal influences likely to affect the supply and demand position in the market under investigation. When this market is derived from or is joined to another, then the investigation would concern itself with all those factors influencing the associated product or service; tyre manufacturers would study car registrations, potential purchasing power for cars, fiscal attitudes towards private transport, the attraction of public transport, government policy on railways and the development of roads, etc., etc.

Special attention would be given to current or possible governmental action which might affect markets. This could include action on prices and wages; direct and indirect taxation; industrial and private consumer subsidies; restriction or liberalization of trade; investment incentives; attitudes towards profits; special inducements to capital outlays for social, economic or military objectives; policies on credit for the private consumption and investment sectors; potential changes in public ownership in industry and commerce; attitudes towards monopolies and concentrations of industrial power; potential legal restrictions, etc. Where local authorities are increasing in importance as buyers, then they would receive special attention.

Trends in wage rates, wage drift, earnings, incomes into households, male and female earnings, and incomes at various age levels would figure prominently in infrastructure investigations.

Studies of birth rates, racial groupings, population distribution, family sizes, age of marriage, sex distribution, educational opportunities, etc., could all provide information on which marketing decisions could be based.

Products sold through retail stores would repay an investigation into trends in the territorial distribution of such stores and their potential uses as outlets for the goods. Economic forces or social habits may make shopping precincts more or less attractive. Local taxes could be of great importance when considering retail costs, recommended prices and profit margins.

A new segment is most profitable if it is discovered by investigation and then exploited; it is less profitable if it is only perceived when it is being exploited by others and their success attracts imitators.

Research into Trends and Segments

Trends within a total market are an obvious field of investigation. Division can be on the basis of industry, types of customer, outlets and different quality and price segments.

Developments in particular industrial uses can prompt product research. The changing importance of different types of retail outlets can affect packaging (self-service), brand policy (multiples), and price policy; the organization of the sales force would be influenced as a greater need for merchandising was indicated, or larger accounts required a higher calibre of selling. Trends in quality segments are a ready-made indication of possible total market trends which might warrant investigation. All segment developments will help advertising and other sales-promotion plans by showing the direction of the greatest potential.

Research into Territorial Distribution

This can be used to show the expected and/or potential sales in different regions of a market. It can indicate declining and developing areas, and this information can be used to assist the location of advertising and to help achieve the best organization of the sales force. Payment and incentives to salesmen should be based on an estimate of the fertility of the area in which they work.

Where an enterprise undertakes the bulk of its own distribution, then knowledge of the territorial distribution of sales is clearly important in the location of depots and the operation of vehicles. When distribution is by independent dealers, the same knowledge can be used when appraising the suitability of the network; a developing area may require additional retail and wholesale outlets.

Research into the Timing of Sales

Time is highly perishable in many branches of selling. The missed opportunities of a peak season cannot be recalled; the profits which have been forgone are lost for ever. Exact information is needed on the timing of consumer buying so that production (product development if needed), distribution, selling to dealers, and advertising can all be scheduled to make the maximum commercial impact. Network analysis may be used to make the achievement of the peak buying time more certain; if the task is impossible within the normal activities of the enterprise, then the relative cost of more expensive but quicker methods will have to be weighed against the profit consequences of not meeting the required date.

It is essential to know the times of final consumer purchase and not that of intermediaries. Regular buying throughout a year by wholesalers, and even retailers, may disguise periods of great variation in the volume of buying by the general public.

Sometimes an irregular incidence of final sales may prompt an inquiry into ways and means of increasing sales in the off-peak season. Attempts may be made to make turkeys a regular rather than a festive meal. Extra discounts may be given to dealers to encourage them to stock and sell goods in the slack period.

THE CONSTITUENTS OF MARKETING RESEARCH – SALES POLICY RESEARCH

Many of the main elements of policy research are covered by product research, but there are important aspects which still merit special attention. Throughout sales policy and promotion research the main purpose is to give guidance on the make-up of the marketing and selling 'mixes'; the effectiveness of each constituent of the 'mix' will be appraised, as will be the combination of the 'mix' itself. Such appraisal is not, however, a purely negative or critical activity, but also recommends possible ways of increasing the efficiency of each constituent and improvements in the total marketing and selling strategies. Three aspects of sales policy still concern us, those dealing with price, credit and distribution.

Price Policy – including Dealer Relationships

With a new product, research is needed to show the 'natural' price valuation given to similar products so that the price of the new product could be in harmony with this 'natural' valuation (often really an 'unnatural' valuation as it is subjected to artificial selling pressures which may distort values). Where the new article is a novelty without precedent, then a similar investigation could be carried out to assess the valuation put on the article by the potential consumers. Inquiries such as these give an indication of the built-in preference associated with the product, and show the extent of any resistance which will have to be overcome where a product is priced in excess of this 'natural' valuation.

Once a product or service is on the market, its price must be made to make the maximum contribution to efficient selling. The relative effects in the long and short term of price reductions as against advertising will have to be assessed. The degree of price and brand susceptibility must be determined. High final prices to the customer which contain large profit margins to dealers will have to be compared in efficiency with lower prices and reduced margins.

The elasticity of demand for the total product and for the individual brand is an important part of this research. The influence of the changing economic position of the customer on demand must also be known. Inelasticity of the total demand may rule out price-cutting as a policy for increasing sales because of the effect on total revenue; advertising might then be preferred. All studies of the likely reaction by consumers to changes in price must incorporate some judgement on the possible retaliatory policies of competitors and the consequent final price situation after all reciprocal action has taken place.

Specific aspects of price policy, such as recommendations of resale prices and profit margins, will require special consideration in dynamic market conditions. Any judgement on the selling efficiency of a policy of resale price recommendations will require studies to be made of the infrastructure of the market, as seen in the attitudes of customers to the purchase of the product in retail stores which do and do not desire such policies.

The relevance of the current price policy and the dealer profit margin it contains to the contemporary functions of the dealer in the sale and distribution of the product should also be kept in mind. Where increased pre-selling now takes place, dealer margins could be reduced; if good design has reduced the need for after sales service, any margin to cover this service is now less necessary; should the dealer be unable or unwilling to recruit the standard of labour to which the profit margin is related, then the margin should be adjusted downwards.[5] On the other hand, where the costs of the dealer have increased through increased rents, rates, wages, etc., then in order not to alienate the wholesaler or retailer, margins may have to be increased.

Recommendations on price policy cannot realistically be made unless they are related to the product cost structure. The existence of efficient, expensive and newly installed equipment may exert pressure to remove any restriction on prices. Such a move stems from a fear of idle capacity and the belief that the more efficient equipment can meet any challenge of price competition.

5. In some cases the profit margin to dealers could be increased to enable them to offer wages which will attract the calibre required for selling and servicing the product.

The same diligence under dynamic market conditions is needed in the industrial field to discover the current priority rating given to price in the motivation 'mix' of the buyer. This could well be a projection of the importance of price in the market which he, in turn, is supplying. It could also be due to a more scientific approach to material costs by the industrial customer. In this rational market, there must be complete compatibility between the thoughts on price and profits of buyer and seller.

Credit Policy

Research must be used to identify the contribution of credit to efficient selling. This may well vary with market conditions: a new model at an increased price may make credit more important; increased competition from credit-backed goods might compel imitation; more attractive cash purchasing opportunities, e.g. on sophisticated food and drink, could necessitate better credit terms for consumer-durable competing items.

Pressure on the working capital of a customer may make the extension of credit into a marginal sales advantage in the industrial market. A similar situation might exist in the supply of goods to retailers. Where goods are equal to private consumers, retailers or industrialists, then good credit terms may create a comparative company-patronage advantage. Where credit is normal practice, then to refuse it may result in a comparative disadvantage. The degree of dependence on credit should also be estimated; central governments and banks, through credit and interest policies, can seriously affect the sales achievements of firms which are too dependent on credit in their selling strategy.

Distribution Policy

Trends in consumer shopping habits and in retail developments would be the bases for recommendations on the distribution policy regarding wholesalers and retailers. Such developments would have to be considered along with their financial implications before realistic decisions could be taken. Where multiple stores are increasing their share of a market, then this might necessitate changes in the policies towards wholesalers.

The importance of distribution and, in particular, stockholding at the point immediately before the retailer might receive special attention if it is discovered that the retailer is unable, for space or financial reasons, to hold large stocks. If analysis showed increased purchases through self-service stores, then this would increase the need to ensure that the product was always on the shelves; this is a distribution problem.

Changes in the product or the range which reduce its complexity might facilitate the use of independent dealers. Such a move, however, should follow research into its feasibility in terms of selling efficiency; the new policy with its obvious cost economies would have to be compared with the selling advantages of using the present sales organization.

Any movement of a product, for any reason, from shopping goods to convenience goods, or from speciality to another category, would require a reorganization of retail distribution policy to match the new classification if sales are to be maintained.

New shopping habits, such as increased acceptance of mail-order buying, the tendency to shop for shops rather than goods, changed social attitudes towards different types of retailer, and the development of 'one-stop' convenience shopping, must all be investigated to determine their influence on a firm's distribution policy.

THE CONSTITUENTS OF MARKETING RESEARCH –
SALES PROMOTION PLANNING RESEARCH

This aspect of marketing research deals with the constituents and make-up of the selling 'mix'. Any selling device must be critically analysed to measure its efficiency in selling. Where products are basically similar and there is some degree of price standardization, then this branch of marketing research assumes added importance. If the total market for a product is inelastic, then research into selling methods could be the true basis of the share of a market enjoyed by an enterprise.

Certain parts of sales promotion planning research have

received attention under other sections as it is impossible to segregate certain sales activities; package policy is related to product research, but it is part of selling; branding is related to outlets policy; dealer relationships are concerned with the price which must contain their profit margin and also the place of the dealer in selling. Certain of the larger selling activities do, however, require treatment here.

Advertising

Attempts should be made to measure effectiveness, in terms of awareness, attitudinal change etc. and of sales, of different types of advertising and different media. Lack of positive correlation between awareness and sales may indicate inadequacies in other parts of the marketing plan, e.g. defects in the product or package, its quality, price or availability due to bad distribution. The contents of advertisements will be based on motivation research and studies of those of competitors. Location and timing will be moved to maximize effectiveness if research shows a different distribution of consumption from that of the past. The importance of the dealer in the sale of the product will be identified to help in decisions on trade advertising and advertising to the final customer.

To be effective, industrial advertising must be aimed at those who are in any way responsible for purchasing decisions. Each advertisement will be framed to suit the knowledge and motivation of each person participating in the decision to purchase; it may stress technical factors, cost-effectiveness or merely prestige; research, often based on a feed-back from sales representatives, will show the current sources of authority for industrial purchasing.

Branding

The retentive brand name of today with the correct connotation may be totally unsuited for the consumer of tomorrow. However, even though brand names should be up to date, changes should only be made with a full knowledge of the loyalty attaching to the old name. The retention of many individual brands by large industrial complexes should be based on such loyalty being a greater contribution to selling efficiency than could be obtained by exploiting the economic advantages of using only one name.

The contribution that the brand name can make to advertising efficiency will depend on its suitability for the type of advertising currently used; a name which is adequate for newspaper advertising may be inadequate when spoken or as a part of a television or radio jingle.

The importance of the promotion of dealer brands is better studied under distribution research in that it is based on retail developments. However, it is also necessary to consider the relationship of various brands in their appeal to different segments of the market, and this would include close study of the effect of dealer brands on manufacturers' brands.

Dealer Policy

It is important to recognize and assess the place of a dealer in the sale of a product; incentives to dealers must be weighed against increased advertising and reduced prices. The strength of consumers to pull goods through dealers with and without their support should be known.[6]

Aid to dealers may have to be positive and not merely implied in the profit margin on the products; assistance could be given to enable the retailer to sell products more effectively.

Personal Selling

Research is needed to discover the contribution that personal selling through representatives should make to efficient sales promotion. If analysis shows that patronage is largely a product of the work of the representative, then greater attention must be paid to the management and conditions of work of the sales force. Where the article, by its nature, requires demonstration of its working and applications, then the personal type of selling will obviously be advantageous.

6. See page 125, 'Condustrial Goods'.

On the other hand, less responsibility will rest on the sales force if the product is unique or has special attractive characteristics which can create strong product patronage. Company patronage arising from the price policy or the general capabilities of an enterprise, e.g. consistent quality, reliability, good credit terms, etc., can similarly reduce the dependence on sales personnel. Highly effective advertising coupled with brand susceptibility on the part of the consumer may also promote sales efficiently without undue pressure from other quarters.

Completely objective analysis is needed to isolate the part played and/or needing to be played by personal selling. This analysis is mainly concerned with the position of the product to be sold and that of the company, but an increase in effective selling on the ground by a competitor might necessitate similar action.

Efficient personal selling stems from an analysis of the true nature of the particular selling function concerned and the recruitment and training of staff to meet these requirements. If the necessary calibre is not readily available, even after training, then other departments may be needed to compensate for the deficiency, e.g. technical advisory departments.

A new type of recruit and training content may be needed if it is discovered that industrial buyers are more concerned with cost-benefits and less occupied by technical knowledge of the product.

Ethical policy and the need to sustain goodwill may influence the method of payment used, with reduced dependence on commission, if it is important to maintain long-term good relationships with customers. Reduced labour turnover of salesmen and associated departments is vital where the main motivation for selecting a supplier stems from the human element in sales.

The organization of sales departments and those service departments ancillary to selling, e.g. sales-production liaison, must be based on the existing market conditions as seen in the needs of customers and the activities of competitors. The setting up of a special product division may be caused by a similar action, or threat of so doing, by an important competing supplier.

Within the market, a new outlet development may require special attention and this would be reflected in the sales organization meeting this new need, e.g. important multiple-store orders.

TOTAL MARKETING RESEARCH –
THE CONTRIBUTION TO MARKETING STRATEGY

Marketing involves 'adjusting the whole activity of a business to the needs of the customer or potential customer'. Therefore, marketing research should be so comprehensive that it covers every activity of the business which can in any way affect present or future attitudes of consumers. A dilatory reply to an inquiry caused by inefficient office organization; the receipt of a reminder for a bill already paid; broken promises caused by bad control of distribution; even the deflation caused by ignorance of the name of a customer and the nature of his business; all can be attributed to inadequate marketing research which has failed to identify and influence the part played by the office, the accounts department, the transport office and the junior office worker or telephone operator. Marketing concerns all functions and employees, and marketing research should be as comprehensive. But it is, above all, vitally concerned with marketing strategy and with identifying, creating or sustaining a comparative advantage.

To perform this creative function correctly requires a thorough and objective self-analysis to determine the current competitive standing of the business, the comparative standing achieved by competitors, the current competitive strengths and weaknesses both in total and in particular elements – e.g. quality, price, good-will, delivery, image connotation, product advantages, etc. – and finally, the feasibility of changing the existing strategy to improve the competitive position of the enterprise. The marketing research function is concerned with a comparative study of compatibility between the use of assets and customer attitudes on the part of competing enterprises, and recommendations on the use of assets or resources to improve competitive standing.

Specifically, an attempt must be made to determine the strength of existing and potential sources of patronage. These may emanate from the product itself, e.g. machine tools may be more efficient, cars more safe, breakfast cereals may have increased vitamin content. On the other hand, patronage may be derived from the company's activities, as when the product is available from many sources. For example, the supply of goods to multiple stores is based on cost, quality consistency and delivery reliability; the sale of components (specified) to a car assembler is based on similar qualities; identical consumer goods may obtain a better point-of-sale display because of a better understanding by the manufacturer of the stockholding and financial problems of the dealer.

In many markets, such as those for emotional goods, the comparative patronage attraction may be created by advertising, i.e. the application of assets to change the attitude of the consumer. Nevertheless, such a use of resources should be based on the patronage strength of competing products so that the motivation can be exploited which gives the greatest return per unit of outlay; this involves consideration of the motivation priorities of current or potential customers and the activities or possible counter-activities of competitors. Thus, if quality has become a top reason for purchasing, then the product may be 'traded up' in quality, price and advertising presentation changed to suit the new situation. But this action would have to be measured against the likely response of competitors. Are they able to 'trade up' more easily and quickly than the firm taking the decision?

The productivity of a marketing decision concerning the use of resources is largely determined by the reaction of competitors. Thus it may be decided to achieve in an industrial market a better position by means of increased expenditure on quality control, but the extent of the comparative advantage so gained is determined jointly by the efficiency of the execution of the change in quality policy and also by the reciprocal action of competitors. The output in terms of comparative advantage may be completely eliminated if the competitor takes similar action. The same reasoning would apply to a policy of price reduction (a sacrifice per unit sold) in response to a suspected increase in price-consciousness; extra margins or aids to dealers might only benefit the distributor if copied by others.

Outlays on product development are in a different category, in that competitor response cannot be instantaneous. Even though the results of such outlays may be equalled by similar action on the part of competitors which would render product patronage neutral, the situation if the product had not been developed would be serious in that the time needed to rectify the position is longer than that needed to change a price, step up advertising, or improve quality control. There is a penalty consequence associated with not committing outlays in most aspects of marketing, but the penalties vary in weight between those which could ruin a firm, e.g. inadequate product development, to those which can be rectified more easily, such as price reductions.[7]

The need to identify a comparative position *vis-à-vis* competitors and patronage motives on the part of customers is particularly important when individual customers represent a significant share of the market, e.g. supplying the industrial market or large multiple retailers. Such a situation would justify the most detailed approach to each customer and to competitors' activities. Attempts must be made to determine the rating or assessment given by the customer to each potential supplier, and this rating must be analysed to determine the importance of patronage sources which currently have priority. Should reliable delivery become a dominant buying motive, then the comparative standing of each supplier to meet this motivation must be assessed. In addition, the supplier may require to reallocate resources to rectify a low rating by the customer to meet this requirement, e.g. increased attention to production planning and control.

The practice of marketing is not based on certainties, and marketing research, to be really scientific, accepts this. Consequently, estimates only can be made on likely reaction from competitors; we are dealing with objectively estimated probabilities. A similar attitude must be taken when dealing with customer rating of products and suppliers; the practice of vendor rating should not be confined to scientific purchasing but should be used by marketeers to discover the strength and weaknesses of their firm, its products, services, and promotion methods relative

7. Although even these may require drastic revision of costs to be successful.

to others and the possibility of using assets to change and improve its comparative marketing position. This is really a marketing audit.[8]

8. See also Part Six.

2. Motivation

WHEN we state that marketing is customer-orientated, we imply that the activities of an enterprise should reflect the motivation complex of the potential consumer. In less than ideal conditions, this will probably mean that the amalgam of qualities possessed by one product will be better or worse in the mind of the customer than that of another; rarely will the two complexes of product qualities and customer motives be identical. The function of selling is to persuade that this identification of the personalities of the product and the consumer is complete or the best available. A drink is easily recognized as possessing the qualities which correspond to the motivation or drives of a thirsty man, but in affluent societies the complex is not complete without added distinction in the drink and the attachment of a price. The liquid may appeal to the basic animal desire to quench a thirst, the added distinction to the need to conform with or emulate others, and the price to the economic position of the consumer and his valuation of the product relative to others with which he could also satisfy his biological and social drives. This is the type of complex of consumer drives to which modern products and their promotion must respond.

The basic drives to quench thirst, to satisfy hunger, to seek shelter, to desire sexual satisfaction, to emulate others, to conform, to be accepted by a group, to quest for security, to cheat death, to enjoy leisure, are all exploited in marketing. Some consumer drives have their basis in the individual, whilst others are the consequence of people living together. Thirst, hunger, shelter, maternalism and sexual drives can exist outside society; emulation, conformity and the herd instinct are clearly only possible when groups exist. Social drives may use the group, of which the consumer is a member, as a term of reference, or the term of reference could be a more advanced group to which the consumer aspires; the 'Jonesmanship' of affluent societies is the most common manifestation of such drives and has been extensively exploited by marketeers unable to sustain demand by appeals to biological needs.

Consumer drives can show themselves in either emotional or economic activity. The need for security and emulation can result in emotional buying beyond economic needs in order to demonstrate the holding of a position in society, but it can also result in economic judgements, devoid of emotion, which are intended to increase the wealth of an individual or business. The profit motives can be justified on emulative and security grounds and can even be extended to cover the desire to be accepted by a group, either at the current level or a higher one than that now occupied. The desire for security and acceptance is displayed by managers in industry when taking rational buying decisions, and also by housewives when buying clothes, and their husbands when buying new cars.

Sometimes the exploitation of a consumer drive may be obvious, as when an entrepreneur responds to the need for rudimentary shelter, food and clothing for a family. However, the existence of subconscious drives, which can only be identified by professional analysis, has led to the use of a more covert or hidden type of motivation. Quality chocolate is sold on an appeal to sex, education and class; cars will be sold on social and sexual grounds, the latter having its manifestation in the physical properties of the car, and the former in the position given to the buyer through its possession; cigarettes are associated with sexual conquest; drinks are shown to give added strength within a group, conformity, masculinity and social standing – in many cases the ability to quench a thirst is ignored.

Motivation research forms the basis for efficient marketing. Appeals to consumer drives can be incorporated into the design of a product or its pack, by shape, texture, colour or size; if the personality of the product can thus be reconciled with that of the consumer, then the productivity of outlays on selling is increased. The decision on price, pack, brand name, advertising contents and even the choice of retail outlets can all appeal to subconscious motivations which are unknown, or only vaguely known, by the consumers.

The psychological extensions to similar products are often

based on these subconscious drives. A brand name may have a class or emulative connotation; a pack may exploit the sexual, maternal or emulative drives; advertising may suggest ways to acceptance by the opposite sex, the herd, or a higher-rated group; the retail store may have a distinct social image.

That product which identifies itself with the most powerful combination of consumer drives will, other things being equal, achieve the greatest marketing success. If all car manufacturers are selling equally convenient transportation at similar prices, the one who identifies his product with the social drive for acceptance or emulation, or with virility, masculinity or sexual strength, would be suggesting a comparative advantage as a psychological extension to his product with considerable emotional power. Comparative advantages are the basis of all successful marketing; if one cannot be found at the conscious or economic levels, it must be sought in the subconscious.

Motives can be divided into conscious and subconscious; rational and emotional (i.e. economic and non-economic). Consumer goods are considered to be sold mainly through the exploitation of the emotional, non-economic drives whereas, in the industrial field, rational, economic behaviour dominates. Although this may be broadly true, even a cursory examination will show the weakness of such a dogmatic categorization.

The decision to buy a washing machine may be as rational and economic as the one taken when a typewriter is purchased by a business; the choice of a particular washing machine may be as objective as the choice of typewriter. Sometimes the decision to make a purchase is emotional, as when a replacement car is to be purchased, but the choice of a particular brand is completely rational or economic, and vice versa. Social pressures may create an urge to possess a certain type of goods in order to conform or emulate, but although this general drive is emotional, the final choice of product from among those available could be more rational and, in certain cases, as when financial forces are strong, it would be based on strong economic motives; on the other hand, even the allegedly completely rational buying in the industrial market can have some of its basis in emotion as managers seek team acceptance, security and emulation.

The debate regarding rational and irrational motivation loses some of its force if the analyst is willing to accept that the buyer obtains extra satisfaction from his purchase of branded, emotionally-charged goods in excess of their real value. In affluent societies which already possess a large stock of material goods, advances in the standard of living may be easier to make along the road of these psychological additions to, and variations in, goods rather than in creating real advances in the product themselves. Branded goods with their artificial idiosyncrasies are more acceptable in those societies which have passed the biological-needs stage; individuals in these societies are looking for social distinction out of goods.

The term 'non-economic' is perhaps a better one than 'irrational'; the difference between the basic product price and the price paid for the amalgam of physical and social satisfaction obtained from a branded product is a measure of the non-economic nature of the purchase – an indication of the worth of the emotional satisfaction which possession creates. The consumer, when buying such a product, is not acting completely irrationally and may be fully conversant with the contents of the amalgam of satisfaction which is being purchased, but, despite this knowledge, he proceeds with the transaction.

Specific motives may be exploited in the consumer market which have their basis in the individual or contemporary society. Thus the desire for health, cleanliness, comfort, possession of property and leisure are all used in the sale of goods to the general public. Economic motivation may be particularly pinpointed by a 'bargain' connotation to the product. In the industrial market specific claims will be made for the quality, price, durability, reliability, economy, labour-saving and cost-reducing qualities of a product; claims on behalf of a manufacturer might include reliability, co-operation before and after sales, dependability under all circumstances, and good credit facilities.

In order to market any product with the maximum effectiveness, it is essential to know the order of priorities given to motives by customers at different times. The constituent parts of the marketing 'mix' should quickly reflect any changed motivation by customers. The more separated the manufacturer is from the market and the greater the time lapse between the conception and the sale of a product, the more important it becomes to set up some research activity to identify customer drives accurately and speedily, so that the marketing 'mix' can be reorientated if necessary.

If washing machines are purchased for economy or space-saving, then this should be apparent in the design and price of the product; should space-saving become more important because of pressure on space in modern houses, then this motive would supersede economy, and design for space-saving might legitimately take priority over price. Domestic refrigerators have been purchased for various reasons as consumer motivation 'mixes' have varied through time; 'Jonesmanship', health and hygiene, space-saving and economy have all been used to promote these products. Television receivers were sold on the basis of reliability when they were first introduced and fear of breakdown was a dominant consumer motive; when technical standards reached an acceptable level, sales emphasis was switched to price, space-saving, and furnishing appeal. Cars may now be sold increasingly on safety qualities.

Dynamic motivation is also apparent on the economic level, in both the consumer and the industrial markets. Price may become more important because of increased pressure on the purchasing power of the consumer caused by: an increase in the cost of living which is not matched by a similar increase in income; a reduction in income; or the desire to purchase a wider range of goods than is convenient with a given income. Pressure on profit margins, no matter what the cause, would create increased price-consciousness by industrial buyers.

The industrial market demands the same close attention to changing motivation as the consumer market. Quality may become more or less important; credit may be less necessary as enterprises become larger and thus command greater financial resources; tolerances may become slacker to accommodate lower prices made necessary by pressure on profit margins; reliability of supplies is more important when the customer is operating a mass-production or progressive assembly line; budgetary control will result in increased sensitivity to prices; heavy committed fixed costs may create extra fear of breakdown, thus demanding improved design of equipment and better after-sales service. It is the function of the efficient industrial marketeer to plan his sales policy to suit the changed motivation of his customers; in this case, owing to the importance of individual orders, this dynamism in the marketing 'mix' is of special importance.

Marketing efficiency is not concerned with maximizing sales but with maximizing profits. Profits are the result of the spontaneous valuation given to the output of an enterprise by the consumer and the cost of changing that valuation by sales techniques. The better the original motivation research, the more closely the product or services of an enterprise will correspond to the desires of the consumer, thus enhancing their spontaneous valuation which, in turn, will reduce the cost of sustaining sales at any given price. Profits are then maximized.

If the whole of the marketing activity, from product development and design to after-sales service, including all sales-promotion planning, is based on research into consumer motivation, then there is a multiple effect on the efficiency of the selling activity. Sales promotion would be planned in such a way as to exploit the complex of consumer drives which has been discovered, but it would be made even more productive because it would be promoting a product which was also compatible with this complex.

3. The Basic Classification of Goods

AN analysis of the article or articles to be sold and the market or potential market is the first step in the solution of any marketing problem. This chapter is concerned with the basic analysis of the goods or service to be sold and the practical significance of the classification of goods into convenience, shopping and speciality categories.

This division of goods is based on their inherent characteristics and the shopping habits associated with them; the latter is determined largely by the former. There is a degree of subjective analysis about the classification, in that convenience goods to one person may be viewed as speciality goods by another, e.g. toothpaste. It is the general attitude to goods which is under discussion here; if the bulk of the market treats toothpaste as a convenience good, then this is its classification for marketing purposes.

CONVENIENCE GOODS

If an article has close substitutes, is purchased regularly, in small amounts of low unit value, and if the customer insists on purchasing with the minimum inconvenience, that article is called a convenience good. These are the everyday purchases of life such as cigarettes, chocolate, washing powders, tea, bread, biscuits, etc.; they are generally basically simple things, liable to be presented to the customer by many manufacturers, each having a product which is virtually a substitute for any of the others. This degree of substitution has important selling consequences.

A further habit of the customer characterizes convenience goods in that they are normally purchased with some degree of urgency; this is possibly a result of the universal availability of the article, made possible by distribution policies based on its convenience classification, which removes the need for the customer to store large quantities.

113

What are the consequences to the sales planner of this classification?

The actual selling of the goods of a particular manufacturer of convenience goods is made difficult because of the lack of any basic differential between his goods and those of similar competing manufacturers.

Given the characteristics of convenience goods the task of building up goodwill and reducing the volatility of customers depends largely on introducing a form of differentiation obvious to the would-be customer. This, then, is the basis of branding, sales slogans, distinctive packages, premium offers, and all the methods and devices used, including price plans, to identify a particular supply of a common article capable of substitution by many others.

The manufacturer of convenience goods must try to remove anonymity. The customer must be convinced, in fact, that a particular manufacturer's article is not a convenience good for which many substitutes are available, but that it has some degree of uniqueness, some special attributes. Volatility is dangerous where heavy investments are involved in production, and in order to reduce this risk the manufacturer must, by some sales device, create some allegiance to his own product.

The irrevocable nature of purchasing increases the anxiety of manufacturers of convenience goods; if a certain type of branded convenience goods is not available at the point of sale, then the sale thus forgone is for ever lost. The sales-promotion activity to remove similarity and anonymity may require a heavy outlay and, unless the total market is expanding, it could involve large funds without any automatic commensurate positive returns; such promotion outlays can easily assume the character of an automatic on-cost due to fear of the consequences of ceasing to advertise, and can become an embarrassment, particularly when there is any recession in overall demand, or if excess capacity results in keener competition resulting in price cuts. It could well be that convenience goods, by their very nature, lead to intense competition, not only on the sales-promotion side to create uniqueness, but also in the excess investment in capacity which could result from the ease with which the main features of such goods can be copied.

The design of a convenience good is important. The ability to advertise convenience goods effectively would be handicapped if it was impossible to point out any features which distinguish the product.

This desire to distinguish the product is also due to customer attitudes which indicate an unwillingness to shop. The visual evidence is that, despite the enormous outlays on advertising etc. to achieve some degree of customer loyalty, this loyalty does not exceed the desire for convenience, and so goods subjected to enormous advertising campaigns are still found in all outlets. This affects the distribution aspects of selling convenience goods; every point where the article is likely to be demanded must be stocked with that product.

In fact, in the modern context of one-stop shopping, the good sales manager must look for all possible or potential points where the article could be sold. Thus, ladies' stockings are now sold in grocery stores; this product was not considered a convenience good, but it has been converted by customer attitudes, largely created by the distribution policies of manufacturers.

This need to distribute to so many points has its repercussions on the choice of outlets and intermediaries, e.g. the use of an independent wholesaler as the only economical way of dealing with the smaller orders. The tendency towards larger retailer units could reduce the need to use middle-men to assist distribution; at the same time the salesman is liable to become more concerned with presentation at point of sale. Basically, however, the sale and distribution of convenience goods does require a large distributive and selling organization to deal with the need for widespread points of sale.

The development of self-service has further increased the volatility of convenience-goods purchasing. It is the essence of such a store that the housewife will buy, not according to any preconceived shopping list, but will use the display of goods as a sufficient reminder of her needs. Unfortunately for branded goods, this does mean that if the particular product is not on view, it will not be seen and therefore will not be purchased – a substitute being taken. The point of sale situation is thus potentially more dangerous than that of the conventional counter-service store, because no brand will be specifically asked for by the customer.

This results in two policy decisions. Firstly, the distribution system must be good enough to guarantee that the article is always available and that any deficiencies in its supply are immediately known. Secondly, the whole plan of creating product differentiation is based on the new point of sale situation; this would give greater attention to packs, merchandising, and the need to pre-sell the product by advertising and branding.

The oldest and most distinct form of product differentiation could be used, price itself. This could, depending upon customer motivation, be a high price to suggest a special type of distinction, particularly where informed appraisal by the customer is difficult, e.g. cosmetics and soap. On the other hand, if motivation research showed a high level of price-consciousness, then distinction could be created by an emphasis on value. The trouble with such policy decisions is that the practice is eminently capable of imitation, with the result that the goods are again equal but on a different price plateau. Branding, advertising and packaging policies do not lend themselves so easily to this process of complete imitation. Another aspect of policy when dealing with convenience goods is the policy towards dealers.

If there is the assumed high degree of transferability from one brand to another, and if the customer is unwilling to shop, then the manufacturer must not alienate the owners of the retail outlets where the article might be purchased. In a market where substitution is so close, then the retailer does not impair his turnover by refusing to stock and sell the brand or brands of an individual manufacturer.

Long before resale price maintenance was outlawed in the United Kingdom, price-cutting had taken place throughout convenience-goods markets. This was partly due to the invasion of the back streets by the multiple retailer, whose branches were now as convenient as the shops owned by the small independent. The consequence was that the housewife could enjoy at one and the same time both minimum inconvenience in her shopping and the keenest prices. Manufacturers then intruded into the practice of price-cutting, operating their own price-reduction plans through dealers on a national scale. No manufacturer can stay aloof from such policies because of the inherent substitution possibilities in the product.

It can be seen that the basic classification of goods is not merely an academic activity; it forms the basis for important decisions in sales promotion, distribution, and price policy. One of the main purposes behind these decisions may be to remove the product from its class and convert it into a speciality good for which people will be inconvenienced and for which they will shop.

SHOPPING GOODS

At the root of the unwillingness to shop for convenience goods was their small unit value, the lack of any need to do so because of the availability of close substitutes, and the frequency of purchases which would multiply the element of inconvenience. Shopping goods, by their very description, are the opposite and give rise to totally different customer reactions and attitudes – with consequential effects on sales and distribution plans.

Shopping goods are of a higher unit value than convenience goods and are purchased less frequently. They could be bought only once every few years, as with a car; once in a lifetime, as with furniture; shoes, clothes, radios, all fall into the shopping goods category. On the service side, tours and entertainment would be included.

If an article is purchased infrequently and has a high unit value, the customer will become more discriminating and will look for a selection from which a choice can be made. This attitude is strengthened by the lack of urgency associated with these goods; they are not consumable items which have to be quickly replaced like food, but are often articles which are only necessary because of social pressures, and these very pressures can lead to even more discrimination before a choice is made. When the purchase is a replacement purchase, the degree of postponability can be so high that the urgency is further reduced.

117

The principal aspects of customer attitude towards these goods is not only a willingness to shop, but a desire to do so, or even an insistence on it.

With shopping goods the important factor is the location of the outlets. Firstly, the number of outlets can be reduced because of the customer's willingness to shop. Secondly, the manufacturer can draw more attention to his product by placing it near to competing products, thus satisfying the desire to choose from as wide a selection as possible.

Individually very few, if any, producers of shopping goods can make a range which in itself is attractive; even if this were possible, the very nature of the likely reaction of customers suggests the need for comparison with the goods of other manufacturers. Manufacturers who control their own retail outlets and are specializing in shopping goods either supplement their retail stocks with other brands, or locate their retail outlets near to their competitors.

This type of goods can thus be restricted to fewer outlets located in recognized shopping centres. Sales staff can be reduced because fewer retailers have to be called upon. Dealing can in most instances be direct, by-passing the middle-man. The organization of sales offices is easier, and the invoice and distribution cost per unit of value of sale is lower than with convenience goods.

Advertising must still be practised. With shopping goods the ability to differentiate the product at the design stage is much easier, because of the more sophisticated nature of the article, and so the advertisement can be aimed at informing about a real difference.

Frequently, shopping-goods markets are subdivided into quality price sections which are not normally found in the convenience field; this could mean that the original design decision was based on catering for a special division of the market, and the advertising then aims at identifying the product with that section of the market. The pre-selling aspect of advertising is more important in the sale of convenience goods than it is here where the point-of-sale dealer activity is still significant. This implies the goodwill of the dealer to help in the promotion of the product, and so the profit margin must be adjusted to promote his co-operation. Price policy for these goods must be a mixture of market and product research and dealer investigation. A price which would appear to be low enough greatly to increase sales may not be able to accommodate the profit margin needed to persuade dealers really to sell the product.

The enforcement of resale prices was often justified by manufacturers because they did not wish to alienate dealers. This fear is the basis of the common mark-up which is still found in many trades. It is still open for any manufacturer to ignore the accepted margin, but this would be a serious tactical decision. The more a product is pre-sold and desired by the public, the more difficult it is for a dealer to refuse to handle it or attempt to discount the claims made in advertisements, and therefore the easier it would be for the producer to reduce dealer profit margins and still retain loyalty.

This analysis might tend to suggest to the reader that the range of substitutes here is as great as with convenience goods. This is not so, but the dealer is frequently able to convince the would-be purchasers that their mixture of needs could be better met by the combined qualities of price, durability, after-sales service standards, etc. of a particular article; the dealer, by changing the outlook of the buyer, can identify it with another product within the range of goods which he himself favours for commercial reasons.

If a manufacturer has produced shopping goods of distinct peculiarities, then the number of outlets can be reduced even further. Sometimes this can happen when a manufacturer has become, either by product development and design or by advertising, associated in the public mind with a particular product or type of product, e.g. Wedgwood pottery, Jaguar and Rolls-Royce cars. When this point has been reached, the article has ceased to be shopping goods and has become true speciality goods possessing some unique attribute.

SPECIALITY GOODS

This is an abused term enjoying an application and usage far beyond its true meaning. True speciality goods have some unique property, particular attribute, or overall quality which distinguishes them from similar products. This can be achieved as a result of patents, product development and design, or the tradition and long-term standing of the producer.

In contemporary marketing the term 'speciality goods' is applied to products that have achieved distinction by creative sales promotion which has produced a psychological extension to a branded product giving it unique properties in the mind of the would-be customer.

In so far as a manufacturer succeeds, either in reality or in the mind of the customer, in achieving a degree of distinction for his product which is reflected in customer attitudes and shopping behaviour, so the product will have achieved, to a lesser or greater degree, the status of a speciality good.

When an article achieves speciality ranking, then the volatility of the sales situation is reduced. The customer will now shop specifically for an item, or will request it of the dealer. Some degree of speciality can even be said to exist if a person consistently chooses one brand but is not willing to be inconvenienced to obtain it; but although this is a useful consumer attitude, it does not produce the same effects on the distribution policies as true speciality goods.

If it is known that customers will seek out a product, then the consequences to the scheme of its distribution are far-reaching and advantageous. Retail outlets can be reduced, perhaps to the point of exclusive franchises. Direct dealing with all retailers is facilitated, with obvious canvassing and sales-administration economies. If the product is particularly unique, then the position of the manufacturer relative to the dealer will be a strong one.

Forecasting the sale of a product is made easier if it can be assumed that the customer clearly distinguishes it from others. There can also arise a degree of inelasticity in the demand for the product related to the extent to which customers regard it as unique.

The granting by the customer of the distinction of speciality goods to a product carries with it great sales advantages in security and profitability; these represent the returns to product research, advances in design or outlays on creative sales promotion.

THE DYNAMIC ASPECT OF CLASSIFICATION

The classification of goods is, like all marketing, dynamic, and so are the policies and plans which stem from this classification. Shopping goods become convenience goods and assume the distributive policies of these goods, while every endeavour is made to lift convenience goods to the higher ranks.

When an article appears to have reached a point where it has assumed the characteristics of another class along with the customer attitudes of this class, or with a little pressure could be profitably made to assume such characteristics, then the producers of the article should reorientate their sales policies accordingly. This has happened to gramophone records, transistor radios, hardware goods, films, paperbacks, small domestic electrical equipment; all of these, and many others, are being sold on a hybrid basis of half shopping/half-convenience classification. This practice has within it its own perpetuation and there could well be an acceleration in the acceptance of these goods as convenience goods as the public become aware of the increased convenience of their location of purchase.

Brands of convenience goods, by active sales promotion, can become shopping goods, although they rarely if ever lose their original identity. They tend to be shopping goods in varying degrees to different people, e.g. soap, special foods, cigarettes, etc.

The economic environment of the buyer must not be ignored in the dynamic aspect of classification. In a period when the market is more price-conscious, brand preference is reduced, and the article that enjoyed some loyalty, which resulted in its conversion to speciality goods, could easily lose its ranking unless the price policy is correctly adjusted to current conditions.

Modern developments in retailing may in the future play a bigger part in customer attitudes than the classification and the branding of goods. The imagery surrounding the modern shop could well suggest that a person chooses a shop and not a product; and that the overall impression of the store is more important than its particular contents. Such a development, when linked with multiple supermarket stores, requires a completely new analysis of distribution and sales policies. Loyalty to a store takes over from loyalty to a brand; people shop for a shop, not for specific goods. The retail store has become a type of shopping goods or even speciality goods.

The increased turnover of multiples has been largely due to the creation of loyalty to a store to which people will go, perhaps with some inconvenience, to purchase convenience goods and shopping goods. The large multiple enjoys a big advantage when creating a speciality image, in that its large catchment area retains patronage to the chain, despite movements of the population.

The sales manager must maintain intimate contact with shopping habits. If the tendency is increasingly to treat shopping goods as convenience goods or vice versa, then tactics must change accordingly. In some fields it may be deemed worthwhile to try to avoid this relegation of the product by a sustained campaign of promotion, whilst in others the more profitable action may be to follow the new customer attitude and accept it.

The technical achievement of modern advertising and printing must not be overlooked when dealing with the classification of goods. The ability to show to perfection and in detail the models in a range of shopping goods, e.g. space heaters and washing machines, could partly reduce the importance of 'full-line' stocking of all products at all points of distribution. Mail-order activities in the field of shopping goods benefit from this exhibition quality of modern advertising and as a result articles are purchased which have not been seen and examined or compared with competing models. Mail order as an outlet for shopping goods is also helped by intensive brand advertising, especially if this is highly informative; when this occurs the customer's familiarity with the company's product is such that mail ordering is less of a risk than it appears at first sight. This example demonstrates the need for sales managers to be abreast of current development when planning the tactics of a selling and distribution programme.

INDUSTRIAL GOODS

The sale of industrial goods is becoming increasingly influenced by the practices used in the sale of consumer goods.

Allowing for the obvious difference in the meaning of unit value when dealing with the two classes of goods, consumer and industrial, certain types do possess the characteristics of convenience goods. The setting up of a standard for an industry, as with A.P.I. (American Petroleum Institute) and B.S.I. (British Standards Institution), does encourage some substitution among products. The same result can be achieved when an industrial buyer specifies exactly the article needed. When such a situation occurs, the patronage decision made by the customer is based more on the ability of the supplier to work to the convenience of the customer than it is to any quality within the product. Although this convenience may include price, which can become an element of differentiation between suppliers, it would also cover such items as dependability, speed in rectifying errors, reliable supplies, etc., all of which are very akin to the concept of maximum convenience.

The modern organization of industry into disintegrated units, with progressive assembly the dominant method of production, has increased the importance of service or the convenience motivation in patronage, as fears of breakdown must be reconciled with minimum stockholding; regular deliveries, minimum stocks and incipient urgency are reminiscent of consumer convenience goods.

Motivation research into rational motives in the supply of components and raw materials could show a strong similarity to the attitudes to convenience goods in the consumer markets. Where a manufacturer sees this to be the case, then sales plans for these industrial goods would be based on the same principles as those governing sales of consumer goods. This would mean an assumption that the product could be made by many, and that the only reason for selecting a supplier is based on convenience, in its economic sense. This would lead to an emphasis within the sales plan of those aspects which were associated with the convenience motivation of the customer. Advertising and all sales promotion would emphasize the distinctive service features of the company rather than its ability to produce the specified article, which is taken for granted. Supply companies in such markets would aim to build up an image which would create the same type of customer reaction as that which exists towards top-class retail stores; industrial buyers would shop for the supplier, not for the goods. This shows up the need for the highest degree of customer orientation on the part of the supplier and the relegation of the product to its proper place.

Equipment would largely fall into the shopping-goods category with its characteristics of high unit value, infrequent purchasing and lack of urgency creating the time and the desire to shop around. All advertising and exhibition work, together with sales-representative activity, should aim at stressing the amalgam of qualities possessed by the product compared with others relative to the needs of the customer. The shopping centre display is achieved with industrial shopping goods by means of industrial exhibitions and advertising in technical journals. If analysis shows the shopping-goods attitude in the customers, then prestige advertising of a non-informative nature becomes peripheral to the sales activity (this does not mean that it is unimportant, but that it could not make up for product deficiencies, or defects in the information about the product).

Speciality goods in the industrial field would have to be truly of this nature. The knowledgeability of the buyers would militate against any attempt to create by sales devices the type of speciality goods found in the consumer markets. The brand name in this field is a mark of identification, not differentiation, which must be within the product itself.

Despite these qualifications, true speciality goods and services are perhaps the most common class of industrial goods. Products may be the result of innovation by the producer, or made for the special requirements of a customer, both perhaps covered by patent registration. Similarly with firms, manufacturers can build up a reputation as speciality units able to produce a certain range of goods to particular standards of perfection; such a manufacturer is selling on the speciality reputation of the firm and should be customer-orientated to maintain this profitable image.

Industrial speciality goods and firms promote their products in the same way as for shopping goods, attention being focused on the unique features of the product or service spectrum of the firm.

'CONDUSTRIAL' GOODS – CONSUMER GOODS
TREATED AS INDUSTRIAL GOODS

A special strategy may be required when consumer goods in a market have achieved a high degree of interchangeability in so far as customers' choice is concerned. A situation could well arise where in addition to this high degree of substitution, there existed a very strong customer motivation in the form of convenience of purchase. In other words, the heavy outlays on brand promotion to create a degree of distinction in the product and loyalty of the customer had failed to counteract the more heavily weighted convenience factor in motivation.

If alongside such a development there was a parallel trend towards greater dominance of the trade in the goods concerned by multiples, then a further complication would arise. Although the article itself is classified as a consumer good, the actual weak link in its promotion is now in the field of industrial goods, in that, although it may have achieved the necessary degree of acceptability, in order that this can be converted into sales the article must be readily available at points of convenient purchase. These latter locations, however, are dominated by multiple units which regard the goods as a component in their trading mix aimed at maximizing profit rather than a source of immediate satisfaction. The motivation of the professional buyer in such cases is totally rational and resembles the approach of an industrial buyer faced with a range of potential suppliers of a common component; he assumes the interchangeability of the components and chooses on non-product bases, e.g. price, delivery etc.

This is not to suggest that outlays on brand advertising are wasted but that they could be if they were at the expense of possible incentives to dealers in another part of the mix; great outlays may be needed to create only a minor change in consumer attitudes towards a brand and perhaps such outlays could be better spent on meeting the more prominent convenience aspect of customer motivation by selling in the product more positively to retail stores. Clearly, any trend towards shopping for shops would accelerate this tendency.

The suggestion is made that when products have reached a plateau of similarity and interchangeability in the mind of the final customer then the emphasis in selling them should move to an industrial approach and the allocation of resources in the mix should respond accordingly.

This category of goods refers specifically to manufacturers' branded consumer goods which must achieve a certain standard of acceptability by the final customer, but whose sales can be frustrated unless this favourable consumer attitude can be converted into buying behaviour through the presence of the goods at the points of sale frequented by these customers for reasons of convenience, price, etc. The increasing power of the retail buying unit demands a correct fusion of consumer-goods promotion and industrial marketing to maximize sales. The classification does not include goods sold to multiples and others for dealer-brand promotion: this is pure industrial marketing to highly professional and rational buyers.

PART FOUR

MARKETING STRATEGY

1. The Marketing 'Mix'

THE basic aim of marketing is to maximize the output per given unit of input into the business, to achieve the highest revenue per unit of overall cost of obtaining that revenue. It is not concerned with maximizing sales, but with maximizing profits.

In much the same way as the production of an article involves mixing together various complementary but at the same time potentially opposing factors, e.g. capital equipment can replace labour but may make the remaining necessary labour more efficient, so the marketeer is faced with an even greater variety of possible combinations of methods from which to select the one which will maximize efficiency and profitability. As with production, the constituents of the mixture may be seen as aiding or replacing each other – as complements or substitutes. A policy of price reduction may be preferred to one involving advertising for the purpose of increasing sales, but the action on price will probably make the advertising more effective, so that an adjustment in one part of the mixture makes another part more productive in terms of output (sales) relative to input (advertising costs). An increased allocation to design activities may result in more effective advertising and personal selling.

Again, there is a similarity to production method in that the marketing 'mix' should be balanced in the same way as an assembly line or the total operation of a plant; a shortage of any element in production can lead to waste, in that the other elements are less productive than they might be; the true measurement of the diseconomies created by the element in short supply is the waste incurred by the other elements in that they do not achieve their potential. The same situations occur in marketing, and the consequences can be measured in the same way.

If a company is involved in a costly sales-promotion campaign and the essence of the claims made is that the product has a comparative quality advantage, then, to the extent that this quality does not meet customer expectations because of inadequate quality control of the product, so the outlay on advertising, packaging and personal selling will be wasted. Expensive packaging and advertising programmes are frustrated if, to cut down distribution costs, inefficient depots and dealers are used and this reduces the availability of the goods to the final customer. Advertising outlays may create awareness of the product and so be deemed productive as communication exercises, but bad correlation with distributors (margins) or price (too high) may reduce their commercial value. Balance of elements is of vital significance in the 'mix' if waste is to be reduced and the productivity per unit of input maximized. The mixture of 'push' and 'pull' allocations must be correct if net revenue is to be optimized: a bad balance is wasteful.

Consistency is needed throughout the marketing of a product and this is the practical consequence of balance between the elements; inconsistency can lead to waste or lack of productivity in the other elements. If a product is to be sold on a high-value or high-class image, then the design of the product and/or the package must embody this image; advertising will be consistent with the image in terms of copy, art work, and media used; a brand name will be chosen with a quality connotation; dealers with the same image will be used; the calibre of sales representatives and their method of selling will be in harmony with the required projection of the product. The strength of the marketing 'mix' is that of the weakest point.

Unlike the production side, the productivity of each element of marketing is greatly affected by outside forces. The balance at one point in time may be completely out of balance at another time; the introduction of a new product by a competitor, a new type of advertising, a different price policy, a revolution in dealer relationships, all create situations which demand an adjustment of the balance of the marketing 'mix'. The marketing 'mix' then must be balanced within itself, but at the same time it must react sympathetically to external changes in the marketing 'mix' of competitors or perhaps to forestall future competitive developments. The 'mix' will also have to be responsive to all the socio-economic factors identified as relevant to the productivity of the 'mix'; many of these factors are associated with customer motivation.

MOTIVATION RESEARCH AND PRIORITIES WITHIN THE MARKETING 'MIX'

The marketing 'mix' must obviously be customer-orientated. A customer buys certain goods and services because the totality of the 'mix' of each of the suppliers has made a special appeal as compared with all other competitors. The fact that there are different 'mixes' from which to choose and that those not chosen by one group of customers continue to enjoy a market for their goods shows marketing 'mixes' reflecting different motivation 'mixes'; these may coalesce into identifiable market segments, each with its motivation idiosyncrasies. The correct marketing policy for any firm is really the 'mix' which corresponds to the segment motivation 'mix' which is considered most profitable, bearing in mind the ability of the firm to meet the demands of the 'mix', e.g. quality demands, and also the degree of competition among suppliers relative to the demand from the segment.

Sometimes the motivations which are given priority by the potential customer are obvious and rational, or obvious and irrational; at other times they may be very covert and highly emotional. It is the duty of all concerned with the allocation of resources in marketing to detect and respond to, not only motives, but also motivation dynamics.

In the industrial market, investigation may show that dissatisfaction with the existing supplier is the main motive for changing supplier; this should be seen by the current supplier as indicating a need to give top marketing 'mix' priority to the removal of all 'unselling' activities, and may lead to an increased allocation of resources to quality control, production planning and control, distribution, etc. The degree of customer dissatisfaction created by a breakdown in supplies is determined by the economic or satisfaction consequences of the breakdown; in mass-production plants the losses may be very great, therefore fear of breakdown or reliability of supplier may supersede all other motives, and the supply firm will make reliability and dependable after-sales service the dominant feature of its marketing 'mix'. The private owner of a car, washing machine or television set will have to be rated as to the importance of reliability of after-sales service by determining the degree of frustration and dissatisfaction, and therefore customer ill-will, caused by a breakdown in the appliance. In both these cases, the marketing 'mix' may be altered to give increased emphasis to complying with the motivation 'mix'; this could mean more attention to design, and direct dealing with the removal of intermediaries and the setting up of depots giving better after-sales service.

Apparently uneconomical allocation of resources to distribution can often be justified in that it enables the manufacturer to respond to the cost-benefit motivation of retailers faced with on-cost and space problems.

To achieve the maximum effectiveness in a market the whole of the company's activities should be given priority ratings in keeping with the motivation 'mix'; activities which appear to be well outside conventional marketing can, on analysis, be seen to loom large in the customer's motives for purchase or for refusing to do so. Increased labour cost or unrest will create a drive to replace it wherever possible, and this should lead to greater expenditure on research and development and design to produce equipment which will exploit this enhanced motivation drive on the part of the customers. Companies using network-analysis techniques will tend to upgrade delivery as a motivation drive; and so production control should be tightened by the supplier. Price-conscious end-markets may require the use of value-analysis methods or variety reduction, and again the marketing 'mix' should respond sympathetically.

The complementary nature of the 'mix' is seen at this rational level in that where the customer is satisfied with the product or service supplied, then the productivity of advertising is increased in that repeat sales are more easily achieved. Sales representatives will not have to spend time explaining reasons for past failures, but can concentrate on further positive selling.

In the more emotional fields of consumer selling, the allocation of funds to an investigation of motives is a fundamental part of the 'mix' itself. The design, colour, texture and quality of a product, together with its pack, may all result from such research.

Sales research, including motivation research, must be used as the basis for the selling aspect of the marketing 'mix' – the selling 'mix' we can call it – the combination of advertising, special promotions, dealer relationships, channels of distribution, branding, packaging and personal selling. At any point in time it is vital to know the relative importance to the customer of these elements within selling and their relationship to product design, quality, credit, etc. If price is increasing in importance relative to brand, or class distinctions are being eradicated, or service at retail point is not expected or needed, then each one should show itself in the emphasis given to price policy, advertising and dealer margins; all are elements with cost contents; all must be scrutinized relative to customer motivation to achieve that combination of outlay which will maximize returns per unit of cost. Marketing 'mixes' are really exercises in cost-effectiveness.

There need not be complete compatibility between each element within the consumer motivation 'mix' and the marketing 'mix', but the net compatibilities must be reconciled. Thus, a higher price may have to be offset by an emphasis on a product advantage which is greater than the price disadvantage. Motivation research remains the basis of 'mixes' even when the net compatibility is being considered, in that it will show the relative strengths of elements and therefore the power (and costs) needed to discount them in the mind of the consumer. It will be concerned with the likely consequences of selling outlays used for promoting the net compatibility in the light of the priorities given to various elements by consumers and their incompatibility with the product or price, etc.

We now consider certain sections of the marketing 'mix', but by no means all of them,[1] beginning with the relationship between the purely sales activity of the 'selling mix' and moving on to the totality of the marketing 'mix' itself.

1. Clearly the combination of elements is too great, and therefore only those are considered which are of special significance in that they show the basic thinking on 'mixes'.

THE 'SELLING MIX' (ADVERTISING, SPECIAL PROMOTIONS, BRANDING, PACKAGING, PERSONAL SELLING, DEALER RELATIONSHIPS)

In so far as the other elements within the marketing 'mix' are insufficient to sustain sales, so the emphasis is moved towards the 'selling mix'. Where products are not completely compatible with customer need, for any reason, then selling must make up for this deficiency.

As marketing becomes more producer-orientated, so selling is increased in importance; where capital equipment is limited as to the range of products or where past policies have reduced the appeal of a firm, e.g. through bad dealer or customer relationships, or inefficiency at any point in the firm's contact with the customers, then selling may be needed in the short run to remedy the situation.

Emphasis on the selling 'mix' allocation relative to other allocations may be justified when there is a degree of similarity among the other elements as between competitors. When a product is specified by a customer, e.g. a multiple or industrial buyer, when prices are fixed, when all other features are equal as between firms, selling may then make the marginal difference, and so it is uprated for allocation purposes.

Selling is more likely to be productive in those fields where customers can be persuaded to change their attitude towards a product – the essence of selling. This tends to suggest that it will be found mostly in the consumer field with its less knowledgeable and more emotional buyers, where the persuasion of selling can be used to affect, not only the type of product bought, but also the quantity. Allocations to selling within the marketing 'mix' will therefore be greatest in the consumer market.

Within the 'selling mix' the priorities vary according to circumstances; brand advertising takes up more of the sales budget in consumer convenience-goods markets than in consumer-durables, and even more where self-service stores dominate. Packaging receives more attention when the article must sell itself, or when heavy movement or storage costs are involved. Dealer mark-ups may be increased when an unknown brand is handled to offset customer reluctance at the point of sale. Personal selling may have to bear the brunt of making a market where advertising is limited or not effective, e.g. industrial goods. The need for the display of complex products or applications at the point of sale, or to respond to cost-benefit motivations, may necessitate large outlays on the recruitment and training of staff for this purpose.

The main principle behind the marketing 'mix' and the smaller 'selling mix' is that the arrangement and allocation of resources should be such as to maximize returns per unit of outlay. Each resource should be used up to that point where any additional outlay would give a lower return than could be obtained by using it elsewhere. Equi-marginal returns on all outlays should be the objective so that any change would reduce the total return, the maximum having been achieved.

The importance of the 'selling mix' varies with deficiencies in the other elements of the marketing 'mix', the degree of equality between competitors as to price and product, and the nature of the product and the customer.

THE BALANCE BETWEEN 'PUSH' AND 'PULL'

The 'push' policy of selling is concerned with moving goods into distribution points, i.e. wholesalers and retailers. This may be achieved by financial incentives to dealers, special retail promotions, with or without financial inducements, etc.; the aim is to directly exploit the immediate economic motivation of the dealer. These activities could be supplemented by other aspects of the 'push' policy such as increased personal representation and merchandising assistance.

The various elements of this method of selling are largely variable in cost and do not represent any large indivisible outlay; the break-even point between outlay and revenue is soon reached if a 'push' policy dominates the mix.

The 'pull' method of selling uses funds to influence final customer attitudes and make the product move through distribution points; to be replaced by profit-conscious dealers. The method is usually by sustained heavy advertising and related promotional activity acting directly on the final customer; normally involving heavy indivisible outlays with break-even points further away, but potentially the profits may be greater.

It is vital that the 'mix' of these two methods is correct. (Additionally, it must not be forgotten that price policy can be used as a part of any 'push' policy; this would necessitate striking a balance between 'push', 'pull', and price.) Over-spending on 'pull' advertising may create awareness and even change attitudes beneficially but sales will not materialize until this results in behaviour; but behaviour often demands physical presence of the product at convenient points of sale. To under-spend on dealer incentives and over-spend on advertising would not optimize revenue even though sheer advertising goals were achieved. Similarly the expenditure on advertising will motivate dealers to respond positively to 'push' outlays. To maximize revenue, both 'push' and 'pull' are usually needed, and in balance.

PRICE AND THE 'SELLING MIX'

Perhaps the most important decision to be taken in marketing strategy concerns the relationship between price and selling activities. The classical way to increase sales was by reducing price, but today this action is often only taken when all else has failed. Another basic decision is the distribution of the proceeds of the market price between the manufacturer and any dealers who are concerned with its distribution and/or selling; although the market price itself may be partly determined by the need to accommodate adequate distributor margins. There could be a basic incompatibility between the value or price put on the product by the customer, the necessary sales figure at this price and the profit margin requirements of dealers. Payments to anyone other than the manufacturer out of the total revenue received for a product represent an outlay by the manufacturer and therefore should be appraised for their contribution to profitability in the same way as any other outlay; a reduced price to the final customer may, as an outlay, be more productive than an inflated profit margin to the dealer.

In all types of selling, from the simple face-to-face method to the complicated means of persuasion of today, a decision must be made on the relative effectiveness of sales effort (and outlays) and price reductions as means of promoting sales. Both methods cost money; the former involves an outlay, while the latter involves a sacrifice per unit sold. At some point in every selling act, the cost of persuasion can become greater than the immediate profit gained by the sale;[2] the marketeer may thus increase his profitability more effectively by reducing price rather than continuing uneconomic selling.

Where capital has already been committed and where, in addition, a certain scale of operation is needed, then marketing is solely concerned with so arranging the price/selling 'mix' that this optimum production figure is reached with the highest net revenue from sales. With highly capital-intensive industries the situation may not occur where the diseconomies of selling more than offset the potential economies of production. This clearly is the situation in many industries today where the production economies of scale are great, and the achievement of these economies is through the use of equipment involving heavy capital outlays. Firms in such industries are faced with the problem of achieving the optimum production/sales figure by the most effective means; such means often come down to a decision on price reductions to achieve the necessary sales figure, or extra sales promotion to obtain the sales needed at a higher price.

A higher price, above the 'natural' or acceptable price, is the creation of sales-promotion activities, and the net profitability of sales promotion can be measured by the extent to which the expected satisfaction of the customer, as shown by the price he is willing to pay for a product, exceeds the cost of creating that expectation in his mind. Sales promotion can continue profitably up to that point where the cost of creating an increase of satisfaction in the mind of the potential customer is equal to the responses in monetary terms of the customer; beyond that point

2. Sometimes this can be justified in the long period in that repeat orders are a consequence of the initial selling activity.

the activity is clearly uneconomic. This increase of expected satisfaction can be in terms of the individual customer or in terms of additions to the market.[3] As the market becomes more price-conscious or less well disposed towards a product, so the margin will be reached more quickly; this in practice will lead to a reduction in price in order to achieve the marginal equality, which was not possible at the higher price, where the cost of persuasion was greater than the monetary return; an outlay through a reduction in price is more productive. This concept is really an extension of the marginal-utility analysis in that, whereas the simpler versions of this theory assume the customer to act rationally and to purchase unemotionally, this extension assumes that an expectation of satisfaction or utility can be stimulated by sales promotion. The marginal concept still exists, but it is now at a higher level of expected satisfaction which is made up of an estimate of the physical utility, if any, of the product, and the desire to obtain the emotional benefits which possession of the product is thought to give. This synthesized psychological extension to the physical product is a distinctive feature of the goods and services making up the standard of living of affluent societies.

Should the socio-economic situation affect the customer in such a way that price-consciousness is dominant, then any margin between the costs of promoting sales and the revenue from those sales will quickly disappear; the cost of creating a psychological extension to the product will soon become greater than the increase in revenue resulting from it.

In the emotional, consumer fields, the possibility of maintaining the demand for a product at a price above the 'natural' one will be greater than in the more rational and price-conscious industrial market. So the main sales-promotion outlays are to be found in the consumer fields where customer estimates of value can be increased beyond the cost of increasing them, and also additional units of demand can be more easily stimulated. The selling/price 'mix' is, other things being equal, dependent on the potential emotional contents of the goods to be sold, the knowledgeability

3. These are the same in that, if the subjective valuation is increased, then more people will be willing to pay a given price for it than before.

138

of the customer relative to the goods, and the drives on the customer, emotional and social or rational and economic.

However, the cost of selling or the adjustment in price may be such that the diseconomies involved more than outweigh any potential economies in the production of the goods sold, and in such cases the cost of the total activity of making and selling additional products must be considered when additional sales are sought. In other cases, apparently wasteful selling is more than offset by savings in the cost of production; expensive advertising can often be justified in this way.

In selling there are certain types of outlays which are indivisible but which must be made if the firm is to sell in a given market; these represent heavy outlays which can only be justified in terms of potential sales and/or fear of idle capacity in production – they are necessary risks. Such outlays are needed if a firm wishes to enter certain markets with heavily entrenched interests; half the money needed may be only one-tenth as effective in brand promotion. Staying in a market may also involve similar indivisible outlays.

In cases where a decision on an indivisible factor must be made, the alternative looked for may be a divisible one, particularly when a firm is unable to finance the indivisible, or does not have the necessary permanent interest in the market to make the investment worthwhile. Among the divisible alternatives are, not only price, but higher commission to salesmen, an increased sales force, and bigger margins to dealers. None of these involves one heavy outlay, as with advertising, but instead they represent a 'step-by-step' type of outlay which is financed out of the actual sales themselves, and can therefore be more easily sustained by the smaller firm.

A similar situation can occur where good after-sales service is needed involving a heavy outlay. Faced with this cost, a company may opt for a different policy and emphasize price rather than service, or it may make changes in distribution and profit margins to place the responsibility for the service on to others.[4]

If there is evidence that advertising is showing increased

4. See the chapter on Budgeting for comparison of the cost situation involved in this type of decision.

effectiveness per unit of cost, then the decision taken on the price/selling 'mix' might be determined by this factor. The small firm, unable to afford the necessary scale of advertising, might then decide to use other sales devices, such as changes in the product, price reductions, or improved attention to customer. This type of situation can occur when national brands invade the market of a local manufacturer.

When we consider the activities of competitors as an influence on price and selling emphasis, then the problem becomes more complex. In markets where the price is fixed by convention or other means, then quite clearly the main burden will fall on the advertising and associated functions; this is the situation in the United Kingdom petrol trade, where prices tend to move in unison, both up and down. The problem is made worse for the petrol marketeers in that nothing which is obviously a comparative advantage can be claimed for this product other than price, and so advertising is needed to create extensions to the product, at considerable cost. From this analysis, however, the attraction of a price-cut by one firm becomes abundantly clear, in that the comparative attraction of one brand is a result of the similarity of price of all the others. Moreover, although the total demand for petrol may be relatively inelastic, the demand for one brand is highly elastic. Certain cut-price companies have benefited by having a 'mix' which is non-conformist;[5] should the rest of the trade retaliate in like manner, then the comparative advantage disappears.

A similar situation may occur in the relationship between price and dealer margins. Where a trade is dominated by conventional margins, a price may develop for a product, which begins to assume the qualities of a 'natural' price in the mind of the public, although it bears no relationship to the cost of production and distribution. This type of marketing situation presents the prospect of a potentially large demand for any manufacturer whose price does not include the conventional dealer margins

5. A 'maverick' sales 'mix' can often succeed, e.g. a non-conformist price, an obvious increase in value, an ethical policy amid unethical ones, but only so long as the 'maverick' description is appropriate; if others join, then the comparative situation is changed.

and can therefore benefit by non-conformity. Where the dealers are still used, but at reduced margins, the selling 'mix' will now be stepped up on advertising to promote a brand which no longer has complete dealer support. Nevertheless such a policy could be supported if the market was a falling one and the new 'mix' was compatible with more economy-minded customers; the customer drive and the advertising together would be relied upon to overcome dealer hostility.

A similar attack on conventional selling in order to reduce prices in elastic brand markets where 'fixed' prices rule might result in direct dealing with the customer; this might require even more emphasis on advertising, personal selling and also, perhaps, outlays on depots and service stations.

In all 'mix' decisions, however, the future actions of competitors must be considered; the possible situation which will obtain when all competitive responses have ceased is of great significance in determining 'mixes' which are non-conformist. If the total demand for a product is stationary, and the price ruling in the market is 'fixed', any advertising or other sales-promotion outlay will have to be financed out of the gross margin available to each firm out of revenue after all non-selling costs have been met. If one firm reduces its price in this situation of potentially high elasticity of demand for any one brand, then the others may have to follow with similar price-cuts. The consequence would be a final 'settled down' position where the firms would have another 'fixed' price, only at a lower level, and sales promotion would then have to be met out of a reduced gross margin. With an inelastic total demand for the product the results would be lower profits for each firm. It is the possibility of such an end-situation which probably determines many 'mixes' and tends to maintain the *status quo*. With durables, however, the total market may be more elastic, and any increase in demand for a brand is not necessarily completely at the cost of other brands.

Here, with increasing price-consciousness on the part of the market, the case for price reduction could still be sustained in view of the degree of postponability of purchase and the extensive nature of competition. This could be applicable, even when all firms incurred the same selling costs and settled down to a new lower common price, if this price was more in sympathy with the market reaction to this product as compared with all the other products on which the discretionary purchasing power could be spent.

Various price/selling 'mixes' can be used in the same market in response to different motivation 'mixes' on the part of customers. Sometimes this might happen in connection with one firm as it changes the emphasis on elements of the total 'mix' to suit different segments and so achieves maximum sales. One segment may have high price, brand susceptibility, and high-class dealer (and therefore margin) characteristics; another may be motivated by economy with little emphasis on brand or type of dealer. The net profit achieved per article in both markets may be the same owing to the extra promotion costs and margins involved in the higher price, though the producer has increased his market by 'mixes' responding to segment motivation.

RESEARCH AND DEVELOPMENT AND THE 'MIX'

The development of new products, innovations and improvements to the existing range, and the discovery of new uses for products can all be of greater significance in marketing than any purely selling function.

An allocation of the appropriate resources to research and development is needed to sustain the sales needed to make past, present and future investment viable. Plant and equipment must make something which is vendible, otherwise it loses its value.

The priority given to research and development should be greater where peripheral design changes are not sufficient to sustain sales. In the industrial field the main motivation to purchase in a competitive economy is the economic advantage represented by the new machine; sales then depend on the technological, or, more precisely, the economic rate of obsolescence of existing equipment; this rate can be accelerated by research and development. The industrial buyer can be made to fear economic ostracism when faced with a new machine which is also available to his competitors.

In all fields of marketing the effectiveness of advertising and personal selling is more likely to be productive if something new and, at the same time, desirable can be shown. Investment in one part of the 'mix' is thus increasing the productivity of others; advertising is likely to make more positive communications; representatives will make more productive calls.

Where a business is not suited financially to devote adequate funds to research and development, then it might abdicate the function and work to the specifications of others; it then markets through a diffcrent 'mix' with 'reliability' and price rather than economic, functional, or emotional product novelty as a main motive for purchase. Others might work under licence, where research and development has failed and sales pressure on production capacity has weakened. Research and development is the basis of product policy and the sustenance of continued sales; the 'mix' must reflect this.

DESIGN AND QUALITY POLICY AND THE 'MIX'

Although a predisposition towards a product can be created by advertising, the commercial outcome of this advertising is not measured in terms of customer awareness, but in profitable sales of the product itself. The more the design of a product and the satisfaction it gives are compatible with customer motivation, then the more productive the selling function will be. Design may play a prominent part in the provision of a comparative advantage, real or imagined, within a product – a vital need if advertising and personal selling are to be effective.

The quality of the product should be maintained by giving this function its proper priority as a marketing activity. To spend money on creating an image which is not sustained because of bad quality control shows the potential diseconomies present when the elements of the 'mix' are not properly balanced; the waste due to an inadequate allocation to inspection is equal to the reduced effectiveness of the money spent on sales promotion.

CREDIT AND THE 'MIX'

When research shows that credit is an important motive in the sale of a product, the 'mix' should react accordingly. This may involve subsidizing credit and would be considered a sales-promotion cost.

Some attempt should be made to assess the productivity of a given amount of money used as a subsidy to credit as compared with the same outlay on other sales-promotion devices. Customer motivation priorities must again be the dominant factor, but, as with advertising and price policy, the provision of this facility by others might create a new situation and the need for a new 'mix'.

Credit extension to dealers may be necessary in order to promote the maximum coverage of a market. In such cases the diseconomies of not extending the necessary credit would include any frustrated or wasted pre-selling and packaging which had occurred because the desired product was not available for purchase. Wherever dealers have a cost-benefit motivation based on a working-capital deficiency, this should increase the priority given to credit extension by the manufacturer.

AFTER-SALES SERVICE ALLOCATION

Where fear of breakdown is dominant, priority should be given to allaying it by setting up the necessary after-sales services in the 'mix'. Unfortunately this may be expensive if it is to carry the necessary conviction. Additionally, the service must be seen to be available before the purchase will be made; the outlay on it will fall into the same priority category as that on advertising. In fact, without the service the advertising might be unproductive because of the obvious defect in sales policy; certainly the repeat sales based on customer satisfaction would be difficult to achieve.

The provision of an adequate after-sales service may be given to independent distributors, but this will then affect the allocation of returns between the manufacturer and the dealer when the end market is price-competitive, in that the dealer will have to receive a bigger margin out of which to finance the necessary standard of service.

THE 'MIX' AND EQUI-MARGINAL RETURNS

Decision-taking in business is always dominated by the concept of equi-marginal returns.

In marketing, this principle would show itself as the main determinant of the marketing 'mix'; the final allocation of resources among the various elements of the 'mix' should be such that no gain can be obtained by further switching resources from one element or activity to another. Money would be spent on each element up to that point where a greater return would be possible if it were diverted to another one. If design was under-financed and excessive outlays went on advertising, then additional finance to advertising would be less productive than if it were used in the designing of new products. If packaging had involved heavy expenditure, but quality control had been starved of finance, again a switch would benefit the overall returns of the enterprise.

Expenditure involves an economic sacrifice which is made, in business, to obtain a return in excess of that expenditure. Thus the balance between price and sales promotion could also be struck at a point of equi-marginal returns; a reduction in price represents an economic sacrifice in the same way as an outlay on advertising. If greater returns can be achieved by reduced prices than by an increase in sales-promotion costs, then the emphasis should move towards this form of economic outlay or cost, i.e. a reduction in price, until the balance between the two elements had been redressed.

The productivity of each factor is a joint one with one or several others. Price reductions would continue up to that point where the return in selling effects equals that obtained from the last incremental outlay on advertising; the two would then be giving equi-marginal returns. At the same time, however, the new price policy might well be making the advertising more productive. It is the end output of the total input which is significant; this will be maximized when the outlays on all the elements of the 'mix' are giving equi-marginal returns.

Such an ideal 'mix' is a difficult one to achieve in reality. The productivity, relative to cost, of a reduction in price can be altered violently if a competitor reduces his prices; advertising productivity is dependent on the counter-activities of others and the changing susceptibilities of the customer.

To maintain maximum profitability through applying the concept of equi-marginal returns in marketing requires the utmost flexibility in allocation of resources within the 'mix' in order to respond to all those factors which influence the relative productivity of each element.

Earlier, we saw that the existence of indivisible factors might rule out certain alternative policies to some firms, e.g. heavy advertising. In applying the equi-marginal concept to such outlays the productivity would be a long-period estimate rather than an immediate one. An estimate would be made of the long-term consequences of the outlay in terms of sales; and in some cases this might take on, like the modern machine investment decision, the more sombre inquiry as to the consequences if the outlay were not made.

MARKETING RESEARCH AND THE MARKETING 'MIX'

At the base of all marketing 'mix' decisions is the vital one that concerns the allocation of authority and finance to the activity which directly affects the ultimate effectiveness of the 'mix' itself; the correctness of later 'mix' decisions is dependent on a supply of adequate information, but this supply depends on the correct initial decision on the importance of marketing research to the 'mix'. Where an enterprise has accepted the comprehensive customer-orientation which is synonymous with marketing throughout this book, then the desire to obtain this orientation to a degree which surpasses all competitors should result in marketing research being given the required authority, and also the finance needed to make that authority fruitful. With the one-man business this would imply a willingness to give due thought to an analysis of his marketing method, whilst with a large organization it could involve the whole apparatus of a specialist department with advisory or functional authority over all branches of marketing from the introduction of new products to the sales plans, and including a continuous appraisal of the 'mix' which contains these elements in order to maintain its effectiveness at optimum level.

2. Sales Policy and Sales-Promotion Planning

THE concept of marketing used throughout this book covers every aspect of the business which, in any way at any point, could influence the attitude of a customer or potential customer towards that business. Within this all-embracing complex, there are two large divisions; these divisions are sales policy and sales-promotion planning.

Sales policy is frequently used as a term to cover the selling activity, and yet its constituents more closely resemble parts of general policy. Sales policy is concerned with the reconciliation of manufacturing, finance and selling to the needs of the customer; whereas sales-promotion planning is devoted to the execution of the sales of a given product or service, and is concerned with changing the attitudes of customers to the benefit of the enterprise.

The design of the product and the quality standard are sales-policy matters and require sales-policy decisions of considerable gravity; whereas advertising, branding and sales organization are the concern of sales planners who sell the product about which the sales-policy decisions were made. It is just possible that some degree of success could occur without sales-promotion planning in almost any field, and in the industrial market this activity has often been ignored without the demise of the enterprise concerned; but it would be difficult for the most inspired sales-promotion plan to rescue, or compensate for, a totally inadequate sales policy.

Sales policy is really that part of general policy which achieves for a business the maximum customer-orientation; permeating activities which, strictly speaking, are not selling activities. Any investigation of sales policy quickly confirms this, in that any aspect of general policy which affects customer attitudes is, by our definition, sales policy. If the reader doubts the significance of such a broad definition of sales policy, then it must be recalled that the end objective of general policy is maximization of profits, but this is only achieved by accepting that the customer, and not manufacturing ability, is the real source of these profits.

Particularly apparent when analysing the various segments of sales policy is the emergence of the trinity of functions: manufacturing, finance and selling. Sometimes all three will be found in one segment, e.g. with range policy; sometimes only two are concerned, as in design decisions. The result of this community of interests or functions in each segment of sales policy is that decisions always require the co-ordination or reconciliation of at least two, perhaps basically opposed, activities. Again the identification of sales policy and general policy is apparent here, in that general policy contains decisions which are arrived at after due consideration of all the factors (departments, activities, functions, etc.) concerned.

Where sales policy is correct, the following company attitudes will emerge. Research and development will be based on customer reaction and market potential. The design of products will be guided by motivation research and the sustenance of markets. Quality control will assume its true purpose of maintaining the name of the firm, rather than being an inspection function. Production planning and control will be seen as a means of meeting customers' requirements in order to maximize goodwill. Range policy will be viewed in its wider selling and financial context, rather than as an aid to batch or mass production.

Clearly, sales-policy orientation of this calibre is incomplete without a reciprocal attitude on the part of the sales-promotion side. Meeting too many variations in the needs of customers must be known to be basically bad for production. The ability to deliver ex-stock must be seen as a financial embarrassment as well as a sales aid. The advantage of eliminating independent wholesalers and retailers must be set off against the financial implication of such a policy. Increased credit extension, easy to justify in selling, must be judged in financial terms as well as in terms of selling effort.

The financial advisers must also play their part in maximizing the profits of the enterprise through customer-orientation. The cost of stockholding of finished goods or after-sales service spares should be judged in terms of comparative sales advantages over competitors. Price policy may have to be unrelated to strictly tenable costing principles to meet the exigencies of a market.

Although integration of sales policy and sales planning is vital, there must be delineation between them for the successful running of a business. At some point in the sales policy making process there must be a definite decision on product, range, quality, credit, price etc. and jointly on the amalgam of these which is to be created by the enterprise. Sales-promotion planning then takes over a known mixture on which it must exercise all its ability and resources to sell most effectively. There is a need for the selling function to know where it stands concerning what it has to sell and then proceeds to do so.

This distinction does not preclude a flow of market intelligence aimed at improving the sales-policy decision; this is supplied by the sales function executive as its contribution to sales policy. But it does imply that once a joint (policy) decision has been taken, then, despite functional reservations, the sales-promotion planning will proceed to give wholehearted support. Thus if range has been reduced against the advice of the sales department, that department must give the new policy total support in the field. Anarchy is the consequence anywhere if individuals are allowed to deviate from 'cabinet'-like decisions because of their own misgivings. Sales policy means what it says – policy.

The correct construction and execution of sales policy needs the maximum co-operation between, and co-ordination of, the constituent functions of the policy, i.e. making, financing and selling. Where co-operation falls short of the requirements for co-ordination, executive decision-taking at a higher level is needed. Organic acceptance of the concept of the common weal of sales policy is the ideal; but in competitive markets this acceptance may require persuasion or even positive enforcement to speed its growth.

It must not be assumed that sales policy and sales promotion planning are independent activities; such a belief would be contrary to the integrated approach which is necessary for successful marketing. The effectiveness of any claim made by any sales-promotion activity must be supported by the standard of quality of product or service provided. Methods of distribution affect relationships with dealers, as does credit policy. Price policy is an integral part of both sales policy and sales-promotion planning.

3. The Constituent Parts of Sales Policy

PRODUCT POLICY
ACTIVITIES CONCERNED – PRODUCTION, FINANCE AND SALES

WHEN a business is launched, it is equipped and manned initially to exploit a creative or original idea, and it accumulates machines, buildings, administrative and technical talent, and managerial skills. The purpose of this complex investment is to meet the demand likely to be generated by the creative idea. Unfortunately, this state of affairs is not likely to continue for very long. The market for the new product or service will be invaded by new competitors. Even if no such invasion took place, the extensive nature of competition, e.g. holidays competing with tape recorders, etc., would result in an increasing threat of idle capacity once the initial demand had been met. From this point onwards the problem is not to bring together and organize equipment and talent, but to create new products, or variations on the existing ones, which will sustain the market and keep the equipment and talent profitably employed. Product policy is now a necessity.[1] The greater the investment represented by the equipment and skill, the greater the need for a scientific approach to the evolution of goods which can be produced by them.

Product policy, especially in the industrial market, may have serious financial implications. A major and complex product development may require a large amount of finance which may be indivisible if the project is to be completed satisfactorily. Such projects often require a considerable length of time during which they are consuming funds which do not have any immediate cash response from the market. In such cases it is absolutely essential that an enterprise should be able to generate a cash flow from its

1. In fact this often refers to an amalgam of product and service support policy. For the sake of simplicity 'product policy' is used as synonymous with this amalgam.

existing products up to the time when the new development will begin to make its contribution to the flow and to profits. This may require expert forecasting to allow the necessary time for such long-term product development whilst the present product range is successful enough to maintain the necessary liquidity and profitability.

The difficulty of sustaining a continuous flow of products and innovations to maintain maximum profitability varies with different industries. Generally, in capital-goods industries the machines and talents of an undertaking are more flexible, and consequently the product spectrum within the reach of the business is wider.[2] On the other hand, such industries do not normally undertake mass or intensive production of goods, and so the fixed costs associated with the equipment and skill will have to be spread over fewer products, although of a higher unit value. The consumer-goods industries, although handicapped by the narrow range of goods available from their equipment and skill, will tend to produce more rapidly per unit of initial equipment, so that, although the potential product spectrum is smaller, this risk is offset by the reduced need to find new products to justify the original investment, the costs of which have been recovered by the mass of goods already produced.[3]

Product policy is concerned with an evolution or flow of products which is compatible with the existing fund of equipment, skills, liquid assets and goodwill of the business and, at the same time, commercially viable. Product policy can also embrace extension or reduction of the range, diversification and segmentation; it must also pay attention to the advantages and disadvan-

2. See the section on Industrial Marketing for deeper treatment of this topic.

3. This connection between type of equipment, method of production and writing-off period is only a casual one. Obviously, there is a distinct possibility that although the number of orders produced in the capital-goods industries will be much less than in the consumer industries, the value of each one will be greater and so will its ability to bear a proportion of initial costs. In the capital-goods industries, the greater flexibility should imply a longer period in which equipment could pay for itself; there is not, therefore, the immediate urgency created by the more specialized consumer-goods equipment.

tages of various range policies, and to 'commonization'[4] and 'customization'[5] within a range. It may require a new identification of the product; thus, organizations have successfully changed their product identity from cinemas to entertainment and so opened up a much larger field and one in which there was a wider spectrum of products to which their assets could be orientated.

The evolution of products may be based on material and skill rather than equipment where the latter is relatively cheap and too rigid as to use. Ship builders may utilize their talent for making living quarters out of minimum space by diversifying into the production of caravans or industrial housing units; there is no relationship between ships and houses except through the type of work involved, in terms of both design and production.[6]

Sometimes the extension of a range may develop naturally out of a 'package deal' associated with the present basic product; furniture companies may extend from beds to occasional tables and to office furniture, the links being commonized components, sales ability, and customers' goodwill and established channels.

In retailing, the departmental and bazaar-type stores, if managed correctly, are good examples of dynamic product policy; they adjust the amount of space and labour and capital allocated to various products to suit current situations[7] – the link is the retail service itself. Radio and television retailers, built up to meet the boom conditions during the growth of these products, may reorientate towards home entertainment in general and/or electrical services, thus opening up new market possibilities; the link is either through the end-product, i.e. home entertainment, or the nature of skill needed, i.e. electrical.

The diversification of products beyond the existing range may be based on an objective definition of the real role of the company. The technique is concerned with identifying corporate strengths and applying these to existing and/or potential markets

4. Common components throughout part, or all, of a range.

5. Variations on a 'standard' model to suit customer requirements.

6. See the section on Industrial Marketing for special treatment of this topic.

7. Sometimes the product spectrum is redefined by considering the real estate aspect of a shop, in which case the site value will cause a change in product, perhaps from public houses to offices.

rather than the immediate product range; giving a wider variety of products for market exploitation. Care must be exercised, however, against over-estimating the medium- and long-term advantages claimed for this technique, although an immediate one may be gained. The weakness of the method is in the commonality of funds of assets or resources held by different companies. Thus, if company X is currently in market A, but, after analysis of its overall capability, decides that it can diversify and enter markets B, C and D, then it is more than likely that there are enterprises at present supplying these markets which will, after a similar analysis, see some relationship between their capabilities and those markets A, B, C and D which they are not currently supplying.

The eventual outcome could well be a complex of market diversification across all the companies now competing across all markets; competing interfaces would be greatly increased and may overstretch capabilities. Nevertheless, the first company to undertake such a product policy would enjoy a market advantage until enterprises with a similar complex of resources followed suit. In any case, the use of company role-definition techniques is absolutely vital to any enterprise faced with an existing or potential decline in current product markets. Like all transferable methods, the speed of transferability will determine the strength of the method as a source of comparative advantage.

In any case, the calibre of decision-taking among competing companies using company-role definition as a basis for product policy will vary: rarely is the definition beyond dispute. Does a company which is currently making lace curtains define its role as a knitter and so look for new knitted goods markets made by the same production methods, e.g. cellular blankets; or does it consider its role to be concerned with the covering of windows and opt to exploit its distribution capability by deciding to make venetian blinds?

Product policy must be able to maintain and inject the necessary flow of new products or variations to sustain demand at its most profitable level. This involves a combination of functions ranging from research and development by the firm itself, through an intelligence system to cover all developments in an identified spectrum within the product capabilities of the firm up to detailed analysis of all the socio-economic factors underlying existing and potential markets for products.

The result of this comprehensive approach might be seen in products being developed at the right time which were commercially valuable because they were based on market intelligence. It could also be seen in an increased awareness of the possibilities created by a knowledge of developments elsewhere; this could result in a realignment of research and/or production to exploit developments seen to have been successful. Companies may seek to manufacture under licence when research and development has been dilatory or has been incorrectly orientated; if the alternative to licensing is idle capacity in an industry with heavy overheads, and the marketing opportunity represented by the new product or process is likely to be short-lived, licensing may be a more compelling policy.

An analysis of socio-economic forces would be used to identify the cause of growth trends; the actual existence of a growth in a sector of demand is an indication that the demand is being met by suppliers who are already in the market. The most profitable point of location in a growth trend is at the beginning, but this involves obtaining a prior warning through socio-economic indicators.

The increasing cost of land and labour relative to capital equipment is a basis for growth of all those devices which replace the former with the latter; mechanical packaging devices, fork-lift trucks, pallets, self-service store aids, all exemplify this. If women are increasingly employed in full-time work, then convenience foods and laundry aids are growth industries. The desire for greater mobility of labour might develop a demand for mobile houses produced by vehicle builders rather than by traditional means. Labour-saving machines are more desirable when labour is expensive.

The expected life of a product in either the physical, social or economic sense should also play an important part in product policy. Where a product has a physical life of five years, perhaps determined by the company's own design and quality policy, then new products will have to be available to exploit the brand loyalty of the customer when a replacement becomes necessary.

Any such new model would require to be equal in all ways with competitors; this, allied to brand loyalty, would sustain sales. If a car has a good physical life of five years, then inability to produce a new model at the end of this span would sacrifice brand loyalty.

Where fashion or social drives determine the life of a product, the cycle of time will be changed, and products will have to be available when required; cars, radio, television, kitchen equipment and furniture all illustrate cyclical trends towards functionalism, convenience, safety, exhibitionism, utility and economy, in addition to the minor trends in colour and shape. Product research will track such trends and incorporate them into new models at a rate in keeping with the demand for them and the action of competitors. Where these trends are powerful, then it may be necessary to augment the physical-obsolescence cycle with more frequent models responding to current taste.

The economic life of industrial equipment may be more or less than its physical life, depending on the rate of technological advance. It can also be dependent on the amount of work performed by the equipment, i.e. whether or not it has paid for itself. Where the end-product sales have been good and technological advance is rapid, then the replacement of equipment is expedited. Product development must respond to and, in fact, should be part of the technological advance itself. Taxation allowances at the time of purchase and during the working life of a machine will also affect the willingness to replace it.

Quality and price growth segments are based on underlying socio-economic causes which the product policy should establish and track. The widening of a product quality spectrum to include a higher-class car should be planned when the basic causes of such a developing trend are discovered; it is less profitable to make the finding later as it would preclude the necessary coincidence of product development and growth of market which is vital to correct product policy. The ability to see market opportunities is not restricted to any one firm and therefore product policy must include a study of existing and potential competition and the ability of the firm to meet this.

In order to perform this comparative appraisal correctly, the firm must attempt to quantify any comparative technical, managerial, financial, commercial or selling advantages it may have over its competitors. There should be complete compatibility between the technical and managerial attitudes or philosophies of the firm and the prospective new markets; looseness of costing and control may suffice in one market but not in another; the make-up of the firm should be able to respond adequately to the needs or motivation priorities of the new market. Appraisal of compatibility or suitability might lead to the abandonment of a possible market because of the greater ability, experience and marketing know-how of a competitor.

No manufacturer should have to ask himself 'Why are we here?' in relation to a market; he should know. The opportunity cost of a wrong decision in product policy is represented by the possible gains which could have been made had the expenditure needed for a market or product development been used more realistically. If a builder of factories decides to set up a plant to produce industrialized family houses but, having done so, discovers that the conservatism and parochialism of local authorities deny him the market, then the builder loses to the extent that the cost of the new plant might have been invested more profitably elsewhere. Better socio-economic research might have avoided the loss.

Product policy is, to some extent, a continuing 'hedge' or insurance against the threat of idle committed assets, and so any product development policy should have as a priority the maximum use of these assets. Each product suggested as a means of sustaining the viability of the enterprise must be considered in relation to the contribution it is likely to make towards the productive use of the assets. A shipyard, as stated earlier, may produce industrialized house units for use in confined spaces, but the contribution such a development would make to total capacity utilization would probably be negligible. The nature of the new product should be such as to utilize total capacity, rather than a part of it; in our example the fitting-out trades and equipment would be occupied, but this would represent a small section of overhead costs and might even unbalance the overall production facility for the continuing main product.[8] Ideally the new product should redress any imbalance or potential imbalance in the use of assets.

Wherever possible, new products should not only make the maximum use of the existing production capacity and skills of an organization, but they should incorporate as much as is possible of the existing product or products. This would enable economies to be made in setting up for the new product and also in the supply of components either during manufacture or after sales, by maximum 'commonization' of components.

One method of entering a new product or quality market is to buy an interest in a business already established in the market. This method has an added advantage in that the existence of current profitability is not upset by the entry of an additional firm. The take-over method also enables a firm to become an accepted manufacturer of a type of product or standard of quality much more quickly; this is particularly so when the present connotation associated with the business is dissimilar from the quality image needed in the new market segment.

Diversification of products out of the existing assets is clearly preferable where this is possible, but the marketing costs, in terms of establishing goodwill, correct brand connotation and trade connections, may be excessive, both in finance and in time. The need to save time and expense by means of a take-over could be considered as evidence that the market intelligence available to the firm has been defective in that it has not given the necessary prior warning of the relative rate of growth of various product and quality sections within the spectrum of the company.

Finally, extreme care must be taken in estimating the strength of a product development as a source of comparative advantage. This would require objective assessment of it as an immediate source, and the likelihood of the strength of the advantage being sustained through time. The transferability of product advantage is critical in any such exercise; this must be assessed, preferably

8. See the section on Industrial Marketing for special application in that field.

by those not emotionally associated with the product development.

If it is seen that the period of comparative advantage is short, then every effort must be made to consolidate the temporary product advantage through top-class support service, so that the patronage of the customer will continue after the entry of competing similar products. It would be financially foolhardy to allocate ample resources to product development or to obtaining a franchise and to under-finance the supporting services; the balance would not be optimized and it would be disastrous if entry of competitors was easy.[9] Product policy would thus be seen as an amalgam of product and service aimed at marketing the most profitable comparative advantage.

DESIGN POLICY

ACTIVITIES CONCERNED –
PRODUCTION AND SALES

'When fishing, it is the fishes' taste in flies that matters.' A well-designed product should combine functional efficiency with ease of manufacturing. All industrial designers should be aware of the production problems likely to be associated with a design or a variation on it; they must reconcile consumer taste and manufacturing facility, but with the implication that positive selling can be used to adjust consumer attitudes to the design if it is not too divergent from these attitudes.

Design should assist sales promotion by introducing a comparative advantage into the product. This might be a genuine advance in the usefulness of the product, an improvement in its durability, or perhaps better value for the money paid for it. In other cases, however, design may merely provide some mark of distinction out of which sales promotion can create a comparative

9. Support services usually contain a high human element, e.g. delivery, quality assurance, after-sales service, and are thus less transferable between competitors. They are therefore potentially more powerful as a source of long-term comparative advantage if appended to good product evolution policy. It must also be remembered that funds must be available to sell the new product.

advantage in the mind of the customer, i.e. a psychological extension to the product. Design might even be said to have financial implications in that if component parts of old and new designs can be made common, then stockholding costs against production and possible after-sales service requirements could be reduced.

The industrial designer may have to work within restrictive terms of reference. Legal requirements may have to be met. Public taste may be influenced by the introduction of a well-publicized national standard, although this does not carry a legal obligation. If a mother discovers that a national standard of safety has been set for prams, fireguards, or flameproof materials, her main drive in purchasing will be towards this standard because it reflects a dominant instinctive desire. Other standards may be set by the industry itself, either by the industry of the designer or of the customer; the need to rationalize on components might be a dominant motive with governmental buyers; the electrical and oil industries are among many with self-imposed standards.

On other occasions, the specification to which a design staff must work could be highly restrictive. Large industrial buyers may lay down requirements which leave little room for initiative on the part of the supplier's design team; in fact, the design activity here is often carried out by the customer, e.g. multiple-store orders and car manufacturers buying-out sub-assemblies and components. Sometimes the specification may be less restrictive in technical terms, but more precise commercially or financially, in that the main motivation is price. This motivation may be self-evident or it may result from an analysis carried out by the potential supplier; both the industrial and the consumer markets manifest this economic characteristic.

When price becomes the main purchasing motive, the design staff must accept this as the main term of reference. Value analysis will be used to achieve savings in the product without impairing its efficiency. This might lead to new, cheaper, substitute materials more in line with the real use and life of the product; new methods of manufacture might result from new designs. Components may be commonized, thus reducing cost of production and also after-sales service. Existing plant may be used for a new model because of design, with obvious savings.

The function of selling is to persuade the potential customer that the qualities possessed by the product or service for sale are more compatible with his or her requirements than those of any competing product. Clearly, then, the more we make the product inherently compatible with these requirements, the easier it is to sell. Motivation research at all levels, rational and emotional, should precede and directly influence design.[10]

The product should incorporate in its design a scheme of motivation priorities related to those of the potential customers; the rational may outweigh the emotional, and vice versa, but even within these two main divisions there are motives of varying strengths which must be identified. Colour, sex, emulation and self-esteem, and social standing are drives which can be exploited by the industrial designer. These may be combined with more rational ones such as convenience, the desire for leisure, value or economy; and, in the industrial market, economics and ergonomics will replace emotions.

Even in the industrial field an emotional content can often be built into a well-designed product. In an industrial market where several suppliers have reached similarity in the rational aspects of their products and services, the final choice might be influenced by a design with an emotional appeal; this might be achieved through the colour, finish or even the shape of the product.[11]

Motivation research should indicate the importance to the customer of after-sales service as compared with price, etc. The good industrial designer will incorporate after-sales service facility into his design to meet the rating given to this by the customer; thus, where fear of a breakdown and the ensuing inconvenience is greater than price economies in the motivation of the customer, the product designed to reduce this fear will be more

10. We shall deal mainly with product design, but the design of a service or of a combination of product and service must follow exactly the same procedure to be successful.

11. With obvious advantages in brochures, exhibits, advertising, manuals, etc.

efficient from a selling viewpoint, even though it may be more expensive.

The continued patronage of a customer is a fundamental part of good marketing; but this depends on satisfaction with the product throughout its expected life, whether it is a television set, car, lorry or machine tool. The owners of television sets and cars become dissatisfied when there is an interruption in the convenience or service they expected from their purchases; inability to maintain and repair with ease could create this situation. The buyers of lorries and machines reckon their dissatisfaction in economic terms; the cost of breakdown and slow repairs is measurable and monetary.

This facility for after-sales service or freedom from breakdown built into the design should be geared to the calibre of person likely to carry out this service. If the service trades within a country or market or industry are poorly manned, then the design must incorporate a standard of maintenance and repairs compatible with the standard of worker available; design tendency might move towards replacement by factory-reconditioned parts rather than repair. Similarly, a car designer might design to reduce the frequency of servicing. The fundamental question is: 'Does bad service or maintenance reflect on your good name?' If it does, then design must act accordingly.

Selling, as we have seen, is facilitated if the product is designed to suit customer needs. This does not mean an abdication of selling, leading to product anarchy as each customer names his needs, but it does require that the correct balance be struck between the design function and selling in order to achieve that product most likely to appeal to the market; so that although selling is still needed, it is not handicapped but assisted. Designers might, by ingenious means, reconcile customers' product idiosyncrasies and easy production methods by a permutation of common parts or by using standard processes. Range and design are intimately connected here.

The design of a product is frequently rendered impossible because of its nature, e.g. cereals, soap flakes, drinks, etc., and in these cases we must use the same scientific approach to the design of the packs which contain them. However, most goods need packaging, so there is always an extension of the design function to cover packaging.

The package designer and the designer of the goods themselves must work together with one objective – complete customer satisfaction. This may involve modification in design to facilitate transport and keep down distribution costs, particularly where profit margins are tight or the market is price-conscious; with distant markets this need is intensified. Similarly, the product should be designed in order to reduce the risk of breakage, especially in markets depending on the maintenance of maximum goodwill, e.g. consumer-durables and industrial goods. Parts of a machine may be made detachable; design may incorporate easy knockdown and assembly, as with furniture; nesting of products should be utilized wherever possible, e.g. sanitary earthenware. All these qualities would also reduce transport costs. Again, we see customer-orientation in price-conscious and goodwill markets.

Design is often required to help in the sustaining of markets where spontaneous demand cannot be relied upon to be perpetual; it merges with product policy. Research and development of new products at the necessary rate may have to be replaced by design changes, often on the periphery of the product. This is design for selling. To the extent that designers can change public attitudes to products by making them utilize social rather than rational terms of reference for purchasing, so they contribute to sustaining sales. If furniture could take its place alongside clothes as fashion goods with social terms of reference, the sales of furniture would be made much easier. The 'cult of this year's model' is good for sales. The use of designs which incorporate components below the standard of the whole with a view to creating dissatisfaction with the product and thus rationalizing the emotional urge to 'buy this year's model' can be easily justified in terms of private interest. This is not to suggest that this practice is, or could be, widespread, but merely to comment on its commercial worth where it can be practised.

If it is necessary to sell to a market for five years in order to cover tooling-up costs, then a design policy to suit this need is justified. A car manufacturer may go through five variations on a basic design theme each time he develops and tools-up for a new model; if he did know $x^5, ^4, ^3$ and ^{2} when introducing model x^1, then, with the social drives within the car market, no one could doubt the commercial wisdom of the policy.[12]

The position of design within the marketing complex is a vital one. The allocation of resources to this function should be based on the real contribution that it can make to increased customer satisfaction and/or capacity utilization. The efficiency with which design is made compatible with the needs, emotional and rational, of the customer is dependent on the use of motivation research to identify the drives associated with the product and the priority of these drives.[13] To the extent that the design does correctly reflect customer motivation so it will enhance the productivity of every aspect of selling; the returns on advertising and personal selling per unit of input will be directly proportionate to the compatibility of the product and the customer needs, other things being equal. The real value of design can perhaps best be seen in the diseconomies which arise where money is spent on sales promotion which effectively draws attention to a product unsuited to the customer's needs.

RANGE POLICY

ACTIVITIES CONCERNED – PRODUCTION, SALES AND FINANCE

Diversification, Segmentation, and Range Extension

Product range policy can take two extreme courses, diversification or simplification. The former lays down no limit on the nature of products which may be made by a company, sold under a brand name, or controlled by a group of producers, or promoted under a family brand name. I.C.I. represents diversification in this sense, but so could a washing-machine manufacturer who developed the production of his fractional horse-power motors

12. If the market for black-and-white television sets has not been saturated in a country, it is commercially wrong prematurely to introduce colour sets.

13. Value analysis must consider the mix of rational and emotional functions of the product before arriving at cost-saving recommendations that undermine emotional returns to the customer.

to meet an industrial demand outside his own needs. Diversification can also be achieved by licensing arrangements or financial links between firms which might culminate in take-overs.

Diversification of all types has a built-in 'hedging' function in that the risk of over-dependence on any one market is reduced; if this market is a declining one, the insurance function is immediate and obvious. Insurance might also be sought in a policy of diversification where a market is dominated by one or a few customers; a common situation in industrial markets.

Can a method be found that will achieve the advantage of diversification without the possible disadvantages of increased overheads, that avoids entering fields in which selling know-how is limited, and does not alienate the production side, which may dislike any form of range extension?

The most appealing solution is a policy of segmentation. This falls short of extreme diversification in that it restricts the product range to a single group, or even a basically single product, e.g. knitwear, cycles or furniture; but it involves a range of quality or price or other idiosyncrasies which caters for different segments of the market.

Segmentation is based on the desire and need to maintain markets large enough to achieve the lowest unit of cost output. The same equipment and administration may be used for all segment products; the variation may be in quality, material, packaging, peripheral design, brand and price. In some instances, the segmentation of product may be a consequence of retail developments, these being the outcome of more basic socio-economic causes, e.g. the development of price/quality segments utilizing, and perhaps provoked by, multiple stores catering for this type of customer.

Each segment has different socio-economic priorities and the variations in the product and its promotion will respond sympathetically to, and thus exploit, these priorities. Social consciousness may dominate, and the response will emphasize brand name, advertising style, choice of outlet, and price.[14] Value or

14. Segmentation can also have the additional by-product of market research, in that it can be a means of identifying growth segments in a total market.

economy motivation would result in an appropriate selling 'mix'. Clearly, provided the product is basically from the same production capacity, administration, equipment, and labour, then segmentation is helping to achieve a greater market and lower unit production costs.

Diversification and segmentation cannot be clearly separated. A manufacturer of traditional carpets may decide to produce and sell tufted carpets on a latex base: the method of manufacture is different, the type of equipment and labour is unlike that needed in the traditional Wilton and Axminster field. From a marketing viewpoint, the tufted carpet may be considered more a substitute for linoleum than competing with other carpets. Some carpet manufacturers might jealously guard their established brand names and refuse to attach them to the new product. The motivation 'mix' of the customer for the new product would have an economy bias, whereas the old market would have its due share of social drives. The product range policy is thus a mixture of diversification and segmentation.

Extension of Variety

When an enterprise decides to sell a range of goods rather than its ability to make goods, then it must reconcile the manufacturing, financial and selling aspects, if the range is to be correct. Sales departments might clearly prefer wide ranges, although this is an abdication of the selling function. Finance controllers may point to the stockholding diseconomies of extensive ranges in both components and finished goods. Production can usually show excellent reasons for limiting the variety of products as much as possible. The size of a batch must be determined by the economics of production, the speed of selling and the cost of holding finished goods; as always in sales policy, the three great activities conjoin.

Additions to a range can be made in order to achieve a more economical scale of production or in response to sales department pressures. The addition of a product must be judged according to its overall implications to the company and not those involved for any one section. Is it compatible with the present asset and resource make-up of the company? Does it redress any im-balance in asset or facility utilization? How necessary is it to the achievement of better production costs? What is the opportunity cost of the new line in production terms? Will the cost of breaks in production of the existing range be more than offset by the market for the new product? Can the existing sales force be used? Do the established methods of distribution suit the new product? Can it use the existing goodwill and brand names of the enter-prise? Will it affect the sales of existing products, i.e. will canni-balism take place? What will be the extra cost incurred in selling and distribution as a result of the new product? Will the selling advantage of the better range offered more than offset this mar-ginal selling cost and any production and stockholding dis-economies which are additionally incurred?

However, even after all these questions have been set and answered, the problem of range in a dynamic competitive econ-omy is far from resolved. The unknown quantity is the likely actions of competitors if an enterprise does or does not introduce the new product.

A new product which largely eats into the sales of competitors' products with little effect on a firm's existing product sales is clearly the desired end; this can be achieved if a segment com-pletely new to the enterprise is the objective. Even here, retalia-tory action could involve entry by discomfited competitors into the new segment. Clearly, some evaluation is needed of the possibility of this occurring through an analysis of the production and promotion capabilities of competitors.

Where a company is considering a new product which is known automatically to involve cannibalism, then the relative profit-ability of the existing and replacement product must be assessed. However, even if it is clear that the replacement product has a lower profitability than the existing one, it may still be good marketing to introduce it, if it is suspected that competitors are about to launch a similar product and that the market reac-tion is likely to be favourable. Thus, although the profit margin on a small economy car may be less than that on the existing range, its introduction would be justified if competitors were thinking along similar lines and customer motivation 'mixes'

showed economy priorities. If the new model were not introduced, then customers might be lost to competitors. The real
drama of product ranges is best seen in this type of industry,
i.e. automobiles, with its enormous fixed costs of production,
promotion and distribution and after-sales service; to decide incorrectly may reduce for some considerable time the productivity
and value of these fixed assets.

Variety Reduction or Simplification

If there were an unlimited variety of products from a manufacturer, then the selling function would be made much easier.
Conversely, the narrower the range of products to be sold, the
greater the need for selling in a positive way. It is when range
policy is looked at, not as a selling matter, but as a marketing
matter, that a less biased view can be obtained. To do this, we
must first examine how the introduction of a reduced range could
in any way affect the attitude of the customers towards our product. How do the manufacturing and financial consequences of
variety reduction affect the end product and its marketing?

Variety reduction or simplification can occur in two main
forms. The most obvious is when a company deliberately reduces
the range which it is producing. The other type is where the
company reduces the variety of components used in a certain
range of end-products; this is sometimes called 'commonization',[15] indicating the use of 'standard' parts for most or all of
the models in the range. From such a policy, certain manufacturing and financial advantages occur which could be of great
importance in the marketing of the product and even in the act of
selling itself.

The most apparent advantage is the spreading of the fixed cost
of manufacturing. This could result in lower prices leading to
greater sales, or to a greater margin between cost of production
and selling price which could be utilized for sales promotion or

15. The terms 'standard' and 'standardization' are best restricted to the
situation which exists when a third party, e.g. B.S.I. or A.P.I., sets up standards of size, quality, performance, safety, etc. which are accepted by the
whole industry; standardization is the term which should be used here.

any other marketing activity. If the customer reaction to price cutting is not significant, then the new margin could be used to increase brand loyalty through advertising; a true selling advantage resulting from variety reduction just as much as the increased sales due to price reduction.

Serialized production, facilitated by variety reduction, can lead to the introduction of simplified inspection procedures and the advantage of more consistent quality; good throughput of standard units may be vital to good quality control. Any policy decision which results in a more consistent quality in the end-product must be considered a selling advantage. The money invested in advertising is largely concerned with creating brand loyalty and the making of claims for a particular product or manufacturer; such loyalty and claims can only be made and substantiated if the product does give the expected performance. Many products are so similar that the only difference in the mind of the buyer is consistency of performance after purchase. A manufacturing advantage, easier quality control, is thus converted into a selling advantage.

A more complex advantage is that commonization of components makes sales forecasting and therefore production planning much easier. It is easier to estimate total sales of all lines than to forecast the sales figures for particular lines within this grand total, but if the individual lines have a high proportion of common parts, then the problem is simplified. This situation can occur in most production-assembly industries, e.g. small computers. The greater the proportion of the lines which are made from common components, the more the estimate of the individual lines resembles the estimate of the total. In practice this means that production of components can be planned further ahead, with the obvious advantages in the maintenance of schedules, delivery dates, etc. – all selling advantages.

If competing products have reached a plateau of similarity, then the most important selling point could easily be the ability to deliver from stock; this is particularly attractive where the distributor is short of working capital or space. A similar situation might occur where a supply emergency had to be met (ability to help in such a case can greatly increase company patronage). The holding of stocks to enable a producer or distributor to offer an ex-stock service does, however, involve heavier financial commitments in stockholding but, with a reduced range of components and/or end-products, the cost of providing this important customer service can be reduced.

If, after investigation of customer motivation and competitors' activities, the sales planners decide that the ability to deliver from stock is rated very important as a selling device, then the company with a simplified range could use the same amount of working capital and space for stockholding as before, but could give a better service because of the greater stocks held per line sold. If the ability to provide this service is not so highly rated by customers, then the company could, after variety reduction, provide the same service as before but at less cost, and possibly reduce price if this is conducive to greater net revenue.

Furthermore, we should not overlook the possibility of greater returns from the research and development function if the people concerned are allowed to concentrate more on the fundamental aspects of the product line rather than complying with individual customer idiosyncrasies. This type of advantage is well illustrated in industrial equipment markets where suppliers can concentrate on the overall economic and technical efficiency of a range rather than the problem of each customer. The long-term profitability consequences of this are only too clear in the rapidly changing product markets of today and/or where product patronage is dominant.

On the pure sales-promotion side, the balance is supposed to be in favour of diversification rather than reduction in range. To what extent is the usual sales approach to this problem justified? Are there any advantages to any of the sales-promotion activities?

Advertising of shopping goods and industrial goods is concerned with informing the potential customer about the special characteristics of a product; such information fitting into an approach which insists on selection before purchase. Unfortunately, the use of informative advertising as a means of persuasion may be made difficult where a wide and varied range is being promoted. Variety reduction by enabling the full advertising

171

effort to concentrate on a more limited range can achieve both an informative and a repetitive type of campaign.

Extensive ranges may require a decision on whether to promote products or brand; a reduced range could achieve both with the same outlay. Brand advertising would stress the name of the product in the hope that at the point of sale the pre-selling influence would affect the choice of article. Informative advertising could carry this pre-selling a stage further by promoting the special features of the product and associating these features with the brand name.

If motivation research shows that the customer rates uninterrupted satisfaction highly, e.g. from a vacuum cleaner, adding machine, a lorry or a machine tool, then the after-sales service given to the product must receive attention equal to this customer rating. Modern standards of living contain a high proportion of complex products. The basic tools of a domestic washday did not require any after-sales service, but as the drudgery has been removed, so the equipment has become more complicated and prone to breakdown. This same reasoning applies to many devices in the industrial field, e.g. automatic control equipment, fork-lift trucks.

People, whether they are ordinary customers buying cars, or industrialists buying equipment, hope they are acquiring a long period of trouble-free satisfaction. The same people, however, would probably tend to assume the possibility of breakdown and, when this does happen, the mental approach of the customer is completely influenced by the speed with which the defect is rectified. Quick rectification of a technical fault can enhance the brand standing to the customer. Variety reduction can play a key part in maintaining the standard of after-sales service needed and can assist in the creation of customer loyalty based on satisfaction. This aid to customer satisfaction could well be decisive; inability to carry out after-sales service is often the most important 'unselling' activity. If the components within a product range have been commonized, then the cost of holding adequate stocks of each component at strategic points in the market is reduced; a given outlay on stockholding will give a higher standard of after-sales component availability.

Additionally, other things being equal, ability to service is to some extent dependent on the variety of goods to be handled; if the range is reduced, then greater familiarity with each type of product should result in a higher standard of after-sales service by agents and the company's own employees. A simplified range can make a contribution to efficient distribution by facilitating the use of agents and retailers to replace direct dealing. The more extensive the range and complex the article, the greater the need to deal directly in order to maintain the necessary standard of product knowledge at point of sale and after. Where products are complex, e.g. computers, then the introduction of a reduced range will be the only means of reducing the technical knowledge needed to handle them. The allocation of the various selling, installation and service tasks between the manufacturer and the independent dealer is influenced by the nature of the range to be sold.

Where conventional distribution economics suggest the use of independent dealers, this has to be considered against the potential sales and service disadvantages which could arise by following such a policy. Simplified ranges, by reducing the knowledge needed at dealer level, would enable the distribution economies of using dealers to be exploited more fully. In the industrial field this is seen in the greater use of agencies and dealers in the sale of more standard types of equipment. In the consumer field it reduces the fear which is involved when the manufacturer of a branded article allows a potential source of goodwill or ill-will, i.e. advice and servicing, to pass into the control of dealers.

It is frequently difficult to recruit salesmen who combine technical ability and know-how with the innate ability to sell. By the very nature of the qualities needed, it is easier to recruit and train personnel who possess the art of selling and can absorb the facts of a product range than it is to accept technicians with little or no selling ability. With a simplified range of goods the task of instructing salesmen in the qualities and functioning of the goods themselves can be made easier.

If it is so obviously advantageous to reduce the range of goods produced and sold – why then is not variety reduction axiomatic in range policy?

173

Range Policy and Economic Conditions

In an economic situation where profits are reasonably easy, there would appear to be no great incentive to incur the marketing problems of variety reduction; the opportunity for greater profit, assumed to be possible if range is successfully reduced, is outweighed in the existing economic climate by the equal possibility of loss if the wrong product decisions are taken. Such environments would tend to support the *status quo*.

Logically, therefore, the value of range simplification might only become apparent when profits became more difficult. The attraction of this argument is enhanced when it is noted that simplication is really a managerial device and incurs little expense. In practice, however, the same companies which see no reason to change their range policy when the economic climate is favourable can generally justify a similar attitude towards change when the market condition worsens. Clearly, when orders are more difficult to obtain, the risk of actually losing orders by refusing to meet special needs will be inflated.

It would seem to follow that any policy decision to introduce variety reduction must be based on the long-term market prospects and not those of any particular moment. A detached assessment is needed of market reaction to the new range, which would be conceived after adequate research into customer attitudes and needs, regardless of special economic circumstances. If a decision to reduce range is introduced, then the whole production, costing and selling activities of the company would be reorientated towards a new policy based on all the price, quality, service, and selling advantages of a simplified range.

It is conceivable that, initially, customer reaction to a new range of products may be unenthusiastic. This could be due to inadequate prior research to discover the needs of the customers and make the new range as compatible as possible with their needs; it could be due to incorrect public relations and sales-promotion plans which have failed to stress the customer benefits of the new range; or, more vitally, it may be due to the price policy of the selling company.

Companies selling a mixed range of products, some with long

production runs and others with shorter ones, may, in order to maximize sales, be inclined to subsidize the price of the shorter run by using some of the economies gained in the longer production run. This type of price policy, which is an extension of 'charging what the traffic will bear', is an obvious deterrent to the introduction of variety reduction policies because it reduces the price differential between the more and less economically produced products. The difference in price might be such that it is less than the customer's assessment of the difference in the ways in which the two products will meet his special needs. Clearly, any research into customer reaction to a simplified product range should be based on the true price, assuming the full share of costs to be borne by each product.[16]

Should the inquiry show a substantial body of customer opinion against the new lines and if there are other sources of supply of equal calibre readily available and under-employed, then a variety reduction policy at that moment may not be the correct decision. This could occur where the advantages, particularly price, were not so pronounced or where certain other factors existed which reduced the attraction even of a substantial price reduction.

If a component is of small unit value as compared with the complex end-product of which it is a part, then the attractiveness of any reduction in price in that component is proportionately reduced. This is even more so where the use of a new component would require any rearrangement of the other parts of the end-product.

The elasticity of demand for the end-product could also seriously affect customer attitude towards possible cost reduction in its manufacture; if the demand is in any way inelastic over small price changes, then the possible inconvenience caused by a newly designed component might more than outweigh any commercial advantage. Should the components be needed in great numbers in the end-product, then the situation increasingly favours the

16. There is an argument for cross-subsidies in that the 'special' of today may help to throw up the 'standard' of tomorrow: 'specials' thus help in product development. Each case would need objective appraisal by the development and marketing functions.

reduced price component. Elastic end-product markets favour variety reduction and consequent cost and price reductions.

The component supplier also has the problem of 'timing' when attempting to introduce a new reduced line of products. The assembler or manufacturer of the end-product may redesign at a different time from that of the component supplier, with the result that the new component may not be suitable for the existing model of end-product. Where a component supplier has a market which is spread over many customers, all redesigning at different times, then the schedule for introducing a new line might be very complicated.

The closest collaboration between the design staffs of both component and end-product manufacturers is vital throughout the period when a reduced range is being introduced; otherwise, the opportunity for selling the component may be lost until the end-product is again redesigned; any new component should be known to the designers when the new model is at its formative stage.[17] The problem is not just a technical one, however; market intelligence is needed to assess the state of the end-market and the likely reaction to any price reduction or increase in servicing efficiency, etc., which might result from the introduction of a simplified component range.

QUALITY POLICY

ACTIVITIES CONCERNED – PRODUCTION AND SALES

A major policy decision is the one dealing with the setting of a quality standard; a decision which shows very clearly the inter-action and interdependence of the selling and production functions and, in fact, demands consistency of action throughout all the business processes.

---

17. Value analysis activities should cover both assembler and sub-contractor through mutual co-operation between design teams.

Quality and the Market

There is no automatic financial virtue in the setting of a high-quality standard for a product; the belief, still held, that 'only the best will do' does not stand up to even the most casual examination.[18] The decision on quality must initially be based on the commercial viability of the suggested quality standard in the light of the current state of the market and the suppliers of that market. Close examination of a market may show that there exists a latent demand for another quality, higher or lower, which has remained dormant because of the goods normally available in the market. Such segments could be well hidden and may require encouragement in the form of emotional advertising before they can be fully exploited. Nevertheless, such a programme may be more profitable than an attempt to break into, or expand sales in, an over-supplied quality standard market. This would certainly be the case where the present market was dominated by heavily entrenched brand names making entry very costly and probably, in an inelastic market, unprofitable. This type of action could occur in the bread industry, or in the supply of clothes, fountain pens etc.; in these cases the tendency has been to go for a higher-quality segment in response to reduced returns in the standard and over-supplied market;[19] but clearly, lower-quality segments can also be exploited, again in response to change in the economic and social environment of the customer. These aspects of quality policy demonstrate its use as a comparative advantage possessed by a product. There are also obvious advantages in identifying quality segments within a market and introducing variations on a product to suit each segment.

18. N.B. In some industries and in some countries there may be legal standards governing quality, such as pharmaceutical products; or there could be a widely accepted standard such as those of the American Petroleum Institute and British Standards Institution; or quality may be governed by the need to prevent legal proceedings, as could occur with foodstuffs. Clearly, such limits on quality standards are commercially obligatory.

19. Assuming the same percentage margin, a move to a higher quality and price range can increase profits. This is particularly appropriate where the profits on the current quality range do not allow any participation in the increased affluence of customers.

The emergence of a successful type of shop catering for a special quality segment could indicate a market which is identifying its quality-price standards with the policy of the shop. Manufacturers could utilize such a development to make an entry into a new market, either by changing the character of their own brand or producing non-branded goods to meet the special needs of the shops concerned. Changes to a higher quality may also be linked to a policy of trading-up: where past or present customers have a greater supply of purchasing power and also desire, for social or other reasons, a higher quality; thus there is a happy confluence of motivation and monetary support for it.

Quality policy in the consumer market must always face the problem of the possibility of ignorance on the part of the final customer and, although consumer intelligence is probably improving, the nature of the goods being purchased is becoming even more complex. In these circumstances the decision on quality and price will have to pay due attention to the quality being an effect of, rather than a cause of, the price. Obviously, there remains a large uninformed section of many markets which still equates price and quality, perhaps via a brand name. In such cases, quality policy could well be governed by the ability to convey quality by peripheral design or finish, etc., the inability of the customer to assess quality correctly, and the returns in revenue resulting from extra sales-promotion expenditure as against the cost of making a better product, assuming that the promotion of brand or product would be needed to offset any lack of obvious quality advantages.[20]

This type of quality decision is likely to be more necessary in the middle ranges of quality; at the extremes, the ability to detect good- and bad-quality goods is obviously likely to be much greater. Thus, though it may be difficult to appraise correctly the quality of tape recorders in the range £25–£45, it would be relatively easy to differentiate between the goods in this range and those below £20 and above £70.

20. The consequences would be that although a lower-quality product is sold for a given price, the net profit may be no higher because of the cost of promoting the image. The ignorant market may be an attraction to those wishing to exploit it, but if too many enter, then competition between them will reduce profits.

Motivation research may show not only a discriminating market but also a need for a quality standard to satisfy a social drive, e.g. expensive knitted goods. Where articles must contain this characteristic, then quality standards will be predetermined by social pressures aided and abetted by discreet emotional branding, advertising, pricing and choice of channels of distribution. Other products not normally displayed or exhibited as symbols of affluence or status may be devoid of such emotions, and quality decisions by customers arc then more rational, being based on need and price rather than social instincts, e.g. electrical appliances.

Quality policy is clearly related to the rate of physical obsolescence of the product. The correct design of a product should result in a combination of parts that are all of approximately the same life, assuming there was a direct correlation between life expectancy and cost of each element; it would be foolish to incorporate a component of a quality standard which was too high for the rest of the assembly unless the extra cost involved was recouped by additional sales. An expensive component, e.g. leather upholstery, might well outlast the normal life of a car and the additional initial price disadvantage created by the use of leather would have to be weighed against the emotional appeal of the component, i.e. leather as against plastic, and the possible distinctive characteristics given to the car by its use. In such cases the emotions exploited may also be susceptible to an increase in price, thus removing the cost/price handicap. Therefore, although some attempt to correlate the rate of obsolescence of the components of a product, so that costs are saved and price is kept to a minimum, will be necessary in the more rational markets, emotional factors may produce a very irregular pattern of physical obsolescence.

Ideally, in the rational, price-conscious consumer and industrial markets, there should be an attempt to reconcile the physical and technological rate of obsolescence. In the field of fashion goods the remark that 'one does not want it to last too long' is indicative of expected physical life being in excess of fashion life; many manufacturers recognize this and produce to quality standards which are governed by this dictum. This, in turn, reduces price and has the effect of perpetuating the customers' mode of thinking at the point of sale, i.e. 'the price reflects the quality I need and the rate at which I shall buy them to keep up with fashion'.

Even in the very rational industrial-equipment market,[21] greater care is being taken to specify quality standards which are closer to the expected technological life of the machine, so that the cost (and price) only covers the real economic life of the article and not the period when it is physically useful but commercially of no value, having been superseded by a better machine.

Value analysis is a specific technique which is concerned with the creation of the product at the lowest cost but still able to perform up to the required standards; such an analysis must cover the quality standards of materials, components and finishes in order to assess their relevance to the end function. The aim is to eliminate waste whatever its form, e.g. by a simplified component, a cheaper substitute material, or a lower-quality fitting, but still to maintain the desired functional efficiency of the product.

This technique must at the same time reflect both the emotional and rational motivation of the customer; just as it would be foolish to maintain an expensive component in a price-conscious industrial market, so it could be bad marketing to remove such an item in an emotional consumer market. The more price-conscious the market, whether industrial or consumer, the greater the need to reduce cost through correlation of the quality standards of the components to that point where their physical and technological or social lives are equal; this involves value analysis and consumer research together.

Quality Policy in Practice and Sales Promotion

Attention has been drawn to the use of sales devices to build up a fund of customer goodwill to enable a business to carry its invest-

21. In the industrial market the term 'quality' as a purchasing motive often means ability to supply consistently at the quality specified. The standard could be high or low. 'Quality engineering and assurance' is a more meaningful functional term in the industrial market: this would contain every facet of a company's activities which influenced the quality received by the customer throughout the period of quality expectancy demanded or hoped for by the customer.

ment risk more easily; prominent among the sales devices are branding and advertising, both intimately connected with quality.

Advertising draws attention to any quality characteristics which the product has to its comparative advantage over others. Branding identifies the maker or distributor and so allows credit to be given for any quality advantage which the product enjoys. The very success of both advertising and branding may result in the undoing of the firm if quality policy is not able to create and maintain the comparative advantages claimed in the advertising or to sustain the quality associated with the brand name which will result in the accumulation of goodwill rather than ill-will.

The setting up of an attainable standard of quality, and then the institution of a quality-control system to meet that standard, must precede any claims made in advertising or the fixing of any brand identification to the product.

As soon as a business has a distinctive name, immediately a bill head is printed, then brand policy has begun. The more that is claimed for a product or service but not substantiated, the greater the disappointment. The more clearly the false claim and the source of disappointment can be identified by branding, the greater the loss of goodwill to the owner of the name. In such circumstances the more realistic policies would be either to set a standard which can be achieved and sell to this standard, or to remain anonymous; as the latter is impossible in most cases, and even the supplier of the non-branded product is known to the dealer who handles it, then the implication is that a realistic quality standard must be set and maintained.

We saw in an earlier section that dynamic quality policy involves reorientation of activities to suit changing conditions in the market. However, such changes might be limited by the ability of the firm to produce to certain standards. An engineering firm, which has always made to a certain tolerance and has the machines and skill only to achieve this standard, might find closer tolerances too difficult. Should such a firm discover that the market for its present standard is declining and that the new demand is for closer tolerances, then the quality-policy decision becomes important to the continued existence of the firm.

The ability of a firm to enter a new quality market could also be affected by its existing image, in that it is currently associated with a particular quality of output. This type of situation might be remedied by the correct use of public relations, advertising and branding. It can even be tackled conveniently by taking over a dominant interest in a firm already established in such a market; this has the advantage of not adding to the number of suppliers of the market.

To say that the quality that the company can achieve is determined by its present set-up is, nevertheless, a static approach to this problem, although realistic in many cases. If a firm does decide to enter a certain quality market, which parts of its activities require to be redirected to meet the situation?

Let us assume that a company wishes to establish itself as 'different', and to suggest in all its sales-promotion activities that it is above the average, and that the extra price charged (price policy may be important in a consistent plan) is reasonable. Such a company is trying to create speciality goods by a comparative quality standard in a market with very close substitutes in both product and price. It will change the tone and copy of advertisements; it will incorporate a new quality concept in its product to distinguish it; but, before any of these take place, it will introduce the means of achieving the quality claimed and also of maintaining it.

On the production side the changes will be many. Commonization of components may be introduced in order to give a more consistent quality standard. In some sections, production or plant layout may move away from the one total unit progressive-assembly type to the more intimate layout of sub-units which, because of the smaller working group, may give greater pride in work, and, in any case, makes mistakes more easily identified and traced. Purchasing will have to be aware of the closer tolerance in all things. The personnel department will introduce a new quality standard when recruiting new workers. The training department will be told to achieve a higher standard of skill and quality consciousness. Perhaps new toolroom aids will be needed to help the calibre of recruits achieve the production and quality standards needed. Quality control of incoming goods and finishes will be working to new standards. Internal inspection will be tightened up, perhaps as to the standards of tolerance and the size of the sample tested.

Any after-sales service would be alerted to a new standard; this might involve removing it from independent distributors, or educating them in their new role; it might mean retraining of the firm's own service depots. Next, a rapid communication service would be needed between each service depot and some central control point which would analyse the breakdowns. This would then be fed back to the plant where appropriate action could be taken to tighten up the internal inspection of a particularly defective part, or to investigate the design or metallurgical aspects of perpetual faults. The company would need to allocate the necessary funds for these important prerequisites of projecting an image of a brand quality.

The sales-promotion activity can now begin. Without the prior work, as shown above, the investment in advertising could be wasted. In fact it could be to the actual disadvantage of the firm because of the boosting of claims which could not be met, and would result in an accumulation of ill-will by the brand name and thus by the company.

CREDIT POLICY

ACTIVITIES CONCERNED – PRODUCTION, SALES AND FINANCE

Without the ability to offer some form of deferred-payment or instalment buying, many articles could never achieve the size of market needed to obtain the production economies of scale. Many new articles would be unable to compete with the existing well-proven and well-patronized ones.

Credit, by expanding a market, can make new forms of production economically worthwhile. Indivisible pieces of investment lead to a new plateau of lower unit cost and thus to lower prices to the customer, higher profit margins, or the use of the higher gross margin of profit to finance sales promotion devices to further the product in the market. We can again see how a sales device, i.e. credit, is closely linked with production methods and facility. It is also obviously linked with – indeed is part of – the financial activities of the firm. The trinity of sales policy is involved.

The extension of credit is necessary in almost every type of selling – the only real exception is where a manufacturer makes to order, and is paid as the order is being completed or on completion.[22] Manufacturers give a limited credit to wholesalers and factors who give longer credit to their customers as one of their services to trade. Manufacturers may give credit direct to retailers. Direct dealing of all types frequently involves an element of credit, from the long-term credit associated with industrial contracts to the shorter-term used for domestic durables.

Convenience goods, which have to be sold at every possible point of sale, present a special case for credit in that the type of outlet through which the goods will be sold is likely to be very short of working capital and perhaps even the means of obtaining it. To sell these goods it may be vital to give good credit to the dealers who handle them.

Credit is a means of sales promotion and, as such, must be considered alongside, and compared with, all other sales-promotion activities. Its importance is in its contribution to efficient selling. In some cases, e.g. cars, the need for credit to be available to the customer is so important that manufacturers will take special steps to make it so. Such a move would follow a motivation analysis which would show the high priority given to credit facilities in car purchase. But a manufacturer should take the analysis even further.

The effectiveness of subsidizing credit sales as a sales-promotion device should be set off against the various other methods, and a deliberate attempt made to achieve some degree of equi-marginal return on each of the sales-promotion outlays. Let us assume that a manufacturer has sustained a brand-projecting advertising

22. Even in this case, the cash flow may indicate large amounts of working capital being put at the disposal of a customer. There is no automatic correlation between the spacing or timing of instalments and the amount of money involved in the manufacturing process up to that point. This may be costly credit where the total order is of high value and interest rates are also high. There may in some cases be very costly pre-production activities such as design.

programme for a range of goods, but reports reduced sales return per unit of advertising expenditure. Consumer investigation may show that, whilst brand awareness and loyalty are better than before the advertising, and the desire to buy the type of goods has increased, sales do not bear this out. An analysis of factors influencing the decision-taking situation may show increased pressure from sources outside this market for the discretionary purchasing power, or economic factors concerning income and the cost of living may have recently become adverse.

The policy recommending itself to the manufacturers could be a cut in prices; but such a move would have to be compared with the alternative of a cut in the instalments paid, brought about by a subsidized extension of credit. Where the analysis shows a greater concern over instalments, or even interest charged, then the latter may give the better result. If the current rate available for investment is 10 per cent (i.e. the opportunity cost of extending the credit), or the credit is being obtained from a bank or finance house at 10 per cent, and the economic charge to the customer should be 15 per cent, then the manufacturer might offer the service at 10 per cent as a sales-promotion device. Assuming a credit of £100 per article over twelve months, this would involve a subsidy to the credit of £5; this subsidy is a sales-promotion cost, and the return on it must be compared with that on a similar outlay on advertising, increased dealer discounts or a reduction in price. There is, however, a qualification to this argument.

Credit is above all a financial matter, even though its influence on sales activities may be considerable. The credit obligation of the business must always be kept at a prudent level – which may occasionally clash with the apparent efficiency of credit as a means of increasing sales. Where the credit is obtained from outside the organization, then additional risk is introduced. Tight control of working capital, involving the achievement of the most advantageous balance between creditors and debtors, can clearly make a useful contribution to the profitability of buying and selling anything.

There are, as stated earlier, certain grand credit restrictions imposed by central banks and governments which make some of the best sales estimates look awry. Hire purchase may be directly controlled by an obligation to insist on certain minimum deposits, which can seriously jeopardize consumer decisions to purchase expensive consumer-durables. Bank-rate charges affect all types of credit; even the company which has its own working capital available to extend as credit sacrifices the opportunity of an increased interest on investments, so that, if it maintains the old credit interest rate, it is forgoing additional profit and subsidizing credit. Logically, the development of larger units, both in manufacturing and in distribution, should reduce the importance of trade credit. At the same time the increasing size of capital-goods projects involves massive doses of credit being available, perhaps over a long period of time.

THE METHOD OF DISTRIBUTION

ACTIVITIES CONCERNED – PRODUCTION, SALES AND FINANCE

The maximization of the value of any product involves provision for making it available in that place or those places where it is most desired at such times, in the correct quantities, and in the proper conditions, as to achieve the greatest profit for the producer. This is the problem of distribution.

When the method of manufacturing requires a heavy fixed-cost commitment, the manufacturer may seek protection for his investment and the maximization of profits by an attempt to control the sale of the product right up to the final customer. Such a policy might be in addition to the more conventional and accepted promotion of the sale of the product through advertising, branding and packaging, and would include direct dealing with the final customer, perhaps through the company's own retail outlets, personal representatives, or some form of mail-order method. All these additional activities may be indicative of an unwillingness to leave the ultimate sale of the products in the hands of independent intermediaries. However, such additional activities should increase the total profitability of the enterprise concerned in that they represent an extension to the production function which should be rewarded.

Policies of forward vertical integration into the wholesale and perhaps retail fields, or any form of direct dealing in the consumer market, may be easy to justify from a selling viewpoint. There may, however, be serious financial implications which more than offset any selling advantage. These would involve the fixed long-term capital requirements for the purchase of sites, stores and equipment, and also the increased working capital needed to finance the longer period between production cost involvement and the receipt of cash for the finished product. This is a sales policy matter, and is not merely concerned with sales promotion; in fact, it could result in such an extension to the firm's activities and their associated costs and risks that it would involve a major general policy decision.

The Elements of Distribution

When production precedes demand, then the function of stock-holding arises; if there are several stages in the distribution of a product then the need to hold stocks in anticipation of demand could be repeated at each stage; manufacturer for wholesaler, wholesaler for retailer, retailer for final customer. Stockholding, or the need for it, plays a leading part in any decisions on methods of distribution, not only because of its prominence in the process, but because of the cost and risk implications it carries.

Modern production methods necessitate the grouping together of large amounts of equipment at central points in order to achieve the lowest unit cost of production. If the economies of production were to be offset by diseconomies of equal magnitude on the distribution side, then the logic of the centralized large location might be questioned. The package and transportation of the goods to the market is an obvious element in distribution, and equally an influence on the reconciliation of the production and distribution optima; good transportation can maintain the reality and credibility of a high technical production optimum, in terms both of the physical condition of the delivered product and also of the increased market made possible by reduced costs of distribution. Distribution, then, includes stockholding and transportation, both of which involve costs and the possibility of varying degrees of proficiency; stockholding also involves risk.

In most markets the final customer will only purchase in small quantities, and perhaps irregularly; but modern production methods require that, wherever possible, large batches should be the basis of operations. Clearly, for the two aspects to be reconciled, there is a need for a function which not only transmits the wishes and orders of the consumer to the manufacturer but also converts the sporadic small purchases into economical batches. The effects of this consolidation function will, however, be equally marked in the economics or costs of distribution itself, in that the cost of processing and transportation per unit of product handled will be reduced in proportion to the degree of consolidation achieved. Specifically, small-value orders are administratively awkward and introduce a high processing cost per unit of sale; similarly the cost of transport per unit carried varies inversely with the total units or value carried. The consolidation function must be added to stockholding and transportation as vital elements of distribution.[23]

Finally there is, in many markets, the exhibition function: the need to display goods for comparison and for persuasion of the customer; manufacturer to wholesaler or retailer; wholesaler to retailer; retailer to final customer. This aspect of distribution fuses with selling, but it is vital if efficient manufacturing and promotion are to be converted into sales.

Distribution – the Financial Aspects

WORKING CAPITAL

In the financially ideal situation a manufacturer would receive payment immediately the goods were made, and with the money received he would reduce his indebtedness; the total working-capital requirements would then be limited to the manufacturing cycle. Where the general practice of a trade is to distribute through independent distributors, then all the distributive activities are performed by others; if the dealers also place orders, then the whole of the marketing of the product, including distribution, is

23. The extension of credit has been omitted because, although universally performed by distributors, it is, strictly speaking, a selling rather than a distribution function; the same applies to selling by distributors.

taken out of the hands of the manufacturer. This situation can occur where industrial suppliers deal directly with customers. Multiple stores may also practise the same method, perhaps placing orders, taking delivery, and paying cash.

In all these cases, the financial obligations of the manufacturer are strictly confined to the working capital needed to produce the goods. Supposing, however, the manufacturer, for good marketing reasons, decides that he will take over some or all of the distribution functions, then his working capital needs will be increased in proportion to the time span of the functions concerned.

This intrusion into the distribution field could cover the middleman function, the manufacturer eliminating the independent dealer and handling the articles up to retail level – a policy decision which can often be justified. The intrusion may go beyond this point and involve entering the retail field in order to deal directly with the final customer; when this occurs the working capital used to produce goods is not recovered until the final sale is made. Should the manufacturer include credit extensions into any part of his operations, then the time span of working capital is increased to the extent of the length of credit given, either to dealer, final customer, or both.

The financial burden of the distribution of goods must be borne by someone; once they are manufactured they represent locked-up capital to some entrepreneur, be it the manufacturer, wholesale merchant, importer, shipper, retailer, or even the final buyer if the article is needed for further industrial processing. Where a large retail organization takes delivery of the goods direct from the manufacturer, it becomes responsible from then onwards for the goods;[24] this will involve setting up depots and stores to hold the goods and the financing of the actual stock-holding right through to the final customer; the manufacturer might also be relieved of transport responsibility to a large extent and the consolidation function will have been achieved by the nature of the order itself.

Manufacturers then might go forward into distribution right

24. A fact which will be represented in the price negotiated between the multiple and the producer.

up to direct dealing; similarly retailers might go backwards to the point of production, usurping functions as they go. What is happening is a reallocation of functions and not their elimination; someone must perform them, and, if they have financial implications, these must be borne by the current incumbent.

In conclusion, when manufacturer or retailer move out of their normal sphere of operations, they are adding to their basic entrepreneurial activity. Manufacturers become wholesalers, perhaps also retailers, even moneylenders. Many vertically integrated organizations have really created an intimate grouping of the various functions associated with the making, distribution and selling of their products. It is not unreasonable to assume therefore that, in addition to the extra profits resulting from the anticipated extra efficiency, these organizations make a profit from the actual performance of the functions themselves which they have taken over from others.

OTHER COSTS

Manufacturers who hold stocks in order to maintain supplies to dealers are often using up valuable space which could be used for production purposes. The higher the cost of land and buildings, the greater the cost of stockholding, not only at immediate post-production point but throughout distribution. Depots frequently must be located within an area of high site value. Warehouses are, however, better placed than retail stores, which must be sited for customer convenience and could mean very high outlays. In many mass-consumption societies, the problem of the fixed costs of distribution, as represented by buildings and sites, is a difficult one because of the pressure on land and the resulting high land prices.

Goods do not move into and out of stock without the aid of labour and perhaps mechanical handling equipment; all the office services will be needed, together with systems to control the stocks themselves. Transport is required between stores. Finally, there are the sundry items such as heat, light, power and insurance for goods in stock. Again the costs must be carried by some entrepreneur; to remove independent dealers does not remove these costs, it merely transfers them.

Distribution – Risk

Inherent in any holding of stock is the risk of loss through theft, fire and physical deterioration, but such risks are minor ones as compared with the risk of market obsolescence. The fear that a product in stock will be outdated before it has been sold is always present when the goods are prone to fashion and changing taste, but today this risk has, in many markets, been extended well beyond this narrow esoteric range.

The perpetual supply of new products is a feature of modern marketing; it is the required method of achieving sustained profits in satiate societies. The rate of product supersession is a major influence on the risk of stockholding, but it is a 'given' factor in the situation, because it is the result of deeper forces.

Furthermore, the product may be replaced in the customer scale of priorities by another which is in no way related to it, except that it is competing for discretionary purchasing power: cars may sell less easily when colour television is initially available; stocks of cars would lose value, not because of new models, but because there was a more attractive way of spending discretionary purchasing power.

In modern marketing, change is a major influence: salesmen like something fresh; advertisers prefer a new product; customers should be pleased with something both fresh and new. This desire for change is not confined to the non-essentials. To produce a new item is often impossible in the field of necessities and so the marketeer falls back on the pack to sustain markets by suggesting a changed product. Package changes can be seen most obviously in the food trade, but they can be applied in clothing, paints etc.

There is also the additional associated source of danger in the ability to communicate effectively the nature of the product change to the potential market. The efficiency of communications within a market is a prime influence on the speed with which existing stocks are rendered less valuable by making the customer aware of the new model or product. Modern means of mass communication by radio, television, and large-circulation newspapers can reduce the market attraction and value of stocks in hours, perhaps minutes.

When a manufacturer is performing the stockholding function, he can run down stocks prior to introducing a new variety. Although a manufacturer aiming at maximizing the goodwill of dealers could introduce some device to inform or compensate the dealer when new models were about to be launched, it does not entirely remove the instability inherent in modern stockholding.

Knowledge of new products and methods is so transferable today that the cost of research and development must be recovered in the relatively short period before competitors imitate; this implies secrecy, and an element of surprise. This secrecy would be more difficult, the greater the number of dealers concerned in the secret; limited numbers of dealers with exclusive franchises and therefore a vested interest in the continuing range of products from one manufacturer would clearly be a better proposition.

Distribution – the Consolidation or Rationalization Function

Where the cost of processing an order remains reasonably constant, there are obvious advantages in maximizing the size or value of orders in order to spread this fixed cost. The processing costs involved here would include the actual canvassing and taking of the order, the administration associated with the order in the sales office and the depot, the making-up of the order, its physical distribution, the rendering of all notes and bills and the keeping of an account, and any after-sales activity such as complaints and returned goods.

Faced with the problem of maintaining contact with a large number of retail outlets, many of them small, the manufacturer might logically turn to some other organization to rationalize his scheme of distribution. This might involve the use of wholesalers, but the same rationalization can be achieved by selling through widespread multiples or even by using the centralized buying offices of cinema chains, hotels, garages, etc. All of these intermediaries will introduce distribution economies into the system by buying in bulk from several manufacturers and making up orders for their customers or branches from many groups of products and brands within groups; this reduces the cost of processing an order from manufacturer to intermediary and thence to the retail point.

Manufacturers may well have a mixed policy to reduce costs to a minimum; dealing directly where the value of an order would justify this and, otherwise, dealing through middle-men. Sometimes the market itself may be segmented by the manufacturer who deals directly for one segment of his market, e.g. middle-quality multiples, indirectly for low qualities, and directly again for top-quality high-value goods.

The analysis so far has been on a pure cost basis; we shall see later that too strict an interpretation of costs, both stockholding and processing, could lead to bad marketing policies. Excess costs in this sphere may be needed to offset potential 'unselling' activities and therefore consequential diseconomies in other parts of marketing, particularly sales promotion.

Distribution – the Policy of the Manufacturer

Distribution policy is governed by the desire to maximize the long-term profitability of the enterprise and, in so far as the independent distributor contributes to this objective, then he will be used. Where, however, it can be shown that no such contribution is made, or that the cost is greater than the marketing effectiveness, the decision to eliminate should be taken and the function would then pass to others more able to achieve the objective of the enterprise.

PERFORMANCE OF THE STOCKHOLDING FUNCTION

If the middle-man is not performing the warehousing function adequately, one of the main reasons for his continued existence as a separate institution would cease to exist and the manufacturer could eliminate him. The manufacturer who is holding excessive stocks, relative to the state of his trade, is conceivably carrying out part of the middle-man's function; such a manufacturer would not consider the reasons for the middle-man not holding stocks; the removal of wholesalers would be regarded as being due to their inability to come to terms with the risks of modern stockholding.

193

Retailers may be compelled by cost and customer factors to hold the minimum stocks per product sold, and to rely on wholesalers for speedy replenishments; but if the wholesaler does not hold adequate stocks of a particular brand, the retailer will be forced to accept substitutes. Where self-service stores dominate a trade, this could seriously weaken the sales of a manufacturer in that this type of selling is dependent on display; the customer must actually see the brand or product. If the wholesaler has been remiss in that stocks of one brand have been depleted and substitutes taken, these substitutes will be displayed by the retailer and then bought by the customer instead of the product brand of first choice. In markets where products are close substitutes, the consequences of faulty supplies to the retail point could be serious to the individual brand owner, but not to the dealers concerned, who would maintain turnover by selling substitutes.

In all cases of marketing, the potential diseconomies of an 'unselling' act must be clearly estimated; in this case the whole complex of sales promotion through advertising and packaging with all the associated costs would be partially wasted by the unselling activity of faulty distribution preventing the product from being on display. The true cost of bad stockholding is this waste represented by barren sales promotion – barren because of a weakness at one point in the selling process.

BRANDED GOODS AND DEALERS

The brand image is part of the complex of activities used to reduce the risk inherent in modern business by creating a degree of loyalty among customers. The cost of promoting a brand image may be very great, and the effectiveness of this outlay is usually determined by the degree to which the branded product meets the expectation of the customer, an expectation built up by sales promotion. One potential weakness in all brand projection is inadequate quality control, and this could affect attitudes towards the use of independent middle-men.

Where a product is fragile or perishable or likely to be affected in any way by unenlightened handling, the manufacturer who has promoted the product has a great interest in the calibre of his distribution. Thus a manufacturer of biscuits could decide to deal directly with orders, which, on purely cost grounds, would be uneconomic.

The solution is not necessarily direct dealing if some other method can be introduced which will achieve the quality standards. The use of exclusive or semi-exclusive dealers with full knowledge of the implications of bad handling, both to themselves and to the manufacturer, might be a solution. Devices such as bulk discounts based on individual orders would be replaced by those based on orders over a period; this would reduce the processing economies, but would lead to less risk of overstocking and quality deterioration.

The cost of promoting a brand name may be so great that the additional cost of maintaining maximum customer satisfaction and goodwill through distribution could be minute compared with the possible diseconomies. More scientific control of stock is, perhaps, easier to impose on oneself than on others.

Consumer-durables, such as cars and washing machines, accumulate goodwill for the brand by giving satisfaction during their operating lives; this will often require after-sales service provided by independent dealers. Quality control must in these cases extend to the calibre of service given in the period after sales, and this could involve entry into the distribution of the product, either to improve the service or to replace it. Exclusive franchises may be given; additional profit margins could be provided to encourage adequate stockholding of spares and the employment of the correct type of skilled worker. Manufacturers might set up their own depots at strategic points to hold stocks against dealer needs and to help in after-sales service. Again, it is a matter of the incremental cost as against the potential diseconomies associated with not doing it in a market where customer satisfaction is based on service from equipment.

In the industrial field the need to set up independent distribution systems occurs less frequently because of the direct nature of most transactions, but it can do so. Thus, in the office-equipment field the need to set up large selling and servicing organizations is based, not only on the degree of competition in the market, but also on the nature of the product and the importance in economic terms of continuous service from the equipment. Typewriters are relatively simple and a breakdown is not calamitous, so they can be distributed and, to some extent, serviced by independents.[25] But even the smallest computers require sophisticated technical and commercial knowledge to sell and maintain, and the consequences of breakdown could be serious; so they are sold direct and are serviced by the selling company.

In the case of both consumer-durables and industrial equipment, the method of distribution is based on customer motivation and the complexity of the product relative to the available ability of independent dealers.

Events in markets where resale price maintenance has been abandoned might suggest that top customer motivation is not service, but price, in that the lack of after-sales service facilities does not deter the customer when the price is cut. Before definite conclusions could be drawn from this, however, the post-purchase reaction of customers would need to be known. Does a customer fail to give service its real priority because it is assumed to be either not needed or it was in the past always available (which would make the customer inexperienced in this motivation)? Also the relative attraction of price and service would be influenced by the standard of service experienced in the past; where this was inadequate, then the customer might rationally choose the lower price.

To achieve a better identity of loyalty and interest, the manufacturer might take over part or complete control of a dealer, in order for his product to receive the maximum sales effort in keeping with customer motivation. Such policy decisions can result from reaction to the effectiveness of existing distributors and their inability to reorientate themselves towards the producer, i.e. they will not sell his product efficiently; or the lack of customer orientation on the part of dealers who are not sufficiently aware of, or sympathetic to, customer motivation.

25. The extent of range is also of importance when deciding on the use of independent dealers in this market; the more extensive the range and complex the product, the more will direct dealing be favoured. See the section on Range Policy.

THE CHANGED NATURE OF POSITIVE SELLING

Traditionally, wholesalers sold to retailers, and retailers to the final customer. Increasingly, however, this has been taken over by manufacturers who live in a state of perpetual anxiety as to the viability of their production resources, and so refuse to abdicate the job of selling to others. Thus, goods are made in response to an investigation of the customers, not on information received from dealers; many are branded and advertised, over the heads of the dealers, directly to the final customer. Middle-men and retailers may thus be reduced to the non-selling activities of stockholding and processing orders, plus display. To the extent that the profit margin allowed to any intermediary exceeds the payment for the functions performed, it is clearly, in such circumstances, in excess of the services rendered. In such a situation the manufacturer is not maximizing profit.

Suppose a manufacturer has created a market for his branded goods and allows indiscriminate handling of them at wholesale level. If the degree of inter-wholesaler competition is great and this is reflected in their operating costs and so in their expected mark-ups, then the manufacturer might be increasing the price of his product to meet the cost of an activity which in no way contributes to the marketing of his goods. In highly price-conscious markets the manufacturer could then take steps to reduce the profit margin at wholesale level, either by setting up his own organization, reducing competition by giving an exclusive franchise, or attempting to reduce the margin now given.

Certain developments have tended to increase the importance of the retail store to the manufacturer, even though the selling activity of the retailer himself has been reduced – these concern self-service stores. The store here acts as a reminder of needs; customers may take substitutes on display and make no verbal indication to the store-owner of their preference for an absent brand, robbing the dealer of any indication of customer preferences. The distribution consequences of this to the manufacturer are many. He must convince the retailer directly of the benefits of holding his products; he will help the retailer to help himself by advising on display, etc.; he may have to supplement or replace the independent wholesaler as a supplier of goods to this type of store because of the fear of a breakdown in supplies.

Self-service stores change the pattern of selling in that functions are reallocated. The article is sold by advertising and branding before entry into the shop, thus reducing the selling function of the retailer; the package is so designed as to sell silently by display within the store, thus further reducing the selling aspect of retailing; finally, the customer serves himself, thus taking over the service aspect of retailing; only convenient display remains of the previous functions of the retailer, but this is vital.

THE STRUCTURE OF RETAILING AND THE PROBLEM OF COMMUNICATIONS

The basic socio-economic forces appear to be in favour of the development of bigger retail organizations; the multiple and the large departmental chain are a result of this. The processing-cost advantage previously held by the wholesaler has now passed to larger multiple retail buyers. Manufacturers' distribution policies should be founded on the existing and future development in retailing and customer habits; if they can discover fundamental forces governing these, then the policies will be even more firmly based.

If, after research, it is observed that a product is being increasingly purchased in multiple stores, then the manufacturer's distribution policy should be modified to meet this change in customer habits; a policy of 'no direct dealing' with retailers would obviously need reappraisal; attitudes towards prices and brands may also be re-examined.

The efficiency of modern production methods is too great for the speed of communication of market intelligence through the traditional channels; the modern production line can make perhaps thousands of products which, owing to an uncommunicated change in the market, now have less chance of being sold. The introduction of intermediaries between the maker and the final buyer creates a communication problem in sales research.

In those cases where a manufacturer controls his own outlets, the necessary machinery can be introduced for continuous appraisal of sales, and the supply of information for production decisions. The quicker the flow of such information, the lower the possibility of wasteful production; this waste is two-fold in that the machines may be making unwanted goods when wanted goods could have been made if the information had been available.

Although vertically integrated organizations are best suited to reduce the time flow of market information, it can still be achieved when an article is distributed through scientifically controlled multiples. The production process in this case will originate from an order obtained by the sales division from a multiple, but this order may be based on a scientific estimate of customer needs and will be controlled throughout the period of production to meet changing customer reaction.

Small and numerous retail outlets ordering through wholesalers present a specially difficult problem when a manufacturer is wishing to discover the turnover of his product at retail point, and special audits may be commissioned to discover the rate of turnover and also the relationship of this to competing brands; however, even this is not as instantaneous as modern production methods require. To outline the process of ordering is to appreciate the likely length of time taken; the period taken for the retailer to decide that the article is not selling; the decision not to reorder from the wholesaler; the period when retailer reaction is registering on the wholesaler; the final reduction in his order to the manufacturer to meet retailer reaction. Where a market is segmented in any way, reaction to different products or quality ranges may be delayed, thus preventing speedy reorientation to meet expanding and contracting segments. The longer the period of communication and the greater the propensity to produce goods, the greater the need to introduce retail audits, direct dealing with retailers, multiple store orders, or even vertical integration.

It must not be overlooked also that, where sophisticated sales methods are used in combination with price policy, the decision-takers require the same type of information as those concerned with production. The success at retail point of various combinations of sales methods must be known quickly so that corrections can be made where necessary and with speed.

DISTRIBUTION INEFFICIENCY AND INDIRECT TAXATION

Basic inefficiencies in distribution can become enhanced by the application of percentage profit margins at distribution points, or *ad valorem* taxes at post-production stages, or both. If a tax of 20 per cent is levied on ex-wholesale price and this price has accommodated inefficiencies within it due to any cause, then the actual tax is increased and so is the ex-wholesale price of the goods. Where any profit margin is a conventional percentage of the buying-in price, then the profit margin has a multiplier effect on the inefficiency; a 45-per-cent mark-up with inefficiency accommodated in the buying-in price would include a 'tax' on the inefficiency. Obviously, cost-conscious producers in highly competitive markets would react very positively to these adverse price moves which might more than offset the economies achieved at production point.

RETAIL STOCKHOLDING

The retailer has a special interest in the possibility of stockholding by others, in that the smaller the buffer stock per line that he holds, the greater the range that he can display and sell per unit of area and capital, and the more attractive his store. The main influences on the buffer stocks held at retailer level will be the cost of holding them, the need to meet customer requirements, and the ease with which new stocks can be obtained; the last factor is directly controlled by the efficiency of their distribution prior to retail level. Where wholesalers perform the stockholding function adequately, the retailer can achieve his objective of a maximum range of goods relative to the space available within the store and the cost of holding them; his shop will be a display and selling point rather than a store.

Where the economics of retailing show an increase in space costs and a need for wider ranges to be displayed in order to attract customers, then the division of the function of stockholding and selling at retail level becomes more important. Manufacturers operating in this type of retailing situation must respond to these economic motivations on the part of retailers, and so arrange their stockholding that they can achieve their objectives of wider display at the lowest cost. If the existing distribution network does not meet these needs because of reluctance to hold stocks, the manufacturer will have to make other arrangements.

RETAIL TRENDS AND SHOPPING HABITS

Retailers must respond to the changing habits of their customers although, at the same time, some types of retailing may trigger off a new desire in the customer of which he has been ignorant, e.g. self-service methods. Similarly, habits may change in the different locations regarded as being normal for certain types of shopping; the small town may replace the city centre when parking becomes difficult; the inter-suburban shopping centre may become more attractive as a place to buy shopping goods; co-operative societies may be considered ideologically wrong as affluence proceeds; multiples and their brands may break through to a new quality-cost stratum; the service element in shopping may be less desired by customers. The list of such changes is endless. It is the job of a manufacturer's sales manager to exploit present and future trends in retailing; he must be able to judge to which type of retail outlet he should be directing his energies and which he can reasonably ignore.

Retailing, like marketing, takes place in an environment dominated by economics, and any analysis of retail trends must begin here, although some trends have their roots in the social rather than the economic fields. Suppose prices are outpacing wages, or direct taxation has been increased, or certain necessities have become more expensive, it is reasonable to assume that under these conditions people will become increasingly price-conscious and perhaps less brand-conscious. Should this occur, customers would shop for those shops where the goods they wanted were more keenly priced; or where, perhaps by means of loss-leaders, etc., they appeared to be cheaper to buy. If a manu-facturer is selling a product which is receiving this type of customer reaction, where motivation has changed because of economic circumstances, then his distribution policy should be reorientated to meet the new situation. This may involve increased distribution through the more efficient outlets; increased use of retailer brands with lower prices, but possibly similar unit returns to the manufacturer; a revision of price policy to allow price cutting by those outlets able, because of their efficiency, to do so.

In cases where the above policies might alienate the sympathy of other retailers, e.g. small-unit traders, an appraisal would have to be made of the net gain or loss in the long period by following each policy. If the basic long-term economic forces were favouring a particular type of retail trader and were to the disadvantage of another, this would clearly help in the decision-taking process.

Retailers must apply the same cost-effectiveness techniques to land, labour and capital as the manufacturer when the relative cost of these factors is changing; the multiple can best achieve the economic employment of specialists, although the voluntary wholesale groups can go some considerable way in this direction by making specialist advice available to their retail and wholesale members. Thus the scientific layout of stores, the correct introduction and use of equipment and close control of the turnover and profitability per unit of outlay on labour, goods, space and equipment are more likely to occur in large organizations where specialist departments have been assigned to these tasks.

The large multiple retail store is better placed than any other retailer in its ability to build up, at a low cost, a local or national image and patronage which is retained within its catchment area; when shopping for shops is a practice among customers, this is an important advantage. To other advantages must be added the willingness of some multiples to relieve the manufacturer of all responsibility for selling his output. On the selling side, there is their realignment of quality-price policies in sympathy with the new distribution of purchasing power, thus maintaining contact with market segments which have become more affluent, and, at the same time, becoming more acceptable to other segments.[26]

Should a society use types of retail store as class indicators

26. Some of their customers may be old customers who have been elevated 'class'-wise, whilst others are older members of this 'class'. Some stores deliberately upgrade their image by using better-class advertising media to maintain contact with customers on the way up and also widen the market appeal at the same time.

and as a term of reference for an individual, then the sales manager must be able to identify the way in which, at any particular time, this is affecting the types of outlets he should be developing. Multiple-store shopping in the United Kingdom has become more respectable, partly due to a reorientation of the quality-price image, thus making them more acceptable to a wider buying public;[27] to omit this type of outlet on account of past associations and images could reduce the market for a product. The position of co-operative societies and discount stores is especially interesting here.

Multiples like the co-operative retail movement, Woolworths, Marks & Spencer, Boots, etc. have always had a national image due to the type of goods stocked, their stores, and the general way of doing business; only casually did they stamp their brand names on the public and yet, in their national coverage, they should be able, by consistency of policy, to present a national image backed by national brands. Manufacturers' brands in the past have enjoyed an advantage because of the extent of their coverage, but the national multiple can compete, not only in coverage, but also in finance, and often has an advantage in price. It seems reasonable to assume that in a price-conscious, increasingly alert market, the amalgam of image and price offered by a multiple will be more attractive than that offered by manufacturers' national brands. This is of vital importance to manufacturers faced with decisions on dealer brands. Certain sets of economic conditions appear to be conducive to dealer branding and the manufacturer must take these conditions as 'given' and work with them.

Before a change can take place in the type and nature of the retail outlet used, as against their organization and ownership, there must be a response or potential response from the public to the change; the successful introduction of self-service stores was really conditional on this type of retailing being acceptable to a

27. Perhaps also because old patrons have risen socially but have retained their loyalties to the multiples; multiples with a 'good-value' image also allow extra money to be made available for other social purchases, e.g. cars.

large enough segment of the market to make the switch worthwhile.[28] The habitual way of purchasing a product can be seriously affected by retail development and, in fact, the nature of the article, for sales-classification purposes, might well be changed from shopping goods to convenience goods. The availability of all goods at all convenience points removes the need, and possibly the desire, to shop. Manufacturers of goods previously sold in shopping centres to which customers were willing to go could well find that their sales were declining because the omnipresence of their type of product had made it into a convenience good. Similarly, the habit of shopping for all types of goods might become a matter of shopping for a shop rather than a particular type of goods. To the extent that customers' habits turn towards particular outlets rather than the brands carried by the outlets, so the manufacturer must watch customer shopping habits more closely.

Other retail developments appear almost inexplicable and certainly unexpected; in such cases the manufacturer must re-orientate distribution policy as quickly as possible after the event. Such a trend is the current rapid expansion of mail-order business in the United Kingdom. Traditionally it has tended to be assumed that there were certain basic reasons why the United Kingdom was not suited to this type of trading, but evidence suggests that either these reasons were invalid or they no longer apply. Perhaps particularly relevant to the case is the universality of most of the branded goods available by mail order, which removes one of the alleged drawbacks, i.e. inability to examine and compare. Also the contribution made by the printing industry to the success of this method of trading has perhaps been underestimated; catalogues have improved beyond recognition. Any manufacturer whose articles would lend themselves to colour presentation might find a useful additional outlet through mail-order retailing. This is even more attractive when the manufacturer is operating

28. It has even been suggested that this type of retailing is particularly well suited to those customers who are lacking in product knowledge and do not like the embarrassment of asking for goods; the situation is similar to the attraction of a self-service store abroad when language difficulties are present.

on a small scale and would find the financing of his own colour advertising beyond his means.

Direct dealing through mail-order or postal sales can also result from a study of the current methods of distribution through retailers and the conclusion that a more profitable segment of the market could be tapped by direct dealing. Where a manufacturer discovers that distribution margins are excessive and would not permit his catering for a more price-conscious segment of the market, then he could decide to deal directly and cut into the distribution profit which is now entirely at his discretion. Such a decision would presuppose no great antipathy on the part of the public towards the mail-order type of purchase. Normally the price differential would have to more than counterbalance the inability of the customer to examine the product; but this is reasonable to assume if the original premise of high distribution profits available as a margin for price reductions is valid.

SELF-SERVICE STORES

When the retail trade in a product veers towards self-service trading, the manufacturer must adjust his marketing policy to meet this. Increasingly the product must be pre-sold by good advertising, brand images, attractive packaging and house style. The manufacturer's packaging policy must be in sympathy with the retailer's problems.

Self-service sales depend on display and so the goods must be seen to advantage. This may involve setting up a new merchandising department to help the retailer; this may be separated from the sales representatives to reinforce the advisory content of the activity. As we saw when dealing with stockholding, the manufacturer may be compelled, because of inadequate stockholding and distribution prior to retail self-service point, to take over some or all of these functions.

Self-service stores are only possible when the necessary extra capital is available and when the customer will accept this informal type of service; this will tend to strengthen the position of the multiples as these are organizations which possess the capital resources needed and do not depend upon a high service content to appeal to the public.

CONVENTIONAL DEALER PROFIT MARGINS

Distribution margins can present a serious challenge to a manufacturer who by building up a brand name, at a considerable cost, can reasonably claim to have removed the selling function of the retailer.

The manufacturer must, however, also consider the importance of the dealer at the point of sale; thus, in selling shopping goods such as consumer-durables where the customer is unable to make an accurate appraisal of the product at the point of sale, the dealer is a key link in the sale of the article and must receive his expected reward.

If a manufacturer with large, modern, and under-employed production facilities had a well-known product and wished to break a traditional profit margin or price level in order to tap a new market and if, on analysis, the trend among the potential customers was found to be towards increased price-consciousness which showed itself in a search for price-conscious shops, then, to the extent that this was the section of the market at which the plan was aimed, the manufacturer has a good case for pressing an unorthodox policy towards dealer margins.

Throughout this book there has been continual emphasis on the 'given' factors of a marketing situation. These should not be confused with entrenched traditional factors such as conventions governing distribution profit margins and methods of distribution. An analysis of the real 'given' factors, those concerned with the socio-economic forces, might suggest that the correct policy to be followed is a break from traditional practice which was better suited to other socio-economic conditions.

There are many successful cases of the non-conformist policy where, merely by being different from the traditional, a manufacturer has acquired a special segment. The dynamic manufacturer when responding to changes in the basic structure of the market will gain because of his better analytical basis for decision-taking.

DISTRIBUTION AND SEGMENTATION

The structure of retailing today does allow the scientific sales planner to use market segmentation to maximize his market, because retailing itself caters for different segments. Investigation may show the development of price-conscious 'shop shoppers' beside a considerable body of traditional brand- and service-minded customers. The use of retailer brands enables the two markets to be exploited almost exclusively. The same policy can be followed in class-conscious markets where joint labelling of goods for particular types of shop could be used to cater for that type of customer who shops for a shop of a different kind. In those cases where mass production is needed, segmentation by retail outlets is a useful policy.

Distribution and Sales Organization

Sales organization must be responsive to changes in distribution. Increased buying through multiples could lead to the setting up of a special department to deal with this type of order; the manning of the department would reflect the size and the importance of the customers, the degree of professional acumen they possessed, and the importance of the order in terms of potential production, distribution, financial and even selling economies.

Regional sales managers may need to redeploy sales forces in order to maintain maximum sales effectiveness in the growing parts of a territory. The emergence of self-service stores might demand the establishment of a specialized merchandising division to assist the distributor in point-of-sale activities; such a division might be kept distinct from the selling division to maintain the notion of advice to help the dealer.

Conclusion

Our theme has been the need for manufacturers to use the same analytical tools on the distribution side as in other parts of their marketing policy. Successful selling requires a deep knowledge not only of retailer trends but of the changing position of the conventional dealer in the sale and distribution of goods. This scientific approach involves an inquiry into possible future developments and their real basic socio-economic causes in order that the sales distribution plan can harmonize correctly with the growth points in the distribution system of the future. Of crucial importance is the fact that this part of marketing is concerned with facing the final customer, without which sales cannot be made; it is an important aspect of customer orientation.

4. Price Policy

In marketing there are some constituents which are exclusively selling functions and which have been referred to as sales-promotion activities. There are others which are much broader in their operation and which affect production and finance; these constitute sales policy. Price policy occupies a special position, being part of both. It is clearly very much a part of positive selling – in fact it is the kingpin of sales promotion. On the other hand, it has, through its relationship to cost, capacity utilization and production, a strong association with sales policy.

To state that a decision is to be made on the price to be charged for a product or service implies that a price policy is in existence. Even if this merely implies an acceptance of the existing demand schedule for a product without any attempt to modify this to the advantage of the firm, it still requires a positive decision to fix a price on that schedule and to accept the demand and revenue which will arise from that price. However, as it is an automatic assumption that such a passive attitude to demand schedules is contrary to positive selling, there has developed the belief that the spontaneous or volitional demand is of little relevance to practical sales promotion. This is not so.

The marketeer cannot escape the part played by economic forces, even though he may appear to do so. He accepts the interplay of competing brands and the competition of all those products bidding for the same funds of purchasing power; he subscribes to the idea of consumer valuations and preference between competing products. What he does not accept is that the demand, the valuation, and the preferences are immutable. He attempts, by positive selling, to increase subjective valuation and preferences, and consequently the demand at any given price. Nevertheless, the state of demand prior to the sales-promotion activity is his term of reference; it is the starting point for decision-taking on the feasibility of economically increasing the demand for the product and so the net revenue.

The more the price decided upon is at variance with the spontaneous valuation put on a product, the greater the sales-promotion effort needed to effect the necessary change in customer valuation. Similarly, the more normal demand at any price is below that desired by the company, the greater the outlay on advertising, branding, packaging, commission and dealer incentives needed to achieve the desired demand. The marketeer does take the demand as 'given', but he does not accept it. Price policy is involved in the deliberate act of creating a demand at the price given and maximizing the net profit of the organization after the costs of creation have been met.

PRICE AND PREFERENCES

The price a customer is willing to pay for a product is not solely a result of that product, but of its relationship to others in the current valuation or preference scale of the customer. When a person pays £75 for a television rather than spend the money on a carpet, he is demonstrating that he prefers the television at that price to a new carpet at the same price; he may prefer both to a new car at £750, available on credit. Marketing, being customer-orientated, must take these preferences and valuations as given, accepting them as a challenge to the positive sales activity which must attempt to improve the position of the product in the preference scale of the customer.

The price of a product must be fixed in relation to the customer's existing and potential scale of preferences and values. The potential value represents the possibility open to sales promotion. This implies a relationship, not only within a generic group of products, but also among all those products competing for the same purchasing power. Sewing machines compete in price with each other but also with furniture, refrigerators, and other goods on which the customer can spend his purchasing power. When we say that a product must be competitively priced, this should assume competition from all products seeking the same purchasing power, and not merely competing brands within a generic group.

The changing range of products available for purchase requires price policy to be constantly under review to determine whether it is reacting correctly to new products, variations on existing ones, and the prices of both groups. At the same time, rapid response to price changes within the same product group is clearly vital.

Credit buying, by appearing to reduce the financial burden of purchasing a product, may introduce an advantage to those goods which can be purchased in this way, to the disadvantage of competing goods; in effect, it distorts the comparative monetary valuations of products on which preferences are based.

Although the exact gross revenue which might be obtained from a future price change can never be known, nevertheless an estimate of this can, and should be, made. Such estimates would cover the elasticity of demand[1] for the product as a whole, e.g. petrol, cars, and also that for the particular brand. The problem of estimating the revenue arising from the price really concerns the likely reaction of competitors to any price change. Although in a branded, 'fixed-price' market the elasticity of demand for any non-conformist brand price, up or down, is probably great, this presupposes the retention of the old price by all competitors – often an unrealistic assumption.

The value put on the product by the customer is not only the result of sales promotion and common pricing policies within a generic group, but also the relationship between this common price and that ruling for other groups of products competing for the same purchasing power. Where a common price of long-standing exists in a market, this may become the 'natural' or accepted price for the type of product concerned, even though it may bear little relationship to the costs of production and distribution, including normal profit. It may be sustaining heavy sales-promotion expenditure and high dealer profit margins in addition to manufacturer's profits. When the market for such a product is affected by the existence of other products competing for the same purchasing power, then the limits of this oligopolistic price policy can be seen; price may have to be cut in order to maintain demand.

1. Inelastic total demand for goods may create a philosophy of 'fixed' prices, any reduction having less than a proportional effect on demand and therefore reducing revenue.

THE CONCEPT OF THE 'NATURAL' PRICE

'Let us assume a selling price which is four times the cost of production.' This is not fiction, but fact. Even allowing for the cost of distribution and a return on dealer entrepreneurial activity, such an increase in price between the manufacturer and the final customer appears to be excessive. Nevertheless, such a price policy could be sustained if conditions were suitable.

The market price must be acceptable to that segment of the demand which it is intended to secure. It might be contended that there is a spontaneous or acceptable price which people are willing to pay for a group of products, e.g. refrigerators, shoes, domestic furniture, boxes of chocolates. If this 'natural' or acceptable price is exceeded by a product,[2] then the customer must be convinced that it possesses qualities in excess of the 'standard' products. Where the qualities are obvious, perhaps even visible, or have their basis in the experience of customers who have communicated their findings to others, then the higher price may be sustained without any, or with little, of the synthesized extensions promoted by sales devices; such innate extra qualities are normally the result of product research, design changes, or company service standards. In those cases where the product does not enjoy obvious comparative advantages, although some may exist, then it may be necessary to introduce them into the mind of the potential customer by means of advertising, branding, packaging and even the choice of retail dealer; advertising is here fulfilling an informative and creative communication role. Exten-

2. Investigation may show that the 'natural' price is tending to undervalue a particular product; this would indicate the possibility of introducing a higher-priced product to exploit this diversity. Movement upwards in valuations may be in a segment of the market and not overall. Thus a reduction in the need to purchase consumer-durables may increase the willingness to spend on foodstuffs or clothes. Any deviation upwards from the 'natural' price for these commodities would be more acceptable, and so less reluctance would have to be overcome by product characteristics and/or creative or persuasive sales promotion. The opposite situation, i.e. a reduction in 'natural' valuation, would have the effect of making even the maintenance of the current price difficult and may involve improved product features or increased sales promotion to sustain the present position.

sions to a product which create comparative advantages may be the consequences of long-term advertising and branding; the long-standing product may be surrounded by a type of mythology or folklore, the new one must create its own.

In affluent societies, the segmentation of markets into sections with particular idiosyncrasies provides a fertile field for the creation of synthesized psychological extensions to the product; sales promotion is used to exploit the desires of customers for special consideration. This is not, by any means, to suggest that all products which are sold at above the 'natural' price are bereft of additional advantages; but there is no automatic correlation between the cost or innate value of these additional advantages and the variation in price above the standard.

The existence of a 'natural' price is sometimes made apparent when goods are priced below it. If the goods are only marginally cheaper, then the customer might buy with an easier mind; whilst, at a lower price, scepticism and unease as to the real value of the product may be created: it is too much of a bargain to be true.

Perhaps the reaction to prices which are below the 'natural' price is the best pointer to the main influence on this price level. The reaction is based on the price normally paid for the product; it is the price usually charged in the market that is the 'natural' price in the mind of the customer. This price may contain profit margins for dealers which are excessive for the work and risk taken; it may also accommodate sales-promotion expenses which are high, and which may have assumed the characteristics of a fixed cost to enable the firm to meet competition and stay in the market.

Customers are conditioned to believe that cosmetics, paint, television sets, gramophone records, foundation garments, domestic electrical equipment, and detergents have a certain price value because the passage of time and the maintenance of certain prices have created this artificial value.[3] The more advanced the standard of living and the more intensive all forms of

3. It is possible that there exists a segment which is determinedly non- or anti-brand – perhaps a more aware segment. This section of a market might then be met by a high-price, high-value, non-heavily promoted range of goods, possibly through a multiple.

non-price competition, the higher the 'natural' price which will be supported by social drives in purchasing, the greater the indifference to price and its relationship to physical valuation, and the higher the intensity of sales promotion exploiting this situation.

In those markets where goods are heavily branded and advertised, it is difficult to conceive of a 'natural' price which is divorced from persuasion techniques; the customer lives in an artificial world and his valuations will be artificial. Should well-known branded goods be reduced in price, well below the standard ruling in a market, then this will be considered a 'bargain' (the main grounds for using these goods as 'loss-leaders'); the suspicion which might be associated with a low-priced unknown brand is removed; the goods are a 'bargain' at the price because it is less than normally charged for the brand concerned; it is less than the 'natural' price.

Where the customer is purchasing on purely economic grounds, as in industrial markets, then the opportunity for prices to accommodate emotional or non-economic elements is perhaps eliminated. The old-fashioned 'cost-plus' industrial price implies an absence of non-economic elements in the price.

Much will also depend on the knowledge of the buyer and the ability to appraise a product at the point of purchase. Again, the difference between the two markets, industrial and consumer, is marked. When goods of increasing complexity exist in the consumer markets, then the facility for creating distorted values in the mind of the unqualified customer is greater. Affluent societies count more of such goods in their purchasing, and so they are again likely to be particularly susceptible to 'natural' prices which bear little or no resemblance to the cost of production and distribution (including normal profit), and to excessive sales promotion to create such prices and variations upwards to meet the special needs of those sections of markets which demand goods compatible with their personal and social idiosyncrasies.

The ability to exploit emotional drives and technical ignorance within a market and so obtain 'inflated' prices does not imply any necessary increase in profitability. The cost of creating the additional value must be met out of the extra revenue obtained.

In addition, the existence of such emotional susceptibility will so increase the attractiveness of the market that increased competition may take place, resulting in additional sales-promotion activity and costs – and possibly even a resort to price reduction as a means to comparative marketing advantage. When the revolution is complete and price is used again as a means of selling, then the existence of intensive fixed-cost selling activities, such as advertising, is a serious threat to profitability.

COSTS AND PRICE

The problem here is to reconcile the mechanical, neat and convenient accountancy approach of a cost-plus system as a basis for pricing and the sophisticated demand-orientated, opportunity-cost-minded, 'awkward to quantify' attack of the economist.

The cost-plus system is not as naïve in its application today as is often contended. The practice has been largely modified to contain varying contributions to overhead costs and/or to profits, and these variations are a reflection of the state of the market relative to the need for the job involved, the opportunity cost of getting and doing it, and the position of competitors' capacity.

It thus often represents a convenient balance between the accountant and the economist; it considers market forces as well as the need to maintain a budgeted coverage of costs and return a planned profit. It is the lack of discrimination in cost distribution and the use of arbitrary units for cost compilation, e.g. man-hours, machine-hours, which blunt its use as an efficient tool.

The cost of production must form the basis of any pricing decision for a new product if only to fix the minimum price needed to justify, at the demand, the outlay needed to make and launch the product. The contribution of the economist-marketeer is the estimate of demand at various levels of price, and the effects of varying inputs of sales-promotion outlays relative to price as a stimulus to sales. The accountant and the economist should then reconcile the two sets of information to optimize net profits given known unit costs at various production levels and the nature of demand at various price levels.

This could lead to a price well in excess of unit costs including promotional response, a policy often followed when it is desired to cream a new market when entry by competitors is easy or where interest in the market is only temporary or both. If a sustained interest is sought and if competition is not to be obviously attracted by high profits, then a lower price will be preferred which might maintain customer loyalty more easily.[4]

Ideally, the revenue obtained from the sale of an article should cover every cost, direct and indirect, associated with its development, production, distribution and selling, and also give a profit. In many cases this ideal can be achieved, but price policies must be evolved for less fortunate enterprises; it is in such cases that the structure of costs may play a dominant part.

One of the main distinctions between the demand and supply theory when applied to manufactured and non-manufactured goods has been that based on the ability of the former to vary supply more easily than the latter, with a consequent effect on prices. On the one hand is a natural commodity, such as rubber, or wool, the supply of which cannot be altered in the short period, and so the price is beyond the control of the producers; and similarly they could not react to higher or lower prices in any positive way. On the other hand, manufacturers could restrict or expand supplies in response to price levels.

Such a view of manufacturers ignores the 'cost of selling nothing' in modern industries with a high proportion of fixed costs. There is a fairly close parallel between a rubber planter, who has invested in a plant with a specialized output, and an investment in the sophisticated equipment of modern industry with its narrow end-product spectrum. Within limits, both the planter and industrialist must take whatever price they can get in the market. If there is excess capacity in an industry, relative to the current demand for the products which can be made by it, then the price may well fall below the total cost of production, but still represents a worthwhile price to the manufacturers. Clearly, such a low price, if repeated, might deter further invest-

4. Reference will also need to be made to all products which are similar or answering a similar need in the market as a means of comparison when launching a new product.

ment in the industry, in the same way as it would the grower of natural products; but in the short period, the maximization of returns on investment demands that any price should be accepted which covers direct costs and makes some contribution to fixed costs. In all such cases, the real consideration influencing prices is the possible alternative course of action; if the price is not accepted because it is below the total cost of production, then no contribution will be made to fixed costs.

The fixed costs of modern manufacturing are completely inescapable as they are already committed in the past purchase of land, equipment and buildings, the furtherance of research, and the expense involved in building up the position of the enterprise. Even the cost of senior management, a recurring one, cannot be reduced in the short period, because of the need to retain people who are conversant with the philosophies, techniques and customer-relationships of the company. Where labour is short, even this may have to be retained because of a fear of permanent loss. What of other fixed costs?

Companies in heavily branded and highly competitive markets continue their expensive sales-promotion programmes in unfavourable circumstances, because of the possible cost of reentering the market at a later date if these activities are interrupted. In these conditions, the continued sales expenditure, or rent, to stay in a market is also considered worthwhile because of the potential losses if expensive capital is idle; thus heavy fixed production costs create heavy fixed selling costs. If market conditions became adverse, then the revenue received might become inadequate to meet the total cost of production, distribution and selling where, because of the relatively fixed nature of all these costs, they could not be reduced.

Heavy advertising costs, which represent an indivisible outlay method of sales promotion, can become an embarrassment if markets become less favourable. If sales costs were related more directly to total sales achieved, such as by reducing price, giving increased dealer incentives, using better packs, or paying increased commission to salesmen, then the embarrassment of the fixed cost in selling would be reduced. The manufacturer who decides to enter a heavily branded market will require to become committed to the cost of entering and then staying in such a market; at times of boom, the decision may be optimistically prejudiced by the economic environment at the time, and extrapolation to a less buoyant situation is needed for a realistic decision to be taken.

THE PRICE OF COMPONENTS

The price of any component, other things being equal, is dependent on the part played by it in the total cost of the end-product and the elasticity of demand for this end-product. Where the component cost is a substantial part of the total cost, and the demand for the individual end-product, although not necessarily for the group of products, is highly elastic, great care is needed to prevent a high component price destroying the end-market to the buying firm. If alternative suppliers are available, or substitutes could be used, this would quickly divert patronage to these sources.

Where an article is used in association with another, a kind of component in use or in application, then a similar reasoning applies. Petrol sales are not greatly affected by an increase in their price because the extent of this increase relative to the total cost of using a car is negligible; the sacrifice, in committed costs, of not using it would far outweigh the extra cost of petrol. All car accessories can be priced in accordance with this dictum – the more necessary they are, e.g. tyres, the greater the strength of the reasoning.

The potential extra profits may be reduced, however, by the need to meet, by price-cuts or sales promotion, the extra competition attracted by the profitable situation.

SEGMENTATION AND 'CHARGING WHAT THE TRAFFIC WILL BEAR'

All price policy implies charging the maximum in keeping with the retention of the goodwill and continued patronage, if needed, of the customer.[5] Nevertheless, there are special cases where the weakness of a customer will be exploited to help the seller to compete more effectively in a more difficult market. This is most clearly seen when a protected home market is exploited to subsidize an overseas market where competition is acute.

The policy of price differentials between segments is founded on the need to achieve the production optimum and so reduce unit costs to a minimum, and also on the presence of a high proportion of fixed costs normally found in these circumstances. The price for electricity may vary with the availability and price of alternative sources of power to the customer and the need to maintain 'round-the-clock' output from the heavy investment involved in power station and transmission plant; it may be cheaper to one firm than to another; there may be cheaper rates when the plant is likely to be under-employed or 'off-peak'. Provided that these lower prices cover direct costs and make a contribution to fixed costs, they are economic because the alternative is no contribution to fixed costs which have to be met; the cost of producing nothing is known and, in this case, high.

The two price segments help each other by increasing the spread of fixed costs. If the lower-price market were lost, the fixed costs met by it would have to be borne by the 'captive' higher-price market. Similarly, the gains of the lower-price market are obviously greater, the more the proportionate share of the costs borne by the higher-price segment.

Before such a price policy can be a complete success, certain conditions must be met. Firstly, the article must not be profitably transferable between segments,[6] because this would undermine the policy. Secondly, maximization of revenue involves an ability to prevent cannibalism; cheap day tickets should capture new traffic, which would otherwise make no contribution to fixed costs, and not that already paying the full fare.

Price segmentation may be practised in conjunction with

5. There are clearly 'unethical' sales where no repeat order is expected; the profit per customer is 'once and for all'.
6. Where the article cannot be stored, then clearly it cannot be transferred, e.g. cheap day tickets, off-peak electricity for light and power (for heating, this is, however, possible), services.

product, quality and brand policies to create different combinations appealing to different segments. This might involve the use of dealer brands in order to exploit a particular segment not touched by the manufacturer's own brand. Again, cannibalism must be avoided if possible; sales of dealer brands should not be at the sole expense of the producer's own brand.[7]

Realistic price policy in high-fixed-cost industries will often involve segmentation and cross-subsidies between segments based on the relative strength of seller and buyer. The railways will exploit goods which cannot travel by road and then subsidize more competitive traffic. Car markets are segmented with idiosyncratic cars based on one model but with varying prices. Many manufacturers will subsidize short-run, high-cost products and markets out of the batch-produced models. In all these cases the art of pricing is the ability to charge that amount which will not deter or transfer the customer to a lower price segment or another supplier. The high price must be as high as possible to provide the subsidy, but not so high as to reduce sales.

PRICE AND THE PRACTICE OF THE MARKET

Many markets, or segments of markets, may have a certain ethos which influences prices in them. Such an environment would normally result in a restriction of price competition either at manufacturer or distribution level or both. If, at the same time, there is price leadership at manufacturer level and also common dealer profit margins, then price competition has ceased to exist between brands within the industry or market.[8]

Price policy in this situation involves a decision on conforming with the general practice or following an individual price policy. Such a decision is more profound than one on mere price level, because it involves general selling strategy. To break such price conventions could alienate not only competitors but also the distributors, and where these play an important part in selling, as

7. Where there is a trend to dealer brands on the part of the public, then this may be unavoidable and must be accepted.

8. Product competition and sales promotion will now be intensified.

with shopping goods, then the decision to 'go it alone' requires lengthy consideration. It is in this type of decision that a knowledge of the infrastructure of the market is vital.

Any form of price 'fixing' presents the problem of whether to conform to the ruling price and practice, or not. In the petrol market the common movement of prices by all the major suppliers makes it possible for the price non-conformist to exploit a price differential as a sales aid – provided that there is no price retaliation.

Decisions to follow a non-conformist price-policy will require readjustment throughout the selling 'mix'. If the price of a brand of petrol is reduced, then advertising can be cut down; but if the price and dealer margins on domestic equipment are reduced, then advertising may be increased to offset dealer alienation and brand indifference at the point of sale.

PRICE AND DEALER MARGINS

Should the product have close substitutes, the willingness of the dealer to display and perhaps positively sell is vital to sales. Any price policy by one company which appears hostile to the dealer may result in an unfavourable bias in his attitude towards the products of the company, to the detriment of sales. If conventional margins exist in a market, it may be necessary to accept these to obtain the necessary distribution and positive promotion of the product.

Where dealer margins are reduced below the normal in a trade, advertising may have to be increased in order to exert customer pressure on dealers. Should the policy involve price-cuts, and the market is highly susceptible to these, then the effectiveness of any advertising which contains an appeal to price motivation is of course increased.

Articles which require the maintenance of certain standards of service both before and after sales may require a larger dealer margin to enable the necessary standard to be achieved. Such cases have frequently been instanced as reasons for the implementation of policies of resale price maintenance to prevent specialist dealer margins from being reduced by price competition.

Where interruption in the service obtained from goods is found to be a major cause of dissatisfaction on the part of the customer towards the particular brand, then ways must be found to reduce or eliminate this at source. Customer frustration with a product may be caused by inexpert advice at point-of-sale or inadequate standards of after-sales service. The maintenance of high dealer profit margins would help to remove one reason for this.[9]

Where motivation research shows a lower priority for continuous service from the product and a high rating for price, then a complete reappraisal of dealer margins may be necessary. The customer, however, may be comparing a price reduction with a poor standard of service and accepting the former; the better and more vital the service, the greater the price reduction needed to offset it in the mind of the customer. The main conflict may be between the need to reduce prices and an inability to contain the conventional dealer profit margins in the lower price.[10]

PRICE AND QUALITY

The scientific marketeer must be aware of the reactions of different sections of the market to price and quality. He must then adjust the price and quality of the product or service which he is providing, to identify it with the appropriate segment, or segments, of the market.

The price-quality relationship of the product will have to be communicated to the segment concerned and this may involve extensive sales-promotion activities to create the correct image; the sustaining of the image in an ignorant market may be partly achieved by the price which will give an illusion of quality. In

9. Such a policy must be supported by close control of the standard of service given by the dealer.

10. A similar accommodation within the end price must also be made for indirect taxation on goods. The total price must be acceptable.

those fields where the customer cannot accurately appraise the products at the point of sale, the price acts as a guide to the quality rating, particularly if backed up by adequate sales promotion.[11] The customer is paying for, and is satisfied with, an assumed extension to the standard quality which may bear no relationship to the actual increase in quality standards. This may not result in any increase in the net profits of the enterprise because of the cost of creating the quality image. Where this is easily created, e.g. cosmetics, then this facility will encourage more entrants into the market and the cost of promotion will be increased by inter-brand competition.

Price-quality relationships, although they may have social connotations, are often based on economic circumstances. A trading-up policy is based on the increasing affluence of the market; companies improve the quality and raise prices in order to participate in the affluence of their established market. If profit margins are proportionate, these policies are the logical way for profit expansion in certain markets.

Obviously, economic forces could also create a need for a lower price-quality relationship. Such can occur when too many demands are made on incomes, either by the cost of living or by the desire to acquire more goods. Cheap records, books, tours and domestic equipment are all examples of markets where this has occurred in the United Kingdom.

PRICE AND MOTIVATION

This is closely related to the last heading and also to brand imagery. In affluent societies the urge to show superiority through the possession of goods is increasingly frustrated by the universal possession of these goods. Distinction must be sought in the goods themselves. A high price contained with other quality

11. There are two assumptions here: (a) that the qualities for appraisal are not too widely varied, e.g. a customer could appraise the relative qualities of really cheap and really dear clothes, cigarettes, cosmetics, etc., but cannot distinguish within the ranges of cheap and dear goods: (b) if repeat sales are needed, then expectation must be satisfied; but this may be difficult to assess, e.g. the 'power' of cosmetics, etc.

characteristics enables the product to appeal to this type of customer.

Sometimes the enterprise may concentrate solely on this type of segment and become associated with it; at other times, a mass-market producer might create a price-quality brand variation on his model to maximize total sales by gaining entry into this segment.

Economic forces, as against the social forces which created the above situation, might dictate that the motivation is based largely on value. Price would then have to reflect this; thus impulse purchases are largely price-motivated.

PRICE CUTTING AND PREMIUM OFFERS

To reduce a price as a means of making a sale must be the oldest method of selling and, although there are examples which illustrate the opposite, it remains a potent weapon in sales promotion. The attraction of the special offer or temporary price reduction is that it enables the same price-cut to be repeated at will, with its associated boosts to sales. The conventional reduction in price, involving a big price decision, only injects one such boost; the novelty of a general reduction only occurs when the price is reduced; it does not maintain its characteristics over any period of time; it reverts to being only a price.

Temporary price-cuts, or special offers, can also be removed or terminated without unduly offending customers; their very nature suggests that they are not permanent. But to increase a price which had previously been reduced might have much more serious consequences on demand; the product is now dearer. The temporary price-cut exploits the 'natural' valuation put on the product by the customer, and does not offend it. To increase prices after reducing them requires new valuations and relative preferences to be established.

In addition a decision to bring in a short-period concession is not so far-reaching in its implications as one to reduce the price of the product indefinitely. Should the short-term decision be correct, it can be repeated, even to the extent of a price reduction with intervals of a higher price, to sustain the bargain motive. Should the decision prove incorrect, then the short period in which it applies lessens the consequences.

Offers may also include goods along with the article purchased. The prevalence of these practices and their achievement of a permanent element in the selling 'mix' of some firms, such as when gift coupons are used, does indicate that deeper drives may be operating. Such offers appeal to the urge to acquire property, but have the added attraction of being an apparent bargain; a double drive is in operation.

Any success of price-cuts, premium offers, or gift and bonus schemes can only be explained by reference to the comparison in the customer's mind of the difference between the present price and the normal one. The latter has, however, in most cases been created by the companies making the offer, sometimes over a long period of trading, at other times by affixing a price label to the product giving it an instant 'natural' price to which the cut price can be compared. The device is ideal in sales promotion because it enables the brand owner, within limits, to create a completely artificial stimulus to sales; he determines the 'natural' price which is exploited by the cut price which he also determines.

PRICE INCREASES AND SALES PROMOTION

The bread was alleged to be different, a point which dominated the advertising. Sales remained stubbornly low. Suddenly, the inconsistency of the promotion was seen in that an allegedly above-standard product was being sold for the normal price. The price was increased, the illusion completed, and sales boomed. It was 'deservedly dearer'.

Increasing prices, unfortunately, is likely to have the opposite effect to that given in the example. There, inconsistency of sales promotion exploiting certain motives was rectified, and this caused the increase in sales; price was now in keeping with the projected image of the product. Price increases usually create hostility, but this can be mollified if advantage is taken of certain techniques which occasionally present themselves.

An enterprise may experience extra pressure on profit margins due to increased production costs, but be unable to increase the price because of the effect on customers who regard the existing one as 'natural'. Any increase would run the risk of alienating marginal customers. One possible way out of the dilemma is to dissolve completely the present concept of a 'natural' price by introducing a new or allegedly new, model. This would permit any price increase to be disguised by the new model; the customer would be faced with a 'better' model at a price in excess of the old model. A new fusion between product and price would take place.

Any reduction in the tax applied to goods can also be used as a means of increasing the price and, again, no obvious sacrifice is made by the customer. If the demand for a product at a given price is high enough to sustain sales at the level needed, then a reduction in the tax on such goods will not be handed on to the final customer. The producer will take the reduction in tax as additional revenue. The intrusion of the Chancellor helps to soften the impact.

Clearly, any increase in price is more easily sustained by an individual brand or product if all competing goods adopt similar policies, particularly where all are close substitutes. Sometimes a wave of price increases may occur throughout an industry, or even the major part of a country; it is difficult to avoid the conclusion that some of these are due to a bandwagon effect. If it is seen that the public has been conditioned to expect a price increase, perhaps by newspaper editorial comment, then reaction is less likely to be hostile to the initial movement of prices upwards. Increases by other firms are then accepted with resignation, as if inevitable consequences of greater forces (the government?). An increase in a raw-materials price can set off a chain of increases in the articles of which they form a part, sometimes out of all proportion to the increase in material costs. An import surcharge can create an atmosphere of expectation of increased prices which reduces the hostility of customers when they occur, even though, again, they may bear no resemblance to the true increase in costs which should have occurred because of the surcharges. Acceptance of such increases does depend on the knowledgeability of the customer,[12] but it would also seem to rely on a certain climate at the time of the increase. From a sales viewpoint, price increases in such conditions are amply justified.

PRICE AND INFLATION

Inflation can lead to a dangerous development of the belief that higher prices will be accepted by the market and that these will accommodate any increase in selling cost. Clearly when inflation ends, or deflation begins, the consequences of the increased selling costs could be serious if they were still sustained and the firm had to meet them out of the reduced revenue resulting from lower prices.

An important possible outcome of inflation is that it enables a product to spread into lower-price segments of a market. This occurs if the price is 'pegged' in an inflationary period. The real price will be lower relative to competing products with increasing prices, and thus it could become acceptable to new customers. The advantage of this method of increasing a market by a real price reduction is that it does not affect the price-quality image held by the existing market because no price reduction in monetary terms takes place. In an inflationary situation this reasoning might support the setting of a higher initial price than would otherwise be the case; reductions to a more realistic level, if needed, would take place through the inflationary process.

RESALE PRICE MAINTENANCE

The practice whereby manufacturers or distributors (e.g. wholesalers with their own brand names), or importers recommend and/or enforce the price and profit margin at which a product will be sold in a section or sections forward from their activity is known as resale price maintenance. It manifests itself in the removal of price competition at the level or levels at which it is

12. Even in the industrial market, with its knowledgeable buyers, this inflated projection of price increases based on increased material or labour costs is experienced.

imposed.[13] In the absence of the means of competing by price, resort must be made by dealers to other devices which range from extravagant shop fittings and displays, through free delivery, to the subsidizing of restaurant facilities.

If there is any ethos existing among the manufacturers in an industry about the normal market price for their type of product, then this will also effectively remove inter-brand price competition. If this is supplemented by resale price maintenance, then price competition is removed at all levels of manufacturing and distribution. Competition will be restricted to product design and sales-promotion techniques. With the pressure on sales generated by the heavy investment needed in many industries remaining high, this can only mean that competition which would have shown itself in price will be diverted into more intensive non-price conflict.

The ability to enforce resale price maintenance may depend on the law of the land, but certain economic factors also play an active part. Enforcement implies fear of retribution by those enjoined to comply; the larger the retail unit involved, the less it will fear the sanctions of manufacturers. The growth of large units, in contrast with the former atomistic retail situation, militates against effective enforcement of restrictive conditions of sale. The threat of reprisals by small dealers against those manufacturers who are inactive on price enforcement is a less meaningful one if trade is tending to move towards price-conscious multiple stores. When people shop for shops, not goods, then the supporters of resale price maintenance have an added problem in the strength of the favoured shops.

The existence of heavy investment behind a product and the threat of idle capacity can lead to the abandonment of price enforcement systems by individual producers. This non-conformity can be prompted by the incipient desire of a growing section of retailers to cut prices. When a manufacturer has

13. Statutes outlawing resale price maintenance do not, as a rule, affect the enforcement of prices by dealers over their own brands; these are self-enforced. Where dealer brands and multiples are dominant in a trade, then conventional resale price enforcement will only have a marginal effect on prices and price competition, as will its removal by statute.

invested in more efficient equipment than his rivals and the price and dealer margins ruling reduce his market to a point below his optimum production figure, then the economic incentive to allow more price competition is increased.

Even where enforcement of retail prices continues, the producer's powers of supply sanctions, or even legal action where it is permitted, will be affected by the general conditions of the trade. Devices aimed at reducing the price to the customer without reducing the prescribed price will go unheeded.

Perhaps the greatest threat to the practicability of resale price maintenance occurs when dealers establish their own brand names, particularly if these achieve a prominent part in the total market for a product. The manufacturer in such cases has no control over prices, which are now fixed by the brand-owner, i.e. the multiple retailer.

The entry of a manufacturer into distribution enables dealer price policy to be directly under his control: companies with their own wholesaling and retail organization clearly have no enforcement problems. Such a policy decision to integrate vertically forward may be prompted by a change in the law reducing the power of enforcement, or economic changes which threaten the viability of policies such as those discussed above. Dealer price maintenance may become a distinct problem, but it could be part of the manufacturer's price policy where the dealers are part of the same organization.

Manufacturers, aware of the breakdown of resale price maintenance, may actually decide to introduce more order into its breakdown as a means of increasing sales. Price-cuts at retail points may be organized by producers wishing to enjoy the perpetual appeal of repeated price-cuts in preference to the possible permanent reduction which retailers might use. Such a policy by producers is an admission of the breakdown of normal price control, and also of the inadequacy of heavy advertising to sustain brand loyalty in the face of price competition.

The degree of distortion to prices caused by resale price maintenance depends on the latent possibility of price competition. Where margins are small, the possibilities are reduced. Small profit margins on a national brand may, however, be sacrificed as an attraction or inducement to potential customers of retail stores; the 'loss-leader' sales device is really a product of the 'natural' price created by branding and enforced prices.

Where dealer margins are high, then this will be an attraction to those retail outlets not now selling the product, to do so; it could lead to a proliferation of outlets dealing with it. This proliferation will be facilitated by the ease with which the product can be handled by the skill at the disposal of the dealers. Resale price maintenance removes the price risk from the retailer; pre-selling and packing remove the selling ability; and advanced technology and/or changed customer motivation may reduce or eliminate the technical skill needed. The supermarket and large convenience store dealing in a wide range of goods are the outcome. The former shopping goods, requiring skill to sell and maintain, have been transferred to convenience goods by changes in the product, which may contribute to revised customer expectations of the product and the retailer who sells it. Large dealer margins will encourage this movement of goods to non-specialist outlets when margins on non-shopping goods have been reduced, but retail costs are increasing; dealers will see shopping goods as potential sources of increased profit to meet their higher costs. Resale price maintenance, which perpetuates large retail profits for specialist dealers, may thus contribute to the demise of these dealers when the product no longer needs the previous level of skilled attention, and can be handled by non-specialists; if these stores also indulge in price competition, then resale price maintenance may be broken,[14] and with it the specialist shop if the market is price-motivated.

The enforcement of a price to enable dealers to give the standard of service needed to maintain the goodwill of the customer for a branded product has already been mentioned. Such a practice does, however, require constant revision to keep in line with the service needs of the product; should these be reduced, or the standard of service available deteriorate, then the dealer margin could be logically reduced.

14. Even if the producers restrict outlets to specialized dealers, the entry of imported goods, with no such policy of restriction, can result in a similar threat to enforced prices and specialist outlets.

The desirability of enforced prices has often been put forward on sales-policy, rather than sales-promotion, lines in that it has been considered necessary to enable modern production methods to be better applied. Estimates of sales based on variable prices are more difficult than those which assume a fixed price, and if such an estimate is the cornerstone of purchasing, production planning and even capacity needs, then there is some logic in the argument. Fixed and working capital costs are also saved if sales are stable throughout a period of time and not subject to the fluctuation which might stem from variable prices and speculative buying (and not buying); equipment or stocks would not be needed to meet exceptional demands, but could be geared to an average, consistent weekly sales figure. Although the force of such an argument is considerable, the true situation may be different in that the capacity may be already in existence and fears of fixed-cost losses may be greater than the potential advantage of better production planning. Additionally, the increased speed with which sales trends can be interpreted into production schedules by the use of computers further reduces the effectiveness, but not the absolute logic, of this contention. Marketing is customer-orientated whereas, in the short period, resale price maintenance based on this argument is producer-based.

When close substitutes exist in the convenience goods field, the dealer may refuse to handle the goods which have been subjected to price-cuts without any action from the brand-owner; this could be more serious if the market is not particularly brand-minded and would not seek the product, and/or where self-service operations predominate which require the goods to be well displayed if they are to be purchased.[15]

Shopping goods with close substitutes are in a slightly better position, because the degree of substitution is not normally so close; there will probably be variation in design and price of a degree which is not found in the convenience market. In addition, the predisposition to shop for these goods could result in a positive search for a reduced-price branded product which had

15. The manufacturer would need to determine the effect of shopping for shops in this case. Do customers shop for this type of shop ?

been well advertised; the inability of the dealer to demonstrate the desired brand might make his store less attractive to shopping-goods customers. On the other hand, the dealer does play a vital part in the sale of shopping goods by advice at the point of sale; if he is hostile to the brand, this may show itself at this crucial point.

Before deciding on the abandonment of resale price maintenance with its guaranteed mark-ups to retailers the shopping-goods brand-owner would need to inquire into the infrastructure of his market, and the trends in retailing associated with it. If the inquiry showed increased price-consciousness, perhaps with reduced interest in the quality of before- and after-sales advice and service, a tendency to shop at multiple stores, and an awareness of the brand and its price attributes, then the abandonment of enforced prices could logically follow. Advertising would be increased to exploit the basic customer attitudes on price and brand preference to offset the possible reaction of those dealers who are alienated by the policy.

Resale price maintenance assumed the characteristics of commercial dogma in some trades. This developed over decades of practising this type of price policy. It would, however, be unusual if the nature of the products, the outlets and the customers had remained constant throughout such a long period. It is certainly questionable whether the practice is naturally part of selling rather than an artificial creation born out of special circumstances. The basis of good marketing is the ability to respond correctly to change, and resale price enforcement should not be excluded from this maxim.

5. The Constituent Parts of Sales-Promotion Planning

ADVERTISING

ADVERTISING is one way of promoting the sale of a product; it is not the only way and it cannot work in isolation. Its usefulness, in terms of sales, in any given selling situation will depend on internal factors over which the company has control, such as the nature of the article being advertised, its price, the maintenance of quality, other sales-promotion activities, the correct selection of channels, production capacity, brand name or names used, the design of the product, and the amount of money and skill employed in the advertising. It also depends on external factors of a socio-economic nature, such as brand and price susceptibility, the material standards and economic well-being of a society, the prevalence of certain social instincts within the potential market, the power and availability of media used to convey the advertising, and the activities of all those suppliers of goods and services which in any way compete with the product. Apart from the first category, all other influences on advertising efficiency are beyond the control of the advertiser.

Advertising assists in the selling activity by drawing attention to those particular characteristics of the article which are most compatible with the motives, obvious or latent, of that segment of the market which is being exploited. Advertising does not necessarily instruct or inform about the total characteristics of the article to be sold, any more than any other selling activity; its function is to identify an exploitable characteristic in a product which distinguishes it from other products and to identify with that section of the market for which this distinctive feature is an attraction. Where a product has no such distinction it may be necessary to create one by means of a change in design or quality policy, a move in price or pack, or even by using a unique form of distribution.[1] This does not imply that complete lack of physical

1. Any claim capable of substantiation by the customer must be true, not only for legal reasons, but to sustain repeat patronage, which is vital to the economics of advertising.

distinction precludes advertising; on the contrary, the basis of distinction must now be made solely in the mind of the customer and will be founded on brand imagery and its development through advertising.

The dynamic conditions in which advertising, like all selling, must take place create difficulties in estimating the likely effects of any expenditure on this type of sales promotion; it is impossible to extricate the single influence from others. A given advertising budget will have varying results depending upon, among other things, the general economic and social situation; the products of competitors, particularly if new ones are introduced; the prices of competing products; and the amount and effectiveness of competitors' sales-promotion activities, including advertising. There are even variables within the control of the firm, such as the nature of the effort of the sales force.

It is more than possible that a good campaign might only maintain the present sales position of the company – a worthwhile result where all other factors have moved against the product. Similarly, a poor campaign might succeed where everything is favourable, and companies may even be lulled into a false sense of security in these cases, only to be aroused when competitors awaken to the situation, or economic chills set in, or both.

It is almost as true to say that it is impossible to measure the effectiveness of an advertising campaign even after the event. The increased productivity of salesmen may be used as a standard, but even this assumes that all other factors associated with customer reaction to the product have remained stationary – a difficult position to hold. There is even controversy over just what constitutes a measure of advertising effectiveness.[2] Should it be sales? Should it be awareness of the advert? Awareness of the product? Attitudinal change? Should sustained patronage be demanded of a well-conceived campaign? Is it an exercise in communication, or selling? Is behaviour all that matters? The difficulty increases when advertising effectiveness in the long term is being considered; thus a campaign to launch a new product or brand should have its effectiveness measured in terms of the long-

2. The measure used may vary with the objective, e.g. awareness is a useful measure if a new product or brand is being introduced.

term hold achieved on customers rather than an immediate impact, but this will only be known in the future, if at all.

Any factual knowledge of the effectiveness of past advertising campaigns could undoubtedly make a useful contribution towards taking decisions on a current advertising programme. This would cover the relative effectiveness of media, copy and timing; it could also give some indication of the relative returns in terms of awareness, or sales, of the several ways of contacting customers; thus technical-press advertising could be compared with direct mailing in the industrial field. Nevertheless, any such information from past campaigns would only be valid and useful in so far as full regard was paid to the environment in which the campaigns took place, and the relationship of these conditions to the present situation.

Comparative efficiencies between selling methods must always be difficult to assess. The consequences of a reduction in price as against increased advertising would be difficult to compare since the two policies must take place either at different times or at different places; unless the times and the places were identical from a selling viewpoint, any comparison could be invalid. Marketeers, however, may not be concerned with small differences in the productivity of different types of selling, because of this difficulty of measurement; but they must be aware of the need to recognize different methods and combinations of methods of selling, and to use that method or combination which, in the circumstances of the market, is likely to be most productive of economic sales. Thus there are certain conditions which can be said to suit advertising, and should these prevail, then, other things being equal, this method of sales promotion should be used.

The Conditions Most Favourable to Successful Advertising
(i.e. likely to give the highest return per unit of input)

Goods are not taken up by the market; they are positively sold, possibly at a higher price and in perhaps greater numbers. Nevertheless, just as every salesman prefers an easy sale, and the theme of the first part of this book was the search for socio-economic escalators, so the advertiser prefers certain conditions to prevail; the nearer the actual conditions are to these ideal ones, the greater the productivity per unit of outlay. This does not preclude advertising when the conditions are less than ideal, but it tends to suggest that other sales methods might be examined as the return on advertising will be less than the optimum.

The inability to be certain of the consequences of advertising makes it more necessary to be completely scientific in our approach to it in order to eliminate unnecessary waste; a scientific analysis of the conditions surrounding the product and their suitability for advertising is the first step.

THE OVERALL DEMAND FOR THE PRODUCT
SHOULD BE INCREASING

This is an obvious condition but it needs to be restated because of its implications where overall demand is not increasing, for example where demand is satisfied and/or inelastic, e.g. bread. Clearly, where the ideal condition is not satisfied, any expenditure on advertising, if successful, is likely to lead to similar outlays by competitors to restore the old position within the market; more expense will thus have been incurred by all concerned with no increase in sales to show for it. Such a situation must lead to reduced profits unless prices can be raised to accommodate the increased cost of selling. In times of boom this type of internecine advertising of a mutually cancelling nature can be supported because of the possible apathy of customers towards price increases, but in times of relative recession or increased price-consciousness the situation can become so serious that the solvency of the firm may be threatened.

It would appear that most advertising in brand-intensive markets tends to assume the nature of an overhead cost. In a rising market this fixed cost is not an embarrassment, because it helps the company to participate in the increased sales. Where a certain level of advertising has become accepted both by the marketeers and by the market, fear of passing from the public mind could mean that all advertisers in a market are compelled by fear of 'losing the place' to maintain their advertising at a level which is uneconomic in terms of the current revenue from sales, but which is economic in terms of the overall fixed costs of production and distribution, and is vital if the long-term maintenance of the brand or product image is considered. The diseconomies of current advertising may be more than offset by the potential losses on fixed capital if advertising were to be cut; the greater the fixed costs of production, the greater the potential losses. Where there is a fear of 'not advertising', the productivity of such advertising must be reckoned in terms of this fear, rather than in absolute sales. The realistic marketing practitioner could even suggest that if the outcome of advertising outlay is the continued existence of the company in times of adversity, this is the ultimate form of productivity.

Nevertheless, the original contention was that the best condition for successful advertising is one where increased outlays on advertising are aimed at increasing total sales rather than maintaining or increasing a share of them; and clearly the productivity in terms of units sold should be greater. In a competitive situation the increasing market could lead to an increase in the supply firms and the creation of extra capacity; this could then lead to more inter-firm advertising and, to the extent that outlays on this were in excess of the potential increase in sales, so the advertising would tend to have reducing returns; the extra market potential being unable to support the additional sales-promotion expenditure which is prompted by extra capacity.

THE POTENTIAL DEMAND AND PROFIT SHOULD JUSTIFY THE OUTLAY ON ADVERTISING

This condition is linked to the first. When a business is considering entry into a market, it must reckon the cost of entry relative to the profitability of entry. Obviously, where the market is dominated by well-established products and brands, the cost of entry[3] is proportionate to the strength of their hold over the market and potential market. Nevertheless, even though the cost of entry

3. We shall ignore the cost of entry in terms of investment needed to achieve the necessary size of plant to obtain low unit cost of production. This cost plus the cost of entry might, and does, lead to restricted competition within a market.

may be considered high, it is possibly justified if the potential market is considerable; thus the case for an apparently un-economic (short-period) outlay on entering the quality-newspaper market may be justified in the medium and long terms because of the increased market likely to result from higher education and more leisure; the cost of the launching campaign for an automatic washing machine can perhaps only be reckoned as economic in terms of the growth potential for the product, this growth being based on socio-economic factors.

Unfortunately the problem is not one of potential sales but of profitability. It is conceivable that the entry of a firm into a market with its extra productive capacity could lead to potential over-supply of that market and/or to an increase in the sales-promotion activities of those already in the market to which the new entrant would be required to respond, with a detrimental effect on the profitability of the whole enterprise.

Marketing plans should be flexible enough to meet varying circumstances. In the above situation a company with advertising myopia might take an uneconomic way of entering a market, whereas one with a better understanding of the other elements of the 'mix' would consider price and perhaps dealer policies as a means of entry in preference to, or along with, advertising.[4]

Finally, special mention might be made of a grander marketing strategy which may be associated with the apparently un-economic entry into a market. A firm which has always been to the fore might launch a campaign out of proportion to the poten-tial market (perhaps even in the medium term) in order to re-establish its position in the market. This could occur where competitors have launched more advanced versions of the product and the company is becoming increasingly associated with the older-type model. The cost of the advertising in such cases should not be set solely against the product, but also against the re-estab-lishment of the name of the company and the consequent reflection of this in the sales of all the products made by the company.

4. It may be wondered whether certain companies would not get a better return on sales-promotion expenditure if they looked for markets abroad which are not so dominated by entrenched brands and therefore not so expensive to enter.

THE ARTICLE SHOULD LEND
ITSELF TO ADVERTISING

It might be conceded that most articles could be successfully advertised. Nevertheless, there are certain characteristics which a product should have in order to achieve maximum returns per unit of advertising outlays. To the extent that the article possesses these characteristics, so advertising will be more or less productive.

(a) *The article must be distinctive and identifiable.* If the goods or service to be advertised possess a really unique quality and are true speciality goods, the job of the advertiser is greatly facilitated; e.g. the original stainless-steel-type blade. The productivity of advertising input in these circumstances should be at a maximum, other things being equal. When the product has no unique feature, advertising will still continue but it will be making 'bricks out of straw' in many cases. The emphasis now is on differences created especially for sales promotion; some of these may be real but absolutely insignificant, and therefore requiring to be built up into important characteristics in the mind of the potential customer; but this involves additional effort and expenditure as compared with the previous situation. Obviously, in most cases resort has to be made to branding and the building up of a brand image or psychological extension to a product which is basically too similar to other competing products – a more expensive matter than merely drawing attention to physical facts. The sugar refiners have spent little on advertising sugar because each brand is too readily accepted by the public as being absolutely identical to all others: any attempt to create differences based on brands would be expensive and, in a stagnant, price-conscious market, certainly uneconomic. If a detergent is produced which does possess clearly observed whitening qualities as compared with other brands, there is less need to build-in this quality by expensive advertising.

(b) *The article should stimulate emotional buying.* The term 'emotional' is here applied to goods which can be associated with irrational, non-economic motives, such as sex, fear of death,

239

paternalism, maternalism, hunger, thirst, class-consciousness, emulation, the herd instinct, cleanliness, etc. Any product which is clearly so associated has an advantage in any selling method, and this includes advertising. Cosmetics and patent medicines are ideal for making people buy goods through advertising. Beer drinking can be projected as an emulation or herd activity; continental drinks can be associated with class groups.

Some products associated in advertising with these basic drives are not *prima facie* examples of products possessing such characteristics. Motivation research has, however, enabled subconscious motivation to be exploited.

It is difficult not to come to the conclusion that many of the social instincts associated with certain goods (e.g. cars, domestic equipment) and exploited by advertisers have been assiduously cultivated by the advertising practitioners themselves. An implication by association in adverts that a certain social group uses certain products will generate greater class group-consciousness which, in turn, will make this motive more useful in advertising.

There is, nevertheless, a difference of degree of advertising productivity. Goods which are by nature emotive, e.g. medicine, insurance, wool, cosmetics, will be instantly good for advertising; goods with which social instincts can be associated through advertising, e.g. cars, domestic equipment, television, beer and cigarettes, will be eventually good vehicles for persuasion; goods devoid of emotional or non-economic qualities will be least productive in advertising. This does not rule out advertising in the sale of certain goods, e.g. industrial goods, but it may relegate this type of selling below other methods. It is largely a matter of the relative efficiency of various means of promoting the sales of goods with different innate characteristics and markets: at one end we may have cosmetics and patent medicines, at the other end a machine tool; advertising is used for both, but the objectives and the expectations of the advertising are markedly different.

It must be remembered that, to the extent that the factors of production and distribution are mobile, then the return on advertising more emotive goods will only equal that on other goods. The intensity of competition is increased when the market is susceptible to sales promotion, thus increasing inter-brand rivalry and sales-promotion costs.

(c) *The article must possess qualities which the customer cannot appraise at point of sale.* Many of the emotional claims made in advertising are incapable of verification at the time of purchase and, in fact, many could not even be substantiated after the product has been used. By association, an article may be linked in the mind of the potential customer with social acceptability, class elevation, sexual power, etc., but the acquisition of such qualities as a result of consuming or possessing the article would be difficult to prove or disprove – it would, perhaps, be too esoteric a matter anyway. Where an article possesses qualities or characteristics which cannot be assessed at the point of purchase because of the technical ignorance of the customer, then the article must be either pre-sold by advertising, sold by positive personal salesmanship, or both. Increasingly such articles must be sold by pre-selling which involves advertising. When a person buys a tyre or a car battery, he buys a promise of satisfaction; the promise has been conveyed by advertising aided by branding. To the extent that complex items make up an increasing proportion of the consumer purchases, so pre-selling on non-technical or pseudo-technical grounds will increase.

Many claims made in advertising articles cannot be proved at the point of sale because of the general 'puff-like' nature of the claim, e.g. the reliable washing machine, the economical battery, etc. If at the point of sale any such claim could be refuted on inspection, the advertisement would not even achieve one sale.

Articles, then, which are initially purchased partly as an act of faith because of inability to appraise completely the claims made for them are suited to advertising.[5]

THE NECESSARY FUNDS SHOULD BE AVAILABLE

If it is considered necessary to spend £$2x$ in order to gain entry into a market and £$1x$ per annum to sustain that interest, assuming a given price level, then it would be inadvisable to assume that

5. The economics of advertising do, however, rely on repeat patronage, which demands that the customer is satisfied with the introductory purchase.

£1x would give you half the expected results and that £$\frac{1}{2}x$ would give adequate sustenance. The effectiveness of advertising is not necessarily in proportion to the money spent on it, and it is platitudinous to state that if the amount available for advertising is below a certain level relative to the state of the market, e.g. one with well-established, entrenched brands, then other forms of sales promotion, perhaps in association with the advertising, should be used. Obviously the smaller the amount at the disposal of the advertising executive, the more scientific he should be in its disposal; but really scientific objectivity may suggest that the amount is inadequate and that more productive returns could be obtained by using the same funds in some other direction, e.g. additional salesmen or payment to salesmen, dealer incentives, etc.

THE RELATIONSHIP BETWEEN ADVERTISING AND PRICE SHOULD BE CORRECT

To the extent that the price of an article is not acceptable or 'natural' in the mind of the consumer for whom it is intended, so advertising and other sales-promotion activities will be required to achieve a given sales. In a brand- and class-conscious market it may be decided to take a segment which is motivated by class instincts, and then to raise the price and create through advertising the illusion of value within the branded product. The potential gross profit margin on the product must be sufficient to support the extent of advertising needed to create the new value in the mind of the customer. If the cost of advertising to achieve the necessary customer reaction cannot be accommodated in the gross profit of the product, there is an incorrect balance between advertising and selling price.

The market reaction to the balance struck between advertising and price is of vital importance in striking this balance. If the market is price-conscious, then there would be a less than normal beneficial reaction to advertising and a better than normal reaction to a price reduction. In markets where there is a degree of oligopoly or price leadership, the impact of using price as a means of selling in contrast to the regular practice of advertising would probably be out of all proportion to the extent of the reduction in price; the elasticity of demand for the individual brand in this type of situation may be very great, even where brand loyalties have a strong hold, e.g. petrol, car batteries, tyres, instant coffee. (If the overall demand is relatively inelastic, the final position of the suppliers may be worsened if competitors retaliate by cutting prices. Total revenue would then be reduced, but, as the cost of selling would remain constant, net profits would be reduced to the extent of the price reduction.)

In certain cases the balance between advertising and price will be more easily struck. If the demand for a branded product over a small price range is relatively inelastic, and the article sells in great quantities, then advertising outlay equal to the total cost of such a reduction is more likely to be beneficial than the price reduction. If the price of branded stout is reduced by a half-penny, the effects on sales might be much less than the use of $5,000,000 \times \frac{1}{2}p$ per day in advertising! Sometimes the extent of the smallest price reduction as a percentage of the price received by the manufacturer would rule out regular use of price as a sales aid, e.g. a sixpenny bar of chocolate can only be reduced by one sixth of its price; translated to ex-works prices, this fraction could become one quarter. In these circumstances increased advertising might be a better long-term proposition.

THERE SHOULD BE CONSISTENCY THROUGHOUT THE SALES OPERATION

Consistency is vital if images are to be made and sustained. The expensive article, highly priced, 'prestige' packed, and advertised in a 'quality' way in class-conscious media, must be sold through retail outlets which will maintain the image. The salesmen employed by a company must confirm and complement the advertising message. Where independent dealers are used, the motivational content of advertising should be projected to them so that the potential customer is confirmed in his preconceived motive (created by adverts) to buy the product; this is the more important, the greater the reliance on the dealer for advice at point of sale. Without this consistency of standards and information, the productivity of advertising will be diminished. The greater the control of the total sales effort in the hands of the manufacturer, the less the risk of inconsistency should be.

THERE SHOULD BE THE UTMOST CO-OPERATION BETWEEN
ADVERTISING AND THE NON-SELLING ACTIVITIES

Design. Effective sales promotion is more likely if the product to
be sold possesses some mark of distinction; if this distinctive
feature also gives the product a comparative advantage, then the
productivity of advertising will be increased. The design may be
functionally better than that of the competing products, a feature
to which advertising will draw attention; advertising is here
informing the potential customer about a real advance in the
product's qualities. Innovations in design may not always result
in real improvements in the product but may still create a potential comparative advantage, perhaps emotional, which can be
exploited by advertising; in this case, advertising is both informing and creating a selling advantage. Design may be required
specifically to incorporate in the product some feature which will
distinguish it for purely selling purposes. Advertising would then
be more productive per unit of outlay.

This need for co-operation can be extended to encourage
designers to consider the contribution that their activity can make
towards increasing sales-promotion productivity. Just as the
choice of advertising media can be dependent on the attractions
of the article to be sold, e.g. if it is coloured it may require a
coloured medium to promote it efficiently, so the type of media
available and their comparative effectiveness should make a
contribution to design. Thus, improvements in colour printing
can be exploited more effectively if the product has received the
requisite attention to colour.

Quality control. Any unconfirmed claim, regardless of its source,
acts as an 'unselling' device; it does not return the customer to a
position of neutrality but to one which might be hostile to the
product which has been the cause of the disappointment. This
disappointment may be economic, in which case the 'unselling'
consequences could be considerable, or emotional, where the
deficiency is more difficult to assess but where the effects may be
equally serious.

Advertising must be based on facts. Any suggestion that a

standard can be expected by a customer must be supported by the enforcement of such standards through adequate quality control. Advertising which is highly efficient in that it creates maximum customer awareness of the product, its name, and its associated qualities will become a deterrent to future sales to the extent that it has succeeded in its task but the product or service has not satisfied the expectation of the customer.

Quality control to satisfy customer expectations is vital if the repeat patronage needed for really successful economic advertising is to be obtained.

Production capacity. Advertising is concerned with creating awareness of, attitudes to, and potential behaviour towards a product in the mind of the customer. Provided these can be associated with the means of acquiring that product, a sale will result. The successful closing of the sequence depends on the ability of the firm to supply at the instance of need to the extent of the need created by the advertising and supported by purchasing power. If the demand so generated is in excess of the production capacity of the company, there is waste to the extent of the unsatisfied demand. Advertising, ideally, should not generate purposeful demand beyond the capacity of the advertiser to supply that demand.

Any exact estimate of the likely effectiveness of an advertising programme would be difficult to make and so there could often be cases where waste occurs. Nevertheless, positive effort should always be made to reduce such waste to a minimum. The availability of localized newspapers, regional commercial television and radio stations, and posters enables potential sales to be kept more in harmony with capacity, and at the same time could bring about a reduction in the cost of distribution by using a market near to the point of manufacture (assuming that there was not a distant market where the degree of effectiveness of the advertising per unit of outlay was greater than any extra distribution cost incurred in the more distant location).

The standard of distribution. Wasteful advertising due to inability to provide the article at the right time at the place where the demand is present is perhaps easier to eliminate than lack of capacity, because the former is basically an organization problem rather than one concerned with physical assets. Faulty distribution can be caused by bad timing of deliveries, faulty transport, poor inventory control at factory and depots, and inadequate control over the stocks of independent dealers such as wholesalers and retailers. Today the completely co-ordinated advertising campaign includes control of distribution and the prior notification to dealers of the campaign and its expected results (this is then used as a sales aid in the sales to dealers).

Inadequate capacity and inability to distribute efficiently to maximize the selling effects of advertising could in some cases lead to an increase in the sales of competitors' products where there is close substitution. This would be the case where the advertising had created a desire for a product or generic group of products, e.g. a 'log-effect' electric fire, a first car, but had not created a deep brand awareness. The irrevocable nature of competitive selling is well illustrated in such cases; the outlay on the competing item is irrevocably spent and if the article is not a regular purchase and of some value, i.e. shopping goods, then the loss is even greater.

Distribution efficiency is essential in order to convert an attitudinal and/or behavioural advertising campaign into effective customer behaviour which will result in sales and revenue; it is a vital link in the chain.

Co-ordination with 'face-to-face' selling. The timing of advertising should be correctly co-ordinated with the timing of other sales activities. The productivity of a representative whose product and firm has been introduced through the medium of a trade or other advertisement might be much greater than where no such advertising had taken place. Timing is essential in such cases. With consumer goods the detailed timing and contents of the general advertising campaign should be made known to the dealers before the campaign has begun. This will not only make the dealer more willing to stock the goods but also increase the sales effect of the advertising by ensuring that the products are available when the customers ask for them (assuming that the distribution function is working correctly). Low allocation of funds to personal selling may also be a cause of wasteful advertising where the full effects of the advertising have not been harvested because the sales force is inadequate.

THE CO-ORDINATION OF ALL FACTORS TO MAXIMIZE EFFECTIVENESS RELATIVE TO COST

Factors spread from the inception of an article to the face-to-face situation of the company's salesmen must be co-ordinated to achieve maximum impact. When a new product or variation on a product is at the conception or design stage, estimates must be made of the time likely to be taken to complete all the tasks necessary before the product hits the market. Alongside this schedule of estimated times should be a parallel one covering all the activities leading up to and including the advertising campaign to launch the product. These two schedules must be brought together at a given date which has been chosen as most likely to result in the greatest impact on the market, considering the likely activities of competitors at that time, and the state of the market for the type of product to be sold.

To achieve the maximum co-ordination at the lowest cost, resort is now made to the technique of critical-path or network analysis. In this way the availability of the product in the right quantities at the necessary place and possessing the required qualities will be completely compatible with the extent and timing of all the sales activities including advertising. Such schedules have always been used by the scientifically organized firms, but the application of statistical method to the process has not only led to a greater accuracy and appreciation of cost comparisons between various ways of achieving a given task, but has required the planners to be more aware of the need for overall co-ordination. To use control techniques for research, development and production, and to omit them in sales is the negation of the concept of modern marketing. To achieve a desire to buy a product, whether new machine tool, domestic gas, or detergent, and then be unable to deliver because of badly phased product development, testing of prototypes, ironing out of production problems, badly organized distribution and after-sales service points, etc., would show a basic misunderstanding of marketing, which is a comprehensive concept concerned with maximizing the profitability of the company. Similarly, to have solved all the problems of production and distribution before the programme covering the training and organizing of salesmen, briefing of dealers, and the large group of activities associated with an advertising campaign have been successfully completed would again be contrary to good marketing practice.

Within these schedules there are certain points at which two paths must coincide. Thus, sales training in the product must be completed so that salesmen can call on dealers at the time when that section of the advertising aimed at dealers is appearing in the trade press; this would precede the main advertising campaign aimed at the public. The placing of advertisements requires adequate notice to the media owners by the advertising agency; once these dates have been fixed, the other production, distribution and sales activities must be organized to meet these dates. (Clearly the acceptance of a date for advertising by the agency should be influenced by the feasibility of its being achieved by the business.) Where the timing of a campaign is of supreme importance, e.g. to catch an exhibition or 'season', then the company may be forced to adopt more costly methods to achieve the date, e.g. sub-contracting of part of the product. This is where cost comparisons become important, any comparison being considered against a background of the need to achieve the given date; the importance of meeting the date would have to be quantitatively assessed by the sales department in order to give maximum assistance to the analysts.

Critical-path or network analysis is the logical outcome of the search for maximum co-ordination between the various functions concerned; conceiving, designing, producing, distributing and selling a product; and, by its additional emphasis on cost evaluation, it helps to achieve maximum productivity of the amalgam of functions associated with satisfying a market, the very essence of modern marketing.

The specific problems of advertising

This book is not concerned with the techniques of advertising, which are best left to the specialized writers on this technical subject; rather is it hoped to show the position of advertising in the marketing and selling 'mix' and its relationship to other activities. Nevertheless, having dealt with the ideal conditions and the need for maximum co-ordination of functions, it is in the nature of things to complete the scientific approach by indicating certain specific advertising problems and the approach to these problems.

No person would deny the great contribution of art and craft to the practice of advertising; the writing of the copy, preparation of the artistic side of an advertisement, the choice of brand name, colour of pack, and even the 'pitch' of media to be used. By definition, such activities are intuitive, although they should be subjected to scientific appraisal, wherever possible, e.g. consumer panels, and, to the extent that they are intuitive, they defy communication from mind to mind, or 'heart' to 'heart', through text-books. For this reason we must restrict our treatment of the problem of advertising to the scientific, and give the other side its due reward.

CHOICE OF MEDIUM

The sole maxim governing the choice of medium for conveying a persuasive message to the potential market is that that medium should be used which will contact the optimum number of potential customers most effectively and at the lowest cost. The optimum number is determined jointly by the costs of promotion, distribution, finance and production. Another medium may be available which could contact a larger market at lower unit cost (but higher total cost) but, from a financial viewpoint, would be wasteful because it was creating a demand which could not be economically satisfied, taking into consideration the existing scale of production and distribution.

Decisions must be made on the optimum production and distribution figures and these must then be reconciled with the sales-promotion optimum to give a figure which, in the conditions of the market and the technical, managerial and financial state of the firm, represents the overall optimum.

The decision on distribution will consider the economics and logistics of the physical disposal of the product; additional customers may be readily available in a wider market which may be covered by an efficient commercial television network or national newspaper, but to supply such customers is, at the moment, uneconomic; more concentrated markets nearer to the place of manufacture might be preferred. On the other hand, the more concentrated market may be saturated with the promotion activities of others, which may result in a high unit cost of promotion that more than offsets the lower distribution costs.

If we assume that a decision has been taken on the size and location of the market, what further factors must be considered before choosing media?

That medium will be chosen which contacts the greatest number of potential customers most economically and effectively. This will involve an analysis of the coverage, in terms of potential customers, of each type of medium; a popular daily newspaper or national television network might contact the greatest number of people per unit of outlay but, if the majority of those contacted are not potential purchasers of the product, then the cost of worthwhile contact might be excessive and this type of medium could be wasteful. To sell expensive cameras by advertising in popular newspapers is uneconomic because too many of the readers have no interest in purchasing such products; this is still true even if the cost per unit of readership is lower than that of specialized journals catering for camera enthusiasts.

The effectiveness of a medium might depend on its ability to carry the most efficient message. This may conflict in some cases with the maxim discussed in the last paragraph. A black-and-white newspaper advertisement may be inefficient for the promotion of articles whose colour is a main motivation or attraction; glossy paper may project a cold impression of products which require a connotation of warmth; informative advertising requires a less perishable medium than non-informative and vice versa. Even if a medium will contact the greatest number of potential customers at the lowest cost, it may not be chosen because of its inefficiency ˋ carrying the correct message; both economy and effectiveness must be satisfied.

A medium may be chosen for the specific purpose of upgrading the merchandise which is being advertised, the higher class of medium being projected on to the product. This is likely to be most prevalent in periods of rising affluence as companies try to extend their quality range and price upwards.

Finally there is the need to optimize the mix of media. Different media may be used for different segments, even at different times, and for conveying distinct aspects of the appeal. It is vital to maximize the overall effectiveness of such media outlays, and to this end quantitative techniques can be of great assistance in achieving the required optimization, provided a clear idea is held of the purpose of each medium in the schedule and its contribution to the total objective, and there exists the necessary information-flow both past, present and future (for control) to make the best use of optimization techniques.

THE CONTENT OF THE ADVERTISEMENT

This is determined largely by the objective of the advertising and the motivation of the potential customer. An introductory advertisement must be informative. An advertisement aimed at meeting new competition will have to carry a message which implies a degree of favourable comparison. Prestige and sustaining copy need not be informative. Occasionally an advertisement may be directed more blatantly at a competitor, in which case there is an element of 'knocking' the competing product or the company which makes it – within the professional standard laid down, and the law of libel.

Planned campaigns could well have a progression of objectives. Awareness of the product or brand may be the initial objective: followed by a campaign to change attitudes: finalized by one aimed at converting the changed attitude into behaviour and so to sales and revenue. Sometimes the objectives may be fused, e.g. awareness and attitude.

Long-term advertising campaigns which can become almost part of the folklore of a market tend to rely more on consistent exploitation of motives directly or indirectly associated with the product, e.g. 'Guinness is good for you', 'Horlicks for night starvation'. Effective advertising must be based on motivation research so that the strongest motives can be exploited in the advertisement; the motive can be rational, as with industrial goods and some consumer goods; it can be emotional and have its basis in the subconscious drives of the consumer; it can exploit fears or potential fears, e.g. 'The tyres you can trust in weather you can't', also fear of old age, death, family insecurity, epidemics; specific situations may be used to drive the customer, such as the education and health of children, and presents for festive seasons.

Increasingly advertising has utilized the findings of motivation research in that products are sold on drives which have their basis in strong instincts which give rise to powerful emotions. Sometimes the emotions are not obviously associated with the product but become so as a result of the advertising; they become extensions to the product created by advertising and other sales aids.

Emotions may also be exploited to attract attention before the selling content of the advertisement can be consumed. Sex, humour and curiosity are used extensively for this purpose in all types of advertisement from the more menial consumer goods to the largest piece of industrial equipment. This use of emotions is not an end in itself, but should lead through the advertisement to greater awareness of the product, its name, properties, suppliers, etc.

The content of any advertisement must reflect the motivation and knowledgeability of the prospect to whom it is addressed. Consumer-goods advertising can be emotional from the point of attraction to the point of selling. Industrial-goods advertisements must be eventually informative or conducive to seeking information; regardless of the use of emotions to attract attention, the content of any information must be devoid of non-economic emotions.

THE LOCATION OF THE ADVERTISEMENTS

Clearly advertising should be used in that area where its comparative effectiveness is greatest and where the productivity per unit of outlay on advertising is maximized; always assuming that the diseconomies of distribution do not offset the economies of advertising.

A further decision is required on whether the advertisement is to be pointed at dealers, the general public, or both. Basically, a manufacturer with fears of idle capacity should prefer to promote his product directly to the final customers: the 'pull' policy. This would generate a demand from below to which dealers would have to respond, and so the distribution of the product, in terms of dealer willingness, would follow from the effects of the advertising. Undoubtedly such an argument has force in that it enables the manufacturer directly to control the cultivation of his product's image and market. Where manufacturer-branded articles are retailed through self-service stores, pre-selling by advertising is axiomatic; this type of retailing is based on the assumption that the selling function is taken from the retailer by the manufacturer.

Despite the attraction of advertising direct to the customer, there are many instances where the nature of the article, the closeness of substitutes, and the special position of the dealer at the point of purchase will require that adequate advertising is directed at the dealers, regardless of the attempts to persuade the ultimate customer by direct advertising. Wherever goods are beyond the critical appraisal of the customer at the point of purchase, and/or there are many close substitutes readily available, and the dealer assists the customer to decide on his choice among the competing products, then the dealer must be adequately briefed on the qualities of the product and its relative advantages; the contents of the dealer advertising should confirm and complement the advertising to the general public. In circumstances where the dealer is important and where the cost of effective public advertising is beyond the manufacturer, then the best results may be obtained by concentrating on dealer advertising and point-of-sale displays.

TIMING

Effectiveness and the elimination of waste are again the keynote when making decisions on timing. The timing of a campaign aimed at the final customer should be scheduled to exploit the times when past experience had shown the greatest propensity to purchase the type of product. Where the product is purchased regularly and at no set time, timing in terms of dates may be less important; but where the product sales tend to be highly concentrated, timing is absolutely vital, e.g. wines during December for Christmas and New Year, toasters and heatproof ovenware before a 'wedding season'. Advertising to dealers must be timed well in advance of the peak sales period so that orders can be received and goods manufactured and distributed to meet the demand created at the time of advertising. It is essential that the manufacturer knows the times of buying of the final customer, i.e. the turnover of his goods in his shops, and not the rate of purchase by retailers; steady buying by retail store buyers might suggest similar regular buying by the public, but it could hide considerable swings against which the retailer is building up stocks on a regular basis.

The above reasoning does not preclude the use of advertising during 'off' seasons; in fact, that there is a regular period of slack demand might be an adequate reason for an advertising campaign to boost sales during this off-peak period. This is particularly necessary when the capacity needed to produce for the peak demand cannot be used for any other purpose and so remains unproductive, e.g. the attempt to boost turkey sales during non-festive seasons.

When a special emergency has to be faced, e.g. inability to meet a sales quota, the emergence of new competition or more active selling by competitors, then the timing of advertising is governed by these events. Other special cases are where the timing, e.g. direct mail, must be co-ordinated with the personal call of a representative; his productivity is likely to be increased if the potential customer has some prior knowledge, either of the product, the company, or both.

Advertising and the Future

Some advertising is highly effective in that it confirms the opinion of the customer about the product or service being advertised; it looks to the past experience of the purchasers. Advertising, however, may be required to consolidate the current satisfaction as a preparation for, or insurance against, a future situation.

If a company is making an article which is a truly unique product, a real speciality good, then it may seem unnecessary to invest in heavy advertising programmes, particularly if the goods are being sold up to the limit of the production capacity. Nevertheless, such advertising could easily be justified and in the long run may be a cheaper alternative, if the speciality goods are capable of imitation. The future situation is more important than the present in these cases.[6] Where potential competitors have greater resources for sales promotion, the need for capitalizing on the present position of the company may be even more important.

The Advertising Budget

There are two ways in which any seller can increase his sales: firstly, better value can be given by reducing price or changing the product; secondly, increased efforts can be made to overcome the reluctance of the customer to buy. The use of the first involves a sacrifice per article sold which, it is hoped, will be justified by the overall profit position. The use of the second method requires the expenditure of economic resources, in the form of advertising, personal selling, dealer discounts, etc., which to the businessman means money. To maximize profits, some attempt must be made to set the promotion expenses at their most economic figure.

Ideally, the amount spent on advertising should be that amount which, in the given state of the market, will result in those sales which are necessary to achieve the optimum scales of production, sales distribution and finance. In such a utopian situation a figure would be synthesized which would represent the reconciliation of all the optima, and this would then become the objective of the advertising. Unfortunately, even such a situation as this oversimplifies the intercorrelations which exist, because

6. It is conceivable that the brand name could become the generic name of the product or type of product with obvious long-term selling consequences, e.g. 'Hoover', 'Mini'. There is a debit side to such a development in that people will begin to divorce the name from the producer and extend it to all similar products to the advantage of competitors who entered the market later.

the optimum figure that advertising is to achieve is contained within the sales optimum which itself contains an estimate for advertising in that it assumes that a certain sales figure will result from a given outlay in advertising. Nevertheless, the idea of synthesizing a figure from the optima of all sides has the merit of being comprehensive. The danger of dichotomy between selling and making is removed, and this is of importance when deciding on the economies of any sales-promotion activity. Thus, assuming a given amount of production capacity which cannot easily be increased and which would require a major investment decision to do so, the company will wish to achieve the lowest cost of production; this may be the maximum output without shift working. The advertising optimum might show such economies of scale that the diseconomies of shift working would be more than offset by the economies of advertising – and so the production and sales figure is fixed beyond the conventional lowest unit production cost position of the company. Conversely the diseconomies associated with achieving extra sales to reach the production optimum may be so great that they more than offset the manufacturing economies – thus the reconciled optimum would be less than the production optimum. All this would assume that the distribution and financial optima were compatible with the synthesized figure; this might not be so, and further adjustment will be needed.[7]

The problem of attempting to determine the amount of money to use to achieve the desired end of advertising remains to be solved. This is probably the aspect of selling least susceptible to mechanical calculation, but some attempt must be made; where the exactness of a science is denied us, the scientific approach is a worthwhile second best, and is the approach we must take.

Past experience of the effectiveness of a given sum in known market circumstances will provide a basis for the calculation; the more accurately we can quantify the effectiveness and the

7. We need not remind the reader that the ability to make accurate estimates of advertising effectiveness to the tolerance implied here would be exceptionally difficult. Nevertheless, to the extent that the principles were followed and the difficulties realized, this could be considered a scientific approach.

multiplicity of factors affecting the past market, the better. A similar analysis must then be made of the current situation, the socio-economic factors, competition of all forms, and the relative position of the company in this competition. This approach may be lengthy and may cover every source of information from the reports of field sales-managers and their men to governmental and trade statistics. Using the basic figures of the known campaigns and their effectiveness in certain conditions, the current estimate can be made by comparison of the tasks to be done and the relative market conditions prevailing.

Advertising budgets may be fixed as a percentage of the estimated gross profit or revenue,[8] which enables the activity to be costed within the bounds of the expected revenue. Such a method has obvious attractions, but merely to state the matter in this way cannot carry the certain inference that it will be achieved. If the price has to be reduced to meet unexpected competition or customer reaction, the outlay on advertising will represent a bigger percentage of the gross margin or revenue, assuming total sales to be the same. Again, the method has an inherent weakness in that the assumed sales achievement is dependent on an outlay which is determined by this assumed achievement; the advertising budget is both a cause and consequence of the sales. Where a certain minimum must be spent in order to enter or remain in a market, then the basic core of the budget may be fixed, and any active determination of this as a percentage of revenue or gross profit is outside the control of the company. Lastly, great care must be taken to guard against the tendency to believe that to state matters in a certain form can convert qualified assumptions into positive inferences: mathematics cannot convert bad management into good.

To the extent that an advertising budget and an estimate of total revenue have been made, it represents a worthwhile means of controlling financial achievement – the real purpose of any budget – but it still leaves unanswered the basic problem of estimating

8. Sometimes this is given in terms of individual items sold, but this is an unrealistic distinction if a given total amount of advertising is really needed in a market, e.g. heavily branded markets, or when launching new products.

the effectiveness of a given sum in a future set of circumstances which may be very dynamic.

When an enterprise is launching a new product or brand, or is trying to carve out a larger share of the total market, then both the problem of determining the appropriation and the effectiveness of it will be increased. Such an action will normally affect the *status quo* in a market, and the reactions of those already in the market will be unknown in exact terms. Any measurement of the effectiveness of this type of campaign will require a long-term estimate of the impact made; in the short period, the outlay cannot normally be justified but, if a place in the market is obtained, then the longer-period consequences may make it worthwhile. It may cost half a million pounds to break into a soup market, the assumption being that the outlay is justified by the long-term growth potential of the market; over the medium or long period the enterprise should break even and then make profits. Clearly, such long-term estimates of the effectiveness of current advertising are difficult, although they must be made.

The illogical nature of treating this type of advertising outlay as a constituent part of a particular budgetary period is borne out by the long-term character of the assumed productivity of the expenditure. It is really an investment and has most of the features of an investment in research and specialized machinery; the results are not positively known and the aim or end-product is strictly limited. Logic suggests that such outlays be written off in the same way as investments in equipment rather than associated with any budgetary period. The output of these advertising outlays can extend into decades; the productivity of any sales-promotion expenditure in future years is clearly affected by the impact made by the initial launching of a product or brand name.

To some extent, all advertising budgets must be based on the activities of competitors even if the object of the exercise is merely maintaining the present market share-out among established brands; if some increase their advertising in a brand-conscious market, others may have to follow. The businessman making decisions on advertising outlays may be faced with problems more pressing and urgent than those of reconciling the optima mentioned earlier, but in essence he will be basing his action on the same principles. If, owing to increased competition, it becomes apparent that a sales target will not be achieved using the given budget, a decision must be taken on whether to increase the budget or cease all advertising. What are the relevant factors in this situation?

The previous diseconomies perhaps associated with a larger advertising budget are now more than offset by the potential diseconomies of not producing a viable quantity; this might render extra advertising potentially economic. The further diseconomies of not advertising would have to contain an assessment of the cost of regaining a share of a market lost to a competitor as against the current cost of staying in that market. The greater the proportion of the costs of production represented by fixed costs, the greater the potential diseconomies of not selling; the greater the brand susceptibility of the market, the greater the cost of attempting to regain a lost position. Thus if an advertising budget of £100,000 has been set aside to promote the sale of 50,000 washing machines (these figures representing the optimum as existing at the time of the estimate) and competitors begin a keen sales campaign, or introduce a better product, then the manufacturer may have to decide whether to spend more than £100,000 in order to achieve his sales target. In the circumstances described above, a decision to exceed the budget might be correct if overheads were high, the capacity specialized, and the market brand-minded; even, perhaps, in those instances where the sales target was still not achieved although the advertising budget had been exceeded. Such a decision would require a quantification of the financial consequence of *not* increasing the advertising budget.

To the extent that the effectiveness of advertising budgets is governed by activities of others – competitors all acting in a set of socio-economic conditions over which no individual company has any control – so the setting of these budgets will fall short of the exactness beloved by the mechanic. The scientific marketeer codifies past experience in detail, and uses this to assist in his current decision; he analyses and compares situations, fixes a budget, and then carefully controls the outcome of his decision, using his analytical powers to change the plan to meet new situations; the speed and correctness of the change being governed by scientific pre-planning aimed at meeting the changed conditions.

To subject budgets to changes prompted by factors outside the control of those responsible for the budget estimate does not in any way reduce the true purpose of budgets as control instruments. If, in an estimate of profitability, certain circumstances have been assumed to exist in a market and these are found to be invalid, the budget which was fixed to meet them will be wrong, and so consequently will the original estimate of profitability. The use of a budget in these dynamic conditions allows the changing condition to become known: the unexpected inadequacy of the budget; the need to extend it at the expense of the estimated final profit; the consequences of not increasing it; and the relationship which will now exist between the revenue from sales and the cost of obtaining them.

ADVERTISING COSTS AND PRICE TRENDS

In brand-conscious markets, there is the probability of intense sales-promotion methods and their consequential costs. To enter and stay in such markets will require that the sales budget is in line with the competitive demands of the market.

Such a situation can result in advertising becoming a fixed cost in the cost structure of the firm; as stated earlier it resembles 'key' money to get in and a 'rent' to stay there. Fixed costs are supportable by an enterprise if prices or markets are tending to rise; they are then more easily accommodated in the gross revenue of the undertaking. When advertising becomes partly or wholly a fixed cost, rising prices might result in an increase in this cost; the buoyancy of the end market and its willingness to accept price increases could encourage this tendency. The real problem of such a fixed cost in the sales structure of a firm will occur when prices are reduced or the total market or market share declines; then the same costs must be met out of reduced revenue. It is conceivable that where the production costs contain a large proportion of fixed costs and the sales structure has within it similar fixed costs, then if the price of the product were cut, the enterprise might be unable to make a profit even if working and selling at full capacity.

The Financial Implication of Advertising as Compared with Other Means of Sales Promotion

Advertising budgets tend to be 'lumpy' in the cost structure of sales promotion; the amount needed to achieve optimum returns is indivisible; there is no linear relationship between input in advertising outlay and output in awareness or sales. On the other hand, alternative sales methods may have a linear relationship between cost and returns and may not involve the large unit outlays needed for advertising: payment to salesmen, margins to dealers, and extra attention to packages, all permit the outlay on sales promotion to be, more or less, in step with the sales achieved.[9] These costs largely are self-liquidating.[10]

Where markets are dominated by advertising, e.g. detergents, paints, patent medicines, foodstuffs, then the alternative methods of sales promotion may become attractive to some firms, not only because of inability on their part to raise funds needed for advertising, but because of the reduced risk involved. To some extent the other methods are self-financing.

Advertising and Governmental Economic Policies

Advertising is essentially an activity which thrives on buoyancy and optimism. If the general ethos of a community is confident, then the conditions are ideal for exploitation by means of persuaders. The converse could also be true.

If, after such a period of confidence and optimism, there followed one of doubt and retrenchment, the consequences to advertising might be considerable. The effects of such a change on the individual manufacturer might require a complete reappraisal of sales methods.

If we assume a curb on prices similar to that attempted under the prices and incomes policy of the 1964–70 Labour Government, then certain conclusions might be drawn about future sales-

9. A price reduction will have the same effect exactly in that the cost, the monetary sacrifice per unit sold, is exactly proportional to the number sold.

10. See the chapter on Budgeting for treatment of fixed and variable costs in sales budgets and the cost implications of 'push' and 'pull' sales policies.

promotion methods. Firstly, the assumption that a continued increase in prices will be able to sustain increased sales promotion is unrealistic. Secondly, the attitude towards incurring heavy overheads in sales-promotion costs will change; the break-even point following a large promotion campaign may be moved further into the future if prices are held back when costs are pressing them. Thirdly, and as a result of the first two conclusions, companies may turn increasingly to less 'lumpy' forms of sales promotion which can be more closely geared to the sales revenue arising at the time, present or future. Fourthly, the need to accommodate the costs of production, distribution and selling into a more rigid price, or revenue, could result in a greater attention being paid to cost-effectiveness; distribution appears to be the one with the greatest potential saving, but the possible wastes of selling could well receive more attention; packaging and distribution economies could become more important; wholesale and retail distribution could be rationalized; and all sales promotion could be more scientifically appraised on costs and contribution to profits. Fifthly, product policy would gain in importance relative to other methods of promoting the sale of the product.

BRAND POLICY

Branding removes anonymity. By means of a name, symbol, device or combination of these, the manufacturer or distributor is identified. Identification is at the core of all brand policy.

Clearly, the very act of selling by a person who is known to the buyer involves branding. The seller is identifiable; any satisfaction or dissatisfaction arising from the transaction will be to the advantage or disadvantage of the seller; he will accumulate goodwill or ill-will; anonymity has been surrendered. The more the seller identifies himself by name, dress, habit or speech, the greater the implication in branding.

It is not necessary to have a brand name, trade mark, distinctive package, or a family design theme through a product range to be involved in branding. Such devices merely produce a deeper involvement in branding and all that that implics. A 'well kent' business name, a distinctive letterhead, an identifiable shop-front, the use of a special type of vehicle in a particular livery: any, or all, of these are brand policy; if they exist in multiples, on letters, shops and vehicles, the marketing consequences of such branding could be considerable.

The extensive use of brand names, trade marks and other distinctive features as a positive sales device is intended to exploit the ability of the customer to identify the product and the manufacturer or distributor. It deliberately sets in motion a sequence of events which, it is hoped, will react to the future benefit of the owner of the brand name. This sequence is identification, expectation of a standard of satisfaction, fulfilment, reidentification and further patronage. Unfortunately the sequence, once triggered off, cannot be stopped to suit the brand-owner. If the expected satisfaction is not fulfilled, identification of the source of this will still proceed, perhaps with more persistence, to the disadvantage of the brand-owner.

Should a company use the same name for a range of products, or by some other means make known the common producer, the effects of branding are increased. Goodwill and ill-will will now be transmitted through the range from goods to goods; from one range to another; from shop to shop within a multiple; hotel to hotel within a group; garage to garage within a chain.

Identification of goods through a name also helps communication between customers, whether industrialists, dealers or the general public. The greater the success of a brand name in identifying the product or range, the greater the ease of transmitting information, good or bad, about the products which bear that name. In the more knowledgeable industrial markets, this is not of great consequence because the supplier is always known,[11] but in the consumer market the use of brand names has revolutionized the knowledge of the customer. It is not necessary for the housewife to know the manufacturer of a branded detergent

11. Emphasis on brand names might, however, have an effect on satisfaction even in this field, dissatisfaction being enhanced by the prominence of the name and the claims associated with it.

by name, merely to know that his products are readily identifiable by a name which she knows: she does not need to know that the Pure Soap Company makes 'Sudso Soap', only that it is made by the manufacturer of 'Sudso'.

Branding allows patronage to exist outside the products themselves; a loyalty is built up to a name. This enables new products to be launched 'piggy-back' on those already known to the customer. Clearly, this is financially advantageous but, as we shall see later, there are risks involved.

Why Branding?

Branding represents a happy marriage of the needs of manufacturer and customer in affluent societies. To the manufacturer it is a form of insurance; to the customer it is a means of satisfying idiosyncrasies.

The insurance function of marketing is concerned with reducing the risk of idle capacity; the total assets of the enterprise must be kept profitably employed. Although branding may have more ambitious ends, this is the beginning of the matter.

The need for the creation of a hard core of loyal customers is a consequence of the heavy fixed costs of modern industry. The fixed element in the cost structure requires its counterpart in the market if long-term profitability is to be achieved. Such fixed loyalty requires something with which it can be certainly identified; the brand name provides the banner for the loyalists. Even though the products may be intrinsically similar to competing ones, the brand name creates the necessary distinction; it is a 'homing device'. The more the products in a market have reached a plateau of similarity, the greater the need for branding to achieve distinction: this applies equally to both industrial and consumer goods.

This loyalty is a creation of the product which meets the expectations of the customer, but it is prompted and its accumulation accelerated by other sales-promotion activities. Advertising introduces a brand; if it also confirms the experience of the customer about the product it is doubly effective. But although branding is assisted by advertising, most of modern advertising depends on branding. In most commercial advertising (advertising for whole industries[12] is a big exception), it is essential that the message is attached to an identifiable article. Often the main means of such identification is the brand name itself. Even products with special characteristics need a name to which these can be attached. Brand names are part of the imagery of the product in the mind of the customer; they are part of the psychological extension.

In affluent societies the standard of living enjoyed is not measured solely by the total value of goods consumed, but by the range of the goods and services available for purchase.[13] Branding extends the range of goods within groups and enables the idiosyncratic drives of affluence to be satisfied. People may firmly consider drinks as a sign of wellbeing; when all in their 'term of reference' group enjoy drinks, resort must be made to a type or brand of drinks to satisfy idiosyncrasies and social instincts. Today, a brand name properly chosen and promoted might become a desirable social acquisition in itself; it must be attached to goods, but it would be difficult, if not impossible, to dissociate the product from the brand name in the valuation given to the product by the customer.

The range of goods of advanced societies contains more and more complex items, many of them beyond the understanding of the buyer and in some cases even the distributor. When such an article is sold, then the customer is thrown on to other terms of reference when making a buying decision. Among these terms of reference, price and brand name will figure most prominently; faith in the brand name is part of the desired end of any brand policy.

Finally, the attraction of branding can be clearly seen when, in heavily entrenched markets, manufacturers take over firms with established brand names, even though, in many cases, they may

12. By definition this attracts attention to a product or service, not a brand, e.g. bread, fish, wool, wood, cinemas.

13. It has been suggested that the wide range of goods available in a supermarket or large self-service store creates a feeling of affluence and wellbeing which stimulates buying. A similar range or even a larger one may be stocked in a counter-service store, but it is not exhibited and therefore does not have the same effect.

be making an almost identical product and do not need the extra production capacity. Although there are other constituents of goodwill in these cases, a lot of it consists of the loyalty attaching to the brand name concerned.

The Economics of Branding

When a company acquires or promotes a brand name, it is hoped to secure any goodwill which the product gives to that name. It will help to maximize returns to the producer. A given input into research, development, design, production and quality control will have its output maximized in that the better end-product or service will be identifiable, for future patronage. The input into these factors will thus have an increased return in the continued patronage. If a company had a large outlay on inspection of an identified product, none of the output of this outlay would be lost in that the goodwill it generated could find an obvious direction. Similarly, with a product which, because of a combination of these factors plus price, gives good value for money, any sacrifice made per article, through price, should result in increased goodwill through the brand name. Brand policy when linked with good sales policy will thus increase productivity per unit of input.

Branding, by creating a distinctive image of a product by connotation, can help to remove the goods from the convenience or shopping categories. This can result in a less elastic demand for the brand which would show itself when its price was higher than intrinsically similar products. Likewise, if the prices of these similar competing products were reduced, this would not necessarily cause the abandonment of the branded product.

The increased inelasticity due to customer loyalty could help to finance the advertising, packaging, and dealer incentives[14] which help to create the inflated value in the mind of the customer. The idea that a brand is different could help to sustain the cost of maintaining this image.

The reaction of the customer to any outlay on brand promotion

14. Where the brand image of a product is sustained by selecting special types of retailer, with associated dealer margins.

must be the starting point in any inquiry into the potential returns from any outlays made. If the customer is knowledgeable and purchases unemotionally, as in the industrial market, then the attachment of a brand name to a product would not be expected to do anything other than identify the manufacturer and increase customer awareness; any supposition that an inflated value might be put on the product would be misplaced. The opposite situation would obtain in many consumer-goods markets, where buyers are less knowledgeable and more irrational in their behaviour. The creative potential of a brand name, as against its use for identification purposes, would probably depend on the ability of the customer to distinguish between the product itself and the image of the product. Obviously much would also depend on the nature of the product; if it had emotive potential, e.g. cosmetics, patent medicines, clothes, and complete appraisal of the true value was difficult, then such a product would be likely to give better returns to creative brand promotion aimed at inflating values. It is not an accident that these are also the qualities required of a product if successful advertising is desired; brand policy and advertising go together.

In heavily branded markets with well-entrenched names, the cost of entry might be so great as to render entry by advertising too costly relative to the potential profit. The need for a distinctive brand image, and so the cost of achieving it, is a function of the rate of potential substitution among products, i.e. their intrinsic similarity, and strength of branding existing in any market. Where a product is basically dissimilar, then the need for and cost of promoting a brand image are reduced. Similarly, where branding is not rampant, there is less need to indulge in expensive brand projection (except to safeguard the future). Brand-imagery creation is largely a reciprocating activity caused by competition among goods and firms all able, or claiming, to provide similar goods or services to the potential customer.

In consumer markets the cost of successful brand promotion might make it an unrealistic sales activity for any but the largest firm. The national branded goods have built-in advantages similar to the multiple store or hotel, or garage; they retain patronage regardless of the location of the customer who does not move out of the market. National promotions, however, may require heavy outlays which can only be supported if the production capacity is potentially large enough to support the supply of goods needed to justify this outlay. In heavily branded markets such an additional supply may so over-supply the market that the new condition would render the entry outlay unprofitable.

Goods which are sold in large numbers have an intrinsic advantage in branding, in that they promote the brand by their own existence and circulation. The assumption that such goods are the most economic for branding purposes because the cost of brand promotion is borne by more goods does, however, require qualification. Clearly, if the goods are of very low unit value, their ability to support any fixed selling cost is reduced. Matches could not support the cost as easily as petrol, or motor-cars, despite the number of units sold.

Nevertheless, if the cost can be borne by more goods, then the promotion cost per unit sold is less, other things being equal. For this reason, family brand names have distinct economic advantages over those supported by only one type of product.

The size of the market also appears to be a determinant of the viability of a brand-promotion programme. Where a market is extensive in size and units sold, there is a greater possibility of branding on a large scale, all the brand promotions being made viable by the nature of the market. The more national the market, the greater this tendency. To ascribe this to the ability of such markets to support brand-promotion costs would, however, again appear to be invalid; these costs could be met equally well out of 100 sales of £10,000 each as four million at 25p each. What is important is the profit potential in a market out of which the cost of promoting a brand in the market can be met and a profit achieved.

Branding and Other Aspects of the Business

BRANDING AND QUALITY CONTROL

Branding is concerned with the identification of a product, and the accumulation of any goodwill associated with the product to the benefit of the brand-owners; this is, however, dependent on satisfaction with the product or service. The degree of satisfaction will depend on two things, expectation and experience. Expectation is in the mind of the customer and is created by the brand name itself and its connotation, the advertising message, the price, and any other promotion activity such as dealer recommendation. It can also arise from experience of another product using the same family name. If the experience of the customer is at variance with the expectations, disappointment results. The disappointment is a function of expectation and experience; the former is dependent on sales promotion, the latter on the realism of this promotion and of quality control.

Already we have discussed quality policy and shown that any quality standard which is set must be realistic and capable of achievement by the company. Any claim made for a branded product will give the brand an expectation connotation in the mind of the customer. Assuming that the quality policy is realistic, then the execution of that policy, and, in particular, quality control, is the main determinant, along with sales promotion, of customer satisfaction with the branded goods. The correct sequence of priorities should be the establishment of an efficient quality-control system and the introduction of branded goods for which claims are made through sales promotion

Wherever close substitutes are at hand to the customer – the usual situation in heavily branded markets – the greatest care must be taken to give complete satisfaction. Quality control here involves the control of the article up to the point of use by the final customer. This involves total control of distribution and retailers and clear indications as to the means of storing and use; where the article is heavily branded and advertised at great expense, it is unrealistic to economize unduly on the distribution of the product if it is perishable or fragile.

Service industries present special problems because of the difficulty of implementing a quality policy. Retail stores may lay down standards regarding the merchandise which is to be associated with a shop or group of shops, but their reputation for service is very dependent on the recruitment, training and management of their employees. The same would apply to the hotel and catering trade, to transport, and to vehicle servicing.

There is less possibility in a service industry of detecting and rejecting the work of an operator before it reaches the customer, because of the face-to-face situation involved and the perishability of the operation. At the same time branding assists in these cases by accumulating faith in an unproven service capability if it has been sampled previously and found satisfactory: its potential here is enormous.

Multiple hotels and restaurants and nation-wide retail stores and garages can achieve large economies in the sales promotion of their brand image because the goodwill of the satisfied customer can be exploited regardless of his new geographical location. But standards of service must be maintained throughout the chain if there is to be an advantage; a disappointed patron carries this disappointment with him wherever he goes and the brand name of the multiple becomes a deterrent rather than an attraction.

Occasionally, a brand name is associated, through advertising, with a claim which can only be implemented outside the direct control of the brand-owner. This occurs when any after-sales service is an integral part of a sale and is undertaken by distributors. In such cases every effort must be made to control the standard of service given, by stringent inspection before any concession is given and by regular appraisal of the service point afterwards. Bad servicing affects the branded goods which are badly serviced, and not merely the reputation of the service point.

A customer who has been attracted to a branded product by sales promotion in a situation where close substitutes are available may not return to a neutral situation if dissatisfaction is experienced. The task of winning back such a customer is dependent on the extent of dissatisfaction and the convenience or availability of substitutes. Where the product cannot be accurately appraised at the point of sale, the suspicion created by the last purchase cannot be allayed even on inspection; this would apply to packaged goods as well as to complex consumer-durables, tyres, components and even some types of industrial equipment: in service-dominated industries, the implications are only too clear.

Branding and Sales Promotion

ADVERTISING

Advertising requires an identifiable product and, as we have seen, where goods are similar, brand names become the main means of identification. When goods possess special characteristics the need to identify them is just as great, if the customer is to be able to seek, recognize and purchase the projected speciality product. The legend of an advertisement must be related beyond all doubt to a specific product and this is made easier if the product is given a distinctive name. Branded goods are promoted to, and bought by, the final customer. Pre-selling articles in this way has been given further impetus by the development of self-service stores. Here the branded goods must sell themselves, they receive no verbal assistance; they attract attention and form a link via the brand name with pre-selling advertising or the customer's past experience of similarly branded products.

Measurement of the efficiency of sales-promotion methods is also made possible by branding. Investigations into advertising methods, reaction to products, and estimates of sales depend on the ability of the customer to identify the product being investigated. Attitude of customers in this case must be towards something tangible; a brand-named product.

THE BRAND NAME

The name itself should be legally cleared before any funds are used to promote it. Care, or legal advice, should be taken to confirm that the name in no way trespasses on the goodwill of another. The productivity of any advertising is so uncertain that waste must always be prevented; to promote a brand name which is later denied the firm is a most blatant form of waste.

The name chosen should be one which will make the maximum contribution to selling efficiency. It should project that image of the product which motivation research has shown to be the most effective in moving customers to buy it. This involves not only the connotation of the name chosen, but also its retention in the mind of the customers per unit of outlay on promotion.

Petrol can be called 'Jet' but not 'Plod'. The brand achieves

271

what the chemist cannot; modern alchemy is at work. Even though 'Plod' would be retentive (it probably would be because of its non-conformity), it could not be used because it has the wrong connotation for the sale of the petrol: it creates awareness but does not favourably affect attitudes and behaviour. The motivation 'mix' of the consumer should be reflected in the brand name in order to achieve the maximum output per unit of input into advertising, packaging and personal selling; all will become more productive because of a name.

Social motivation may show itself in names with class associations, such as 'Gleneagles', 'Braemar', 'Windsor Velvet'. Economy needs may produce 'Thrift'. Subconscious drives may give us 'Leisure', 'In', 'Family'. Suffixes, such as 'extra' or 'deluxe', are ideal appellants to the desire to be better than the crowd. The dropping of the well-established trade name 'Standard' by a car manufacturer shows the degree of non-economic judgement which is involved in this socially conscious field with close substitutes.

Trends are also apparent in brand names, and today in the United Kingdom it is the turn of the pseudo-scientific or technical-sounding name such as Morris 1100, — 1800, Renault 4L, Gibbs S.R., Raleigh R.S.W. 16 (Raleigh Small Wheel 16 in.). Continental holiday experiences with their associations give us Cortina, Viva, Capri, etc. Sometimes a brand name may achieve a profitable connotation during its lifetime and may be resurrected and serve a different model at a later date.

Where one family brand name is possible for all goods produced by a firm, the economies are considerable. The very incidence of the same name appearing on a range of goods will have a greater impact. There will be cross-fertilization of promotion within the range; advertising one product will highlight the brand name and indirectly promote the sale of all the other goods of that name; familiarity is important and this is increased by family branding; goodwill is also more easily transferable from one product to another where one family name is used. Finally, it must be remembered that in markets where brand names are well established, the establishment of a new name, and even the retention of the position of an old one, are very expensive. Clearly, such finance as is available for this purpose should be as concentrated in its application as possible in order to make the greatest impact. Economics would clearly suggest that the use of one name should always be the golden rule; unfortunately there are many marketing arguments against this simple maxim.

When a family name has been in existence for a period of time and has built up an image and a fund of goodwill, there is some risk inherent in allowing a new product to assume that name, no matter how well the product has been tested in the field. Such reasoning may lead a firm to use a new name for such a product. But the very nature of a product may preclude the use of the name already used by the business; there may be differences of character, use, market, price and quality between the new product and those already sold.

Where products are dissimilar in nature, then, other things being equal, it would be wrong to use the same brand name to cover all types. If a brand name has been selected to give the correct rational or emotional connotation for one type of goods, it may project the wrong image for another; the use of the same brand name for laxatives and after-shave lotion by a manufacturing chemist might serve as an example of wrong brand names. Where a family brand name has become associated with a quality common to all products regardless of their nature, such a name is consistent with good marketing provided that the firm does this as a deliberate act of policy, c.g. the quality/value connotation of St Michael, the wholly British solid connotation of B.L.M.

SEGMENTATION

Segmentation of a market enables us to produce a basic product with variations to suit identifiable sections of the market; the variations may be geared to quality, basic materials used, performance, price, customer emotions, distribution patterns, etc., and such segmentation usually requires the use of a different brand name for each segment.

Segmentation on a quality basis should be based on different and distinct brand names wherever there is a social attachment to any of the names; it would be folly to sell a high-price article through good-class stores with an obvious class-conscious market bearing the same brand name as another similar line which appealed to the price-conscious customer. Quite apart from the reduced satisfaction which would be experienced by the class-conscious buyer, there is an obvious danger of cannibalism of one article by another. The more accurately a brand name is identified with the desire of a particular segment, the less likely it is to appeal to other segments.

Sometimes the difference in inherent quality may be almost non-existent. This type of situation could occur where a manufacturer supplies large retailers with goods under their own brand name and at the same time markets similar products under his own brand name. This policy can be supported under the following conditions:

1. Where there is a need for a large market to achieve the economies of scale with specialized equipment.
2. Where fixed costs form a high proportion of total production costs.
3. Where the particular type of retail outlet is increasingly being shopped for by your customer when buying your type of product.
4. Where the retailer wishes to tap a price-conscious market which would necessitate cutting the price of the national brand product, thus perhaps alienating other retailers who did not wish to sell on price.
5. Where the market for the two products, the national brand and the dealer brand, is reasonably distinct, either owing to shopping habits, e.g. 'class' stores and multiples, or to ignorance of the true inherent qualities of the goods, or both.

Dealer Brands

Clearly a manufacturer producing for dealer brands is engaging in market segmentation based on shopping habits and/or price-consciousness. Dealer brands do, however, draw to the retailer any goodwill the final customer may associate with the products bearing the brand name, and, to this extent, the bargaining position of the manufacturer may be reduced.[15] This is particularly so where the product is supplied to the specification of the retailer and can be obtained with ease from other manufacturers. Nevertheless, the manufacturer might well be attracted to dealer brands for the following reasons:

1. Where the cost of entering a market with well-established brand names is greatly reduced if this can be achieved via the existing goodwill of a retail chain. Sometimes this may be done on a joint-label basis, such as 'Made exclusively for Cannons by Jacques of Mythwick', rather than a simple sale of non-branded goods to which dealers attach their own brands.

2. Where the trend of shopping habits is too strong to hold back. Thus, in the United Kingdom children's knitwear and ladies' foundation garments are increasingly purchased from multiples, toothpaste from variety stores, and cakes and biscuits from multiple grocers. If the production capacity is specialized, following the trend may be the only alternative to idle costly capacity.

3. The multiple order, by assuring that a given proportion of fixed costs has been met, enables a more positive price and profit situation to be known on the remaining capacity and the 'own' brand goods it produces.

4. Where the firm wishes to abdicate the costs, risks and problems of marketing in heavily branded markets and concentrate on production. The multiple will assume the responsibility for design, quality, quantity, and dates of delivery. The manufacturer then shows his ability to meet these specifications, together with price, more ably than his competitors. Company patronage motives take over from product patronage as a reason for choosing a supplier.

However, the manufacturer, before entering the dealer-brand

15. Goodwill still remains, but it is now on the part of the retailer for the manufacturer; this is commercially just as useful in dealer-brand markets. This goodwill is based on the satisfaction of the final customer, but also on the standard of delivery, quality consistency, overall co-operation, and price of the manufacturer.

market, would have to satisfy himself as to the permanence or otherwise of this market. The large multiple retail stores possess certain innate advantages in the development of dealer brands. They are strong enough to obtain the necessary consistent-quality supplies of goods from the manufacturers at the proper price, without which dealer-brand promotion is impossible; their very size and/or multiplicity is, in itself, a promotion device which will make the name common tender without recourse to expensive advertising.[16] Finally they have the financial and promotional ability required, the latter being available because their scale of operations makes it worthwhile.

Economic and trading factors can also play a vital part in the development of dealer brands. The pressure of increased operating costs may force the enlightened retailer to seek profitability from the extra turnover which would be created by lower prices. Perhaps the only way to execute such a policy is for the dealer to introduce his own brand over which he has complete price control. Should the price of national brands not be controlled, either because manufacturers do not support such policies or by default in the execution of them, then the price cutting which may result could reduce margins to a level inadequate to meet increased operating costs. The attraction of the dealer-branded goods is that the buying-in price is lower, thus enabling the retailer to reduce his price to the final customer while still maintaining an adequate profit margin per unit sold to meet the higher operating costs which he is facing.

Dealer-controlled prices should be able to respond more quickly to economic conditions, both national and local, not only because of the extra margin in which a price manoeuvre can take place, but also because the decision-taking area is smaller than that involved when a manufacturer takes decisions on national brands with extensive promotion, including some indication of price. The extra profit margin on dealer-branded goods, which is so important to the whole price strategy, is due both to the lower buying-in price and to the absence of sales-promotion expendi-

16. At the point of sale, dealer brands may be better known than is apparent elsewhere, and, where shopping for shops has developed, this type of familiarity with brand is vital.

ture as compared with that of the manufacturer with a national brand.

To be successful, all retailing policies must be completely in harmony with the desires or latent wishes of the customers. If dealer brands are to receive a stimulus because their prices are below those of national brands, the customers must be responsive to price motivation;[17] price-consciousness, as against brand susceptibility, is a vital aspect in the promotion of dealer brands. In those markets where the national brands of manufacturers are well established, price differentials will have to be sufficient to offset brand loyalty for these brands. The less price-conscious the customers, the greater the price differential needed to attract them to dealer brands.

It is not necessary for dealers to project an image of cut-price policies; sometimes a multiple will promote a brand with a good value connotation, rather than one of cheapness.[18] Scientifically based retail policies are aimed at exploiting a segment of the market which is, like all segments, distinguished by its motivation 'mix'; people with a particular socio-economic 'mix' shop for the shops which cater for it.

From the manufacturer's viewpoint it is necessary to analyse the infrastructure of retailing in order to discover the likely impact of dealer brands, so that a realistic policy towards them can be introduced. Where there is a distinct threat of the dealer brand making inroads into the sales of the manufacturer's own brand, these more basic economic factors will determine the issue. If there is a positive influence towards the development and acceptance of dealer brands, inroads could well take place; the alternative to supplying dealer brands could be a reduction in sales.

17. In some cases, this could show itself in customers taking relatively unknown but cheaper brands where dealer brands are not sold. These unknown brands could offer a similar profit margin to the retailer, being bought in at a lower price.

18. It could well be that a multiple following a consistent quality policy could begin to build up a loyalty from a discriminating segment which wished to pay a more than average price for well above average quality.

Special Problems of Brands and Stockholding

Assuming a given demand for a product, there is no guarantee that an additional brand name will increase the overall demand; it may merely eat into the demand for other similar products. A dealer faced with the need to satisfy the wide range of requirements of his customers may thus have an increased pressure on his storage space and on his working capital without any automatic commensurate increase in sales. Where a society regards the range of possible purchases as a measure of its affluence, and where customer sovereignty has been pandered to by creating an infinite number of variations to one product, the distributors are in a particularly vulnerable position.

Manufacturers who produce a number of different brand names for one type of product are increasing the problem of stockholding at distribution point. Frequently, rationalization of production and distribution may result from take-overs within an industry, but the brand names are perpetuated even though the articles are identical in every other way; this type of rationalization, although it results in a reduction in the variety of goods made and so creates production economies, does not result in a reduction in the variety of goods sold: the dealers' stock problems remain the same.

There is much that can be said to support the use of several brand names by one manufacturer in that, where group loyalty is great and the group names are known to the customer, the consumer can remain loyal and also change, thus satisfying two types of consumer motivation. Nevertheless, such branding does increase the problems of distribution, and where this activity is becoming more costly because of inflated real estate values, this extra cost and the possible alienation of dealers may more than offset the advantages gained by brand proliferation.

Brand proliferation which is not accompanied by increased turnover may compel the distributor to hold a lower stock of each brand handled in order to reconcile customer expectations of choice, space restrictions, and working-capital economy.[19] Such a

19. Some strong multiples may solve this problem with their dealer-brand policy in that they will limit the brands held to, say, three, one of

valid policy by the retailer may put an extra burden on the organization responsible for stockholding at pre-retailer point whether wholesaler or manufacturer. If wholesalers are used, some incentive may be needed to encourage such stockholding which, if the total market is not expanding proportionately, will mean lower trading profits to the manufacturer per article sold.[20]

PACKAGING

'The pack protects what it sells, and sells what it protects.' The double function suggested in this quotation is an improvement on the original basic idea of a pack being merely a container to protect goods in transit. Nevertheless, this definition is still deficient in that it does not include the contribution that the pack can make to the economic efficiency of distribution as against the purely physical aspect of the delivery of the goods to the customer. The relative importance of these three functions, protection, selling and distribution, will depend upon the nature of the article which is packed, the method of selling, the state of the market, and the general economic circumstances surrounding the sale and distribution of the product.

The Economics of Packaging: the Grand Background

In so far as the pack is an aid to efficient distribution, it must help to make the maximum use of the factors of distribution. The more costly these factors are, the greater the economies which can be achieved by an efficient pack making greater use of a given amount of resources: a well designed pack will make greater use of transport, thus making the transport more productive; similarly it could replace expensive labour, or make any labour which is used more effective. The value of a pack depends not

which is a dealer brand, one the market leader, and the other the brand of the suppliers of the dealer brand: it could be part of the deal.

20. This might well be achieved in that the distributor margins remain the same, even though the increased selling and stockholding performed by the manufacturer would provide a valid reason for reducing them.

only on itself but also on the factors of distribution which it displaces or with which it is associated.

National economies are subject to trends in the relative costs of the factors of production and distribution: labour and land may be cheap, and capital relatively dear; or labour and land dear, and capital relatively cheap. Clearly, in so far as packaging tends to replace labour by capital and makes a better use of a given amount of land, the economies of packaging are intimately bound up with the trends in the relative costs of land, labour, and capital.

In a mass-consumption society, the cost of land and labour tends to be high relative to capital, and this would suggest that in so far as packaging helps to utilize more machinery – in the form of pallets, packaging machines, fork-lift trucks – replaces labour in factories, self-service stores and warehouses, and makes the maximum use of land, e.g. by better use of warehouse and shop space, then packaging is making a useful contribution to the economics of distribution. This is being achieved by substituting the cheaper capital for the dearer labour and making land use more efficient. Transport is a combination of the factors of distribution but it requires a special mention.

At a point in time, an economy will have a given supply of transport services in the form of docks, railways, roads, rivers, the vehicles using them, and the labour and management operating them. This supply of transport services cannot be increased in a short period of time, and therefore, if it is inadequate to meet the needs of the moment, transport is relatively scarce and consequently expensive.

The value of packaging in developed societies is great because it makes better use of, or replaces, the scarce and expensive factors – labour, land and transport. The value of a good pack will be greater, the more costly the factors it replaces and the more it replaces these factors.

Specific Economies of Packaging

THE INCREASE IN THE SIZE OF THE MARKET

The better the pack, the greater the contribution it will make to keeping down the cost of distribution and the delivered-to-customer price of the product, and so, other things being equal, increasing the size of the market. This is an economy super-imposed on the obvious one that a well-protected product is more likely to reach distant customers, which will, in itself, increase the geographical extent of the market and normally the size of that market. Wherever the production optimum is high, this will be a big influence on centralized plant location to achieve the scale needed to attain the optimum. However, the viability of centralized production could depend on the contribution made by the pack towards achieving the necessary market without dis-economies in distribution offsetting the economies of production.

THE SPREADING OF THE FIXED COSTS OF PRODUCTION

This is due partly to the increase in the size of the market pre-viously mentioned, but also to the greater ease with which packs can be changed as compared with changes in the design of the product. If a machine has a technological life of five years, it may be easier to maintain demand for its output over five years by means of package changes rather than changes in the product. This is clearly the case where design advances are 'difficult', if not impossible, as with packed foods.

THE INSURANCE OR SECURITY FUNCTION OF PACKS

Packaging complements advertising and branding in helping to create a body of loyal customers for the product; it assists in the promotion of a brand image and a degree of differentiation without which this loyalty could not exist, e.g. cigarettes.

Packaging Costs as a Factor in the Total Cost of Production and Distribution

PACKAGING AS A COMPONENT

The importance of the relationship of the cost of packaging to the total cost of production is the same as that of any component part. If the cost of the packaging, including materials, equipment and labour, is only a small part of the total cost, and the elasticity of demand for the product is not high, then variations upwards in the cost of packaging will not be particularly injurious to sales. The converse is also true. In those industries where close substitutes are readily available to the customer, and brand loyalty is fickle, the elasticity of demand for one particular brand may be considerable although that for a product as a whole is limited; in such cases, greater care must be taken in assessing the possible consequences of variations in the cost of the pack.

THE TRUE COST OF A PACK

The contribution which a pack might make to distribution efficiency should be set against any apparent extravagance involved in the simpler concept of packaging cost as a percentage of the total cost of production; the economics of transport and warehousing utilization may more than offset diseconomies elsewhere. A cheap pack which is economically attractive on initial inspection may have diseconomies directly attributable to it, such as bad utilization of vehicles and pallets, and increased breakage leading to loss of customer goodwill. The greater the amount of money used in promoting brand identity, the greater the potential diseconomies in a package which might create ill-will.

The more correct view of packaging cost would cover its effects on the delivered-to-customer price of the product and the elasticity of demand for that product. Even this better view, however, is not adequate because it omits any reference to the selling function of the pack; high initial costs of packaging may be more than offset by the contribution the pack makes towards the more efficient selling of the product. Selling is a sequence which is finalized at the point of sale; at this point the pack should not break down the previous build-up in the mind of the customer. A cheaper pack might have serious effects in a packed-food market made up mainly of self-service outlets and with well promoted close-substitute competing products; the diseconomies would equal the outlay on advertising and selling which was wasted because of the 'unselling' activity of the pack at point of sale.

THE PROBLEM OF MATERIAL COSTS

Again, the cost must not be considered in isolation; material is used with equipment and labour. The economies of material must be set off against any potential diseconomies in packaging-equipment cost. Similarly, the use of certain types of pack material might preclude the use of the most efficient types of mechanized handling.

A factor which must always concern the package designer is the extent to which the material used is a raw material for industries outside packaging. Where pack-material costs form a high percentage of total production costs and the demand for this material is mainly created outside its packaging use, any change in this outside demand could have serious repercussions on the cost of packaging. If tinplate or plastics are used for packaging by a firm in a highly competitive market, with other firms using other types of material, e.g. glass, then any relative movements of these raw-material prices could be very important in changing the competitive positions of the packaged products.

PACKAGING AND INDIRECT TAXATION

Any *ad valorem* tax on goods levied on a value affected by the cost of distribution will in turn be affected by that cost. When goods are subjected to purchase tax at wholesale level, then the price at this level will contain elements derived from transportation and warehousing: if these represent 10 per cent of the wholesale price and the *ad valorem* tax is 25 per cent, the cost of transport and distribution becomes 10 per cent plus $2\frac{1}{2}$ per cent, i.e. 10 per cent plus 10 per cent $\times$ 25/100. Clearly any defect in packaging design which results in increased distribution costs is enhanced by the tax; and conversely, good packaging will reduce the indirect tax.

Where distribution costs account for 25 per cent of the retail price, any sales tax could be materially affected by saving or dissaving resulting from good or bad packaging; with products which have a high elasticity of demand, this is obviously even more important.

In the export market, where the cost of the transport element is likely to be much greater, the need to consider the effect of packaging on import duties etc. is of paramount importance.

DECISION-TAKING IN PACKAGING COSTS

At the outset some attempt must be made to quantify the importance of the pack in sales promotion and the possible diseconomies of poor packing. The contribution made by a pack is normally complementary to other forms of sales promotion, and this would involve consideration of the potential effect of good and bad packaging on the productivity of these other forms of sales promotion; this might show itself in a bad correlation between awareness of a product and the sales of that product if the commercial consequences of advertising effectiveness have been reduced by bad packs. At the same time, the importance of the pack relative to other forms of sales promotion would have to be considered to determine the appropriate outlay of funds on packaging relative to advertising, dealer margins, personal selling, and perhaps even the design of the packaged products. The situation is dynamic. Self-service stores increase the need both for advertising and for packaging; poor-quality labour at retail point enhances the need for packaging to be instructive, etc.

The potential waste of other sales-promotion activities is great if packaging is inadequate; this is the true measure of possible diseconomies. In markets with close substitutes, the demand for a particular brand might be highly elastic. In such circumstances the total economy of the pack must be carefully studied so that the selling price can be kept to a minimum. Unfortunately, it is in such circumstances that the pack is used to create distinction between products.

Certain decisions must be taken on the amount of money which it is best to spend on packaging relative to the risk of loss (from any cause). It could be presented as in Figure 1. Curve LL represents the percentage of goods lost at different packaging cost levels, assuming that the more spent on packaging, the lower the percentage losses.

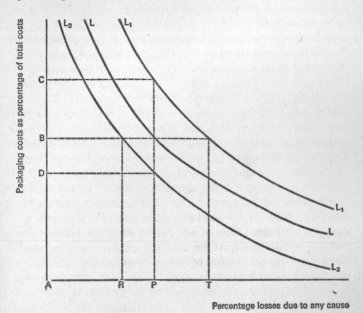

Figure 1. LL represents relationship between packaging costs and losses. L_1L_1 represents deterioration in transport or handling or inferior pack. L_2L_2 represents improved transport or handling or superior pack.

The first decision concerns the relative importance of the costs of packaging, goodwill and the size of the market. Where large outlays have been made to create brand loyalty in fickle markets with close substitutes, fear of sales losses due to damaged packs would be considerable. Attempts would have to be made to assess the potential 'unselling' power of bad packaging and the cost of removing this disadvantage; a point would then be struck which would reconcile the two to the best advantage of the seller. This solution does, however, omit any reference to the need to maximize markets in order to reduce unit costs of production in high on-cost industries. Where mass markets are needed and the customer is price-conscious, then the advantage of a lower-priced product might outweigh any loss of goodwill due to faulty packs; the cheaper pack might then be favoured.

If we assume a reduction in the overall efficiency of transport or a lowering of the efficiency of the pack, L_1L_1 would represent this new situation. At AB level of packaging costs, the percentage losses have increased from AP to AT. To reduce the losses to the old level AP would require an increase in packaging costs to AC. The decision on this increase in costs would depend upon the importance of price as a factor in selling and the influence of frustration to customers in terms of goodwill. If price is important, then the costs would be kept at AB and the additional losses borne. If the market is highly branded and competitive, the extra cost to AC might have to be carried in order to sustain the market. In the sale of industrial goods, the acceptance of the higher cost of packaging would tend to be automatic because of the fear of loss of goodwill if goods were delayed or damaged.

Where the overall efficiency of the pack and the distribution system has been increased and losses reduced, the new situation is represented by L_2L_2. Now for the same outlay AB the firm would suffer a lower percentage of losses, i.e. AR; or it can reduce its outlay to AD and sustain the same losses. Again, the importance of price and the maintenance of goodwill would decide which point would be taken up. Clearly, in both this and the preceding cases, the two points are not exclusive; a firm might decide to settle for some in-between position.

A better design of pack has the same effect on costs and losses as the situation shown by L_2L_2 in that it is more efficient in its use of transport and is less likely to sustain losses; thus, the unit cost per unit of loss is smaller.

All package designers must take the conditions in transport and at depots, transit points, docks, etc., as given; if these are below the ideal standard, the package engineer designs accordingly. Means of lifting, nesting designs, and reasonable weights in multiple packs, are based on an analysis of the journey of the pack. Clearly the use of test packs, laboratory testing, and tests on journeys should be made wherever possible.

The Qualities Required of a Pack[21]

THE PACK AND MANUFACTURING

Wherever possible, and without seriously affecting the performance of the packs, packs should be reduced to the smallest range of size and variety.

The variety reduction of packs can lead to economies in machine utilization where machines cannot handle variable shapes or materials. Purchasing can also benefit. Stockholding costs are reduced in that the amount of stock held per unit of production can be reduced. Variety reduction should also lead to better use of mechanical handling, warehouse space and transport.

Throughout any feasibility study of variety reduction in packaging, the total function of the pack must always be considered. There is the possibility of a clash of interest between the sales need for different, distinctive packs, and those of the manufacturing and distribution sections. Where price is important, a policy of variety reduction can be reconciled with better selling, but where loyalty to a product is based partly on package distinction, reconciliation of all sides is more difficult; good pack design does this.

THE PACK AND DISTRIBUTION

In industries where distribution is a large part of the total cost of the product the importance of packaging as an aid to more efficient distribution is increased. This would occur where distant markets were needed to justify a certain scale of production but where excessive distribution costs would make the product too expensive. Where the article is of low unit value, the position is clearly doubly susceptible to high distribution costs.

21. The development of a suitable pack may be a lengthy process, and the time likely to be needed should be estimated and included in any time scale which is drawn up for the launching of a product or the need to meet a critical date. It would be an important element in any critical-path analysis, particularly for those goods where the pack plays a dominant part in distribution and selling. Time may be needed, not only to design a pack to meet the demands of physical distribution, but also to test its acceptability to dealers and to those concerned with sales promotion.

The importance of the pack in distribution is largely dependent on the cost of the factors of distribution. Where transport, labour, storage space and retailing costs have increased, the importance of the pack is also increased to the extent that it helps to reduce the need for these factors or makes them more productive.

This contribution of the pack to the economies or efficiency of distribution can also be considered a real selling function, not only because it affects costs and price, but also because the cost-saving ability of a pack can affect the dealer's attitude towards stocking and displaying the product. When, in affluent societies, the customer demands a wider selection of goods at retail point from which to make a selection, the pack should assist the retailer to meet this need at the lowest cost in space and labour. Specifically:

1. Packs should be so designed that they convey the product to its destination in the desired condition. This involves the full knowledge by the designer of the actual conditions of distribution which will be met by the package: the climate, transport standards, handling skill, availability of mechanical aids, etc.
2. The pack should assist in the maximum utilization of space in vehicles. Multiples of the pack should facilitate good palletization; multiples of pallets should fill a vehicle or container.
3. The pack should help the mechanization of distribution wherever the mechanical means are cheaper than labour.
4. Packs should make the maximum use of the high on-costs which are met at dealer level. High site values demand a more stringent use of space; a well designed pack which enables higher returns per square metre of space helps to meet the cost-benefit motivation of the retailer. In self-service stores, the easily stacked pack acts as a means of storage and display at the same time. Informative packs remove the need for intelligent customer counselling; packs designed to sell remove the need for employing real sales people at retail level. The pack should also incorporate qualities which help to reduce costs at middle-man point. Packs should be in multiples based on the size of orders normally placed with the wholesaler in order to reduce labour costs. Packs should

be distinctively marked as to contents to assist in speed of handling.

5. Packs should be adequate to maintain the product in good condition throughout distribution and the shelf life within the retail store.

THE PACK AND SELLING

Where a product cannot be designed, e.g. flour, the pack takes over the design selling function. Pack changes are often used to create an illusion of a new product both for the general public, and also for dealers and salesmen. Packaging is part of the attempt to create a distinctive product to which customers can be loyal. It is a major means of identification. Specifically:

1. The pack must be integrated with the whole plan to promote a brand image. The nature of the pack must be consistent with the advertising. Quality advertising and brand names must have quality-type packaging. Basically, the pack is part of advertising.

2. The pack must be the correct size, shape and colour to exploit customer motivation. Customers irrationally project the colour of the pack to the contents within. Bargain-type packs appeal where motivation is more rational. The shape or texture of a pack can be used to exploit certain basic drives. Motivation research is a basic tool of good package design.[22]

3. The pack should be the correct size for the size of the unit for which the purchase is made, e.g. average family, and the life of the contents once opened. Cereal manufacturers must bear in mind the average family and the period of time over which their product will remain at the quality expected by the customer once the pack is opened.

4. The pack should respond to irrational motivation on size and price. Impulse purchasing should be exploited. Even non-impulse purchasers are often so influenced, making them un-

22. It has even been suggested by researchers that the customer in a large self-service store, faced with such a wide selection of goods, is longing to be rescued, and welcomes the distinctive pack which saves her. Suppose they all try to save her!

willing to lay out more than a certain sum of money at any one time, e.g. toothpaste and jam, where larger, more economical sizes may not be easy to sell.

5. Where the customer is concerned with labour saving, the pack should become a convenience pack; tubes and aerosols are obvious examples.

6. The pack must maintain the product at the quality standard expected by the customer as a result of any advertising and branding. This would cover both shelf life in distribution and the period of time usually needed to use it. The maintenance of quality standards in all packed goods is most important because of the unwillingness on the part of the customer to 'try it' again when close substitutes are usually available; the contents of a pack cannot usually be inspected to offset a past, disappointing experience.

7. The pack should be such as to make the maximum contribution to reducing the price to the customer; this is achieved through manufacturing and distribution economies.

8. Where impersonal selling is concerned, as in self-service stores, all the selling qualities needed by a pack are increased. It has been said that, in these conditions, 'the pack should shout at 20 yards'!

THE EXTRA COST OF PACKAGING AS A SELLING AID

The cost of the pack as a selling aid is a completely variable one. These costs are incurred for each pack as it is made, printed and used, to the extent that any additional costs exist for selling purposes over and above those which are necessary for the pack to carry out its usual function. The selling function of the pack is really self-financing out of the price received for the product and does not involve the on-cost risk associated with heavy advertising outlays, which must justify themselves in later sales.

This cost advantage of using the pack as a sales aid is most useful where the total demand for a product is inelastic and where there is pressure on profit margins, both of which could make heavy advertising commitments embarrassing. The marginal nature of the cost of selling via the pack should also be attractive when there is pressure to contain total costs within a given price.

THE NEED FOR DESIGN CO-OPERATION

Where goods are designed, e.g. consumer-durables such as refrigerators, television sets and industrial equipment, the design of the product must always be in sympathy with the design and problems of packaging in order to achieve the maximum customer goodwill through undamaged goods, and also to achieve economies in distribution. Slight changes in design to remove, or make removable, protuberances can result in more efficient packaging. Attention to packaging on the part of industrial designers can result in products which can 'nest'. Packaging and product designers are concerned with the same problem – customer satisfaction; packaging helps to convey the designed product to the user, as an immediate source of expected satisfaction, either emotional or economic or both.

THE PACKAGING OF INDUSTRIAL GOODS

The packaging of industrial goods is primarily a matter of conveyance in good condition to the point of use. The pack is, however, a selling device to the extent that a bad pack would lead to reduced sales.[23]

Raw-materials suppliers are often chosen because of their ability to maintain delivery of consistent-quality goods; packaging should respond to this top motivation. Packaging of components really begins with the use of rust inhibitors in the machining process and ends when the article reaches the assembler. Articles which go in quantities must be considered as a packaging problem when in multiples, not in solo.

The packaging of large pieces of equipment is only as good as the weakest point; damage to a small section may prevent the use of all the equipment. Packaging has the responsibility for complete customer satisfaction, given the means available to the customer for lifting and moving the equipment; means of attaching lifting tackle is a packaging design activity – fork-lifts are not omnipresent.

Among the factors influencing the purchase of industrial

23. Although it can carry prestigious signs on the outside which can be sales devices whilst it is in transit, e.g. by rail, on wharves, etc.

equipment is a consideration of its likely economically useful life relative to its cost. Today, this is an increasingly important factor because of the rapid rate of technological obsolescence which may render a machine obsolete in a relatively short period of time. When making a decision on purchasing industrial equipment, the buyer must assume a date when its economic life will begin; this is usually related to the date of delivery. In other words, the machine is assumed to be productive from that date until some future date, when it will be likely to be obsolete in economic terms in that a better machine has become available. Any untoward occurrence which reduces the commercial life span of the machine could seriously jeopardize its chances of profitability where technological progress is rapid.[24] Such an occurrence would be acting upon a top economic motivation and would react accordingly on the person responsible for it. Bad packaging can be responsible for this type of reaction; industrial package designers must be aware of this top economic motivation of customers and must meet it exactly.

THE SALES ORGANIZATION

Organization for Marketing

All organization structures are based on the functions necessary to achieve a given objective. If an enterprise wishes, as an objective, to secure the highest degree of customer orientation, this should be reflected in its formal organization structure, which will be based on marketing in its widest sense.

If marketing is taken as the dominating influence on organization structure, this will be seen both in the types of functions considered necessary for the enterprise to achieve maximum customer orientation, and also in the relationship of these functions to each other. Production planning and control is usually present in most modern industrial units, but the authority of this function, its manpower strength and its equipment should be influenced by the importance of company patronage motives on the part of

24. There is also the deep-rooted feeling that the competitive advantage which was to be won by using the new machine is being denied to the enterprise – to the advantage of competitors.

customers in particular markets where the goods themselves are equal; if prompt delivery then becomes a top motivation, production planning and control will become the source of an influential comparative advantage, and should then receive the appropriate authority and responsibility.

Sales-production liaison is vital as a concept or attitude of mind in all customer-orientated organizations, but this may result in the setting up of a distinct department aimed at reconciling the two activities in the fields of research, design, customer advice, order priority, and production planning and control. Where product policy is of extra importance, then product research, including research into consumer needs and reactions, should receive extra authority and funds. If quality standards are a top customer motivation, quality control should embrace inspection within the plant and a system of communications to detect and analyse any quality deficiencies after sales; the function would be staffed, financed, equipped and given authority commensurate with the preoccupation of the customer with quality. If continuous service from industrial machinery is important in the motivation 'mix' of customers, the organization structure will show increased recognition of after-sales service departments.

Where a research function exists to appraise the marketing activities, the location of such a department and its allocation of authority and responsibility presents special problems in that it is required to pass judgement on an organization of which it forms a part. The problem is made worse if the function is within a particular department, such as sales, in that it will be examining the work of associates and appraising the ability of superiors; it may even be considering policies based on its own recommendations.

Establishing a marketing research department responsible to the general manager is a possible solution; with very large multiple units, such a department could be external to all units but available when needed. Such a solution does, however, lack the intimacy with day-to-day progress which is achieved when the function is integrated. Marketing research is a continuing process aimed at recommending quick adjustments to enable the firm to meet the present and immediate future; it is not solely concerned with large-scale infrequent investigations. From an organization viewpoint the function might be conveniently divided into the continuous feed-back of day-to-day occurrences, and the deeper probing of detached analysis.

Traditionally, organization structures still accept the division between making and selling, the distinction between production and sales; but the more the non-selling functions are organized in sympathy with the motivation of the customer, the more successful the sales division will be. Essential to any good organization structure is the existence of good channels of communications between the two sides, either formal or informal, which can re-create the common-weal concept of good marketing. When the product and service amalgam offered by competing firms is equal, then recourse must be made to achieving a comparative advantage by positive selling. Thus, in many markets where equal production facility is easily achieved, the whole emphasis of the company organization structure moves to the non-manufacturing side. Distribution efficiency may be tackled as a source of distinction. But resort must usually be made to large-scale sales departments to create product distinction and consumer loyalty; this section becoming more important than all others in the structure.

In order to obtain the maximum selling impact for the non-selling functions, the organization of the sales force must be correctly based. It is vital to persuade customers to try even the finest products and services – the sales organization is designed to achieve this – after which the customer orientation of the total marketing organization will consolidate the selling.

Organization for Selling

The general principles of organization are as applicable to the sales department as they are to any other section of an industrial undertaking, but certain difficulties arise which are associated with the dynamic environment in which the department must operate and the social and intuitive content of the selling activity.

As with all organization-building, the objective must first be determined. Unfortunately, the nature of the organization which will be needed to achieve this objective is influenced not only by the ability and finance within the undertaking, but also by the activities of other enterprises. Intensity of competition affects the sales organization created to meet it. Sometimes, even the objective of the sales organization is not easily established; it could involve more, or less, concentration on a market to extract as many sales as possible or to allow these to be generated over a longer period of time; a given potential in a market could be exploited quickly or slowly, and much would depend upon the imminence and strength of competition. The size of an order could well be dependent on the frequency of calls which, in turn, may be determined as much by fear of the availability of alternative supplies as of the desire to optimize sales per unit of cost. Obviously, the greater the number of calls to be made, or the more intensive the selling, the greater the sales force needed.

The importance given to personal selling in the selling 'mix' is a basic influence. If it is decided that personal attention by employees of the company is an important means of achieving efficient selling, then the sales organization will be staffed in the appropriate manner, in terms of both the quantity and quality of the manpower used. Less dependence on advertising may result in greater reliance on personal selling.

Sound organization practice considers that, wherever possible, specialization should be introduced. In selling, specialization could be by function, product, type of customer, outlet, market, or segment of market; but in all cases it must be economically justified.

This use of specialists is liable to problems of split loyalties and incursions into the unity of command and responsibility. These are problems which occur in all organizations, selling or otherwise, when specialists are introduced; but in the selling situation the defects and problems may be greater because of the intuitive content of the selling activity. A work-study engineer may be able to demonstrate that his contribution to an objective is beyond doubt, whereas the advertising executive might find such an exercise more difficult. Where judgements with a possible basis in intuition replace facts, there exist grounds for friction between line managers and functional specialists.

All organization structures should be based on functions, not personalities. Even in normal organization structures, this principle is often difficult to apply because of the desire to make the fullest use of the capabilities of all employees, particularly executives. Where executives or specialized labour are difficult to obtain, there is an added incentive to adjust the organization structure to suit the available personnel. In selling, the desire to 'bend' this principle of organization may be very great.

The development of a social bridge between the sales representative and the customer may be so much a part of the person performing the operation that special adjustments may have to be made if the salesman is promoted. It may be necessary to incorporate a non-managerial activity, personal selling, into the function of a manager; he may still retain for some time some of his own personal accounts. The non-transferability of the social bridge is the cause of this transgression of one of the basic principles of organization structure. The problems of recruitment, training and promotion all arise to some extent in selling because this basic principle is broken – out of apparent necessity.

The extent to which any principle is broken will create problems which will require common sense and tact to remedy. In selling, functions, responsibility and authority must all be defined so that each person will know his position exactly. If such definition is difficult and there is the possibility of overlapping of functions, responsibility and authority, there should be a clear realization of the weaknesses involved. Similarly, where authority and responsibility are difficult to equate, considerable managerial skill is needed to identify responsibility for a particular occurrence; thus, the position of line managers in charge of the sales force is difficult to appraise when their activities are influenced by centralized advertising.

Because of the special nature of selling and the dynamic framework in which it must operate, deviations from the principles will occur; these must be recognized and allowed for in any realistic implementation and operation of organization structures in selling.

Factors Influencing the Organization of the Sales Force

THE METHOD OF DISTRIBUTION

If a sales organization is completely responsible for selling and providing the product to the final customer, it must contain all the activities required to do so. Mail-order businesses will need extra attention to office administration, stockholding, distribution and advertising. Direct door-to-door selling would require a large sales force. Selling and servicing any type of equipment will necessitate the establishment and manning of the necessary force and service facilities.

The decision to eliminate any intermediary between the manufacturer and the final customer will consequently increase the sales burden of the manufacturer. However, where the whole of the distribution and selling of a product is taken over by another enterprise, such as a multiple store, there is a reduction in the size of the sales organization required. Trends in retailing may require the addition of a merchandising section to assist the retailer.

The nature of the product may determine the possibility or otherwise of using independent dealers which, in turn, will affect the size of sales organization needed. Where the article is complex or the range extensive there may be a reluctance to leave the sale of the product to anyone outside the organization.

Generally speaking, the method of distribution for industrial goods is more direct but is confined to fewer potential customers, so that relative to the number of orders the sales organization is large, but relative to the total value of sales it might be very small. In the consumer market the situation varies as manufacturers make to order, supply multiples, deal through wholesalers, sell and distribute direct to retailers, and market the product directly to the final customer.

THE VIABILITY OF SPECIALIZATION

Many of the basic influences on sales organization structure would seem to suggest the introduction of specialist sections to handle particular functions, products, markets, segments with special needs, or customers of particular importance to the enterprise. The list of potential specialist activities is endless. There could also be further sub-divisions, e.g. product divisions may be sub-divided into industrial and non-industrial, and then further sub-divided with a division for dealing with important accounts.

Specialists in any sphere should only be introduced if the activity can economically support them. In practice, the decision may not be so clear-cut.

The introduction of a specialist department may be based on an expectation of results from the department which would in turn justify its introduction. Sales may increase more rapidly if a new product promotion department is introduced, and this would justify its establishment, although at present sales might not warrant such a degree of specialization. Specialization may justify itself rather than be justifiable.

This does not completely invalidate the principle that specialization must be viable before it is introduced; it extends this principle into the future to cover potential viability. Such an extension is true to the nature of selling, which is a forward-looking activity.

Sales volume in itself is not enough to support a specialist department unless it is associated with value. A machine-tool manufacturer might, with complete justification, introduce a specialist sales force for each type of tool he sells, even though the number sold and the size of the market are small; the value of the sales and their potential profitability would combine with other factors, such as the nature of the article and the customer, to make such specialist treatment economically worthwhile. On the other hand, breakfast foods would require enormous unit sales to make any specialist treatment of the product viable, because of the low unit value and profitability. There are occasions, however, where even though value and profitability do not exist as a basis for specialization, it is still introduced.

Thus, if specialization appears to give a marketing advantage to a competing product, an enterprise may have to reciprocate in like manner. The consequence of not reciprocating may be a reduction in the share of the market and of profitability. Specialists can thus be justified on grounds of security in competitive markets.[25]

25. Naturally, such a position would not be tenable in the long period if the sales situation did not improve; but the incidence of committed costs in

We must now consider some of the basic influences which provoke a demand for specialization within the sales organization but, throughout any discussion of these influences, the comprehensive viability of specialization must always be uppermost. 'Half-way houses' to full specialist treatment exist when the economic support cannot be given; specialization is then made to suit special circumstances. Where an organization cannot afford to support a distinct sales force for each product, it can introduce specialist managers to advise the force on the sale of each group of products.

SPECIALIZATION – FUNCTIONAL

Advertising, marketing research, new product promotion, merchandising, packaging, sales-production liaison, personnel management and sales training are some of the possible fields of functional specialization within a sales organization. The existence of any functional department will be determined by need and viability.

If self-service stores are of increasing importance in the sale of a product, then advertising, packaging and merchandising specialists may be needed, even with the same sales and potential. In markets where there is a heavy flow of new products, it may be necessary to give special attention to the launching of such products if the proper market impact is to be made: new product promotion departments might result. A shortage of suitable sales personnel may demand the introduction of more advanced personnel and training techniques; this would be more important, where personal selling had increased in importance in the selling 'mix'.

Specialization on a functional basis may be made possible by supporting it with more than one type of product, range of goods and brand name, or even extending its application beyond one company to an association of companies. Thus, a department for marketing research may be possible as a continuous service only if it is available on a group basis. Merchandising may be supported by different products and brands.

production, distribution and perhaps selling might make the maintenance of such an apparently uneconomic position worthwhile.

Functional specialization can exist, if it can be supported, within any of the specialist sub-divisions which follow. Any combination of sub-divisions could be used to meet special requirements.

SPECIALIZATION – THE NATURE OF THE GOODS

The more complex the nature of the goods to be sold or their application, the greater the need to allow them specialist treatment. This may require the recruitment and training of skilled representatives, but the need might be met by the provision of a department to provide and supplement the technical knowledge of the representative. The more knowledgeable the customer, the greater the need to match this knowledge.

It may be impossible to recruit and train people able to handle effectively a full range of complex items. The organization of a sales force might thus be influenced by the availability of selling ability relative to the complexity of the products and the knowledge of the customer. This is related to the next aspect of specialization, to which we now turn our attention.

SPECIALIZATION – RANGE OF GOODS

The more diverse the range of goods to be sold, the greater the need to break it down into specialist sections. If a range of foodstuffs is being sold, then as this is a reasonably homogeneous group, no special treatment within the group would be needed; the addition of wines to the range may require a fresh look at the matter. Lace clothes and furnishing fabrics can be sold by one man, but the addition of nylon blankets to the range would break its homogeneity.

With many diverse products it is usual to find that the markets, customers or outlets for the products are also dissimilar; thus, there arises a double reason for specialization; the wine will be sold through licensed premises, the nylon blanket in different shops.

In the sale of office equipment and machine tools, an easy case could be made out for using specialist staff, even though identical customers may be served and there would be duplication between calls; typewriters, simple adding machines and computers are sufficiently dissimilar even when sold to the same customer, as are machine tools for production, and equipment for a tool room.

Specialization for goods can range from complete divisions for each product, each with its own sales force and functional departments and services, down to the use of product managers who will advise the common field force and the functional departments of the special needs of each product. The degree of specialization will depend on the principles previously stated.

The use of product managers will imply that the sales force is considered able to sell all the products in the range when assisted by the special service of the product manager. Advertising and new product promotion, where they exist, would have to work harmoniously with the product specialist.

If a product manager is made responsible for the promotion of his product, it may be difficult to reconcile the authority needed with the maintenance of the accountability of the sales manager and any functional specialist. Where a number of product managers are involved, the situation is even more potentially creative of managerial problems. The position of the individual salesman may also be particularly awkward as he receives different streams of advice for each product, of varying qualities, but is directly under the control of another manager, the sales manager. On the other hand, if the product manager has no authority and is only advisory, then the organization may not get the full return from his employment; line managers may frustrate advice given by the specialist, particularly as the activity contains some intuitive elements which depend on judgement.

Functional authority for specialists will reduce authority elsewhere; staff authority might reduce specialist effectiveness. The position is particularly acute in selling, because of the problem of identifying responsibility for sales achievements, favourable or otherwise. A specialist, whose advice is taken with unfavourable results, can often justify his advice by the dynamics of the marketing situation. If the recommendations of the specialist result in an improvement in sales, it is difficult to separate this cause from others, such as better personal selling.

Where managers are introduced for any type of specialization in marketing, the same problems of defining and identifying responsibility and authority will occur; the normal managerial problems are exacerbated by the special circumstances of selling which make it difficult to identify cause and effects of any particular specialist contribution and/or socio-economic influence.

SPECIALIZATION – RANGE OF MARKETS

Certain market demarcations are obvious, and sales organizations should respond to the special needs of each segment. Home markets differ from overseas markets; industrial from non-industrial; the public sector from the private sector; male from female in the clothing and cosmetics industries; initial equipment components from replacements; domestic, industrial, and marine in the supply of paint; hotels and private customers in the market for domestic equipment; oil may be purchased for lubrication, transport, and for central heating.

In the above example each market is split into segments with distinct purchasing characteristics which may be based on taste, fashion, use, knowledgeability and sanction for purchasing. In the private sector, the buyer may only be answerable to himself; in the public, democratic control of buying could reduce the power of the buyer. Selling industrial goods to processors would exploit their profitability to the buyer; whereas selling to a local authority would not necessarily have such motivation. The financial, legal and sales-promotion aspects of marketing overseas would require to be in sympathy with conditions which, perhaps, do not exist in the home market.

Sales organizations should change when changes occur within a market which show new or potential developments. Where there is a tendency for the national income to be reallocated towards public or private capital-equipment purchases, any sales organization which did not change accordingly would fail to achieve the necessary customer orientation.

SPECIALIZATION – RANGE OF CUSTOMERS

In the industrial market, analysis of the total sales may show trends and potential trends for various, identifiable types of customers. Tubes may be purchased by oil exploration companies, refineries, shipbuilders, local authorities, and constructional engineers, each one having special technical problems and needs, each one demanding, if possible, a separate sales organization. The development of products to meet the special needs of each group is made easier if specialization exists in the sales liaison system. The article stays basically the same, but the application varies with each type of customer; it is used for oil-prospecting by one customer, transporting oil by another, for making lamp standards and water systems by another, and to fabricate masts by yet another. The customers for seats could be classified according to use, and this might give separate sales divisions or specialist managers for seating in education, catering, hotels, entertainment, homes, churches and transport.

In industrial goods, different customer usage will create different cost-motivation complexes. Specialization of the sales force to match customer segmentation should foster a better understanding of the motivation of the specialist customer.

In the market for consumer goods, the idiosyncrasies of customers may coalesce into segments; this may result in a policy which is matched by a similar arrangement in the sales organization, particularly if the segmentation also has retailer distinctions which cater for it.

Where individual orders are of particular importance to an enterprise, this alone will justify the establishment of some specialization in the sales organization. The greater the strength of any individual customer, or group of customers, in a total market, the more important is it that they receive special treatment. Consumer-goods manufacturers may have a special department to sell to multiple stores or voluntary wholesale groups. Tyre manufacturers may have a separate department for selling initial equipment in very large quantities to car manufacturers, and another department for handling the large orders of the national transport fleet owners.

The tendency towards centralized purchasing which might result from take-overs, the large scale of industrial and commercial undertakings, the setting-up of nationalized industries to replace individual companies, and increased buying by government departments and public bodies could all create some degree of monopsony in their several markets. In extreme cases, the sales organization and all activities associated in any way with customer satisfaction would have to be orientated to one or a few large customers. The dynamics of industrial and commercial organizations demand a constant watch on the importance and potential importance of individual orders.[26]

SPECIALIZATION – RANGE OF OUTLETS

This reason for specialization, range of outlets, is similar to that contained in the last section, but it deserves special attention in the light of certain developments in retailing and wholesaling.

Already special treatment by the sales organization has been suggested for large retail orders. Where self-service stores dominate a market, sales organizations should react with merchandising departments to advise the retailer in the new techniques of his trade; such departments may be kept separate from the selling activity in order to establish their advisory capacity in the mind of the retailer.

A manufacturer might, as a matter of policy, only distribute through wholesalers, but would back up such a policy by direct canvassing of retailers. This would require two distinct sales forces selling to each type of outlet. Segmentation of a market might have a parallel in the outlets policy. The production of a higher class of knitwear could require a new sales force because the outlets where the customer expects to purchase are different from those previously used by the manufacturer. A special department may be needed for selling school, college and club regalia, which might be sold through retail outlets that are 'superior' to those normally used in the sale of the main line of the company.

SPECIALIZATION – HISTORICAL CAUSES

Large companies or industrial complexes may display their origins or the consequent take-overs in their sales organizations. Where the range covered by an industrial complex is diverse, the logic of the sales organization is obvious; it is geared to meet the

26. Project divisions may be established with project managers for each large project: this would involve an organizational change of the whole organization.

needs of distinct products, customers or markets. In other cases, it may be due to the desire on the part of the new owners to retain and maintain the goodwill associated with the former companies.

Duplication of sales organizations can occur when the companies taken over supply similar or related products – a motor-tyre manufacturer might take over another one making identical and related products, or a domestic-equipment manufacturer may extend his range by take-overs, but the final complete range is reasonably homogeneous and would not justify specialization. The maintenance of duplicated sales forces may be warranted by any goodwill attaching to the companies or products; but additional support for an apparently uneconomic sales organization may be found in increased intensity of selling.

When distribution systems are maintained in duplicate form, further examination is needed to justify it. If a dealer is a vital link in the goodwill of a company, this may be the reason for his survival after the merger of the manufacturing interests. Where distribution systems are linked with after-sales service depots, the potential diseconomies of duplication could be substantial; the cost of maintaining duplicate machinery, staff, and stocks of spare parts would have to be outweighed by the goodwill allegedly associated with the previously separate and distinct products and distribution networks.

Rationalization of manufacturing activities may result in a range of products which are more similar to each other than those of the previously independent companies. Unfortunately, this more economic organization of production may not have a similar counterpart in distribution. Individual brands within the product range may be considered to enjoy special loyalties even though the products themselves are no longer unique. Where this occurs, the previous network of distributors may be retained, and this may compel the retention of a sales organization large enough to maintain contact with the disproportionate number of retail outlets relative to product idiosyncrasies. In time, the system of distribution and sales organization should become more realistically in keeping with the true needs of the enterprise as the old brand loyalties become diffused.

THE TERRITORIAL ORGANIZATION OF SALES FORCES

Eventually, all sales organizations involve territorial breakdown. Where there is no justification for specialization, where the product or market range is homogeneous, the sales organization may be based completely on geographical divisions and sub-divisions. Apart from the obvious separation on a geographical basis between home and overseas markets, what are the other main influences on territorial division?

Logic, supported by statistics, often suggests that political boundaries should be ignored when defining sales territories within a market, but this may be too drastic. Political boundaries may form borders between groups of customers with certain idiosyncrasies even within one country, and this may suggest that special treatment is needed. Scotland, apart from being reasonably convenient as a sales territory, also has customs, traditions and a national ethos which might justify separate treatment.[27]

Despite the last qualification, that of regional sentiment, territorial organization should be made on a basis which can be quantified. Current sales provide an obvious basis for territorial sub-divisions, but potential sales may give a better one. However, much would depend on the strength of competition; if this were weak, then the force could be kept small and the sales potential exploited gradually; whereas if competition were strong, or potentially so, then quick intensive sales action might be needed.

When the sales establishment has been discovered and the territorial sub-divisions identified, the need for supervision can be linked with territorial requirements as a basis for organization. Pyramiding could proceed from the base upwards – from district to region to national levels.

Physical convenience must also play a part in sales organization. Once a certain point has been reached, communications may become too difficult for efficient management, and so a sub-division may be set up, even though its size is below the average for the organization. The span of control of a sales manager is influenced by the nature of the work to be done and the physical conditions under which it is done. It is also affected

27. Regional advertising specialization may be similarly justified.

by the method of payment, in that less management may be necessary where payment is mainly by results; the men will then be jointly managed by monetary incentive and the manager. Similarly, the lower the rate of turnover, the wider the span of control which the manager can satisfactorily achieve; high labour turnover will require perpetual induction and perhaps training of new entrants, and it will also prevent the building up of team spirit and mutual understanding within the sales force; ethical policies may also be more difficult to pursue.

The physical convenience aspect is again seen in the allocation of territory to a salesman. If the current or potential custom is widely scattered, more time will be spent in unproductive travelling between calls; the ratio of non-selling to selling time will be higher. If the sales obtained or considered possible are deemed to be worthwhile to the company, then the size of the territory and the quota expected of the salesman should reflect the inconvenience of the distribution of the customers. Regions of concentrated custom will require more men per unit of area, and the return to salesmen should reflect the relative convenience of their location. Although, in all cases, studies should be made to increase the effectiveness of salesmen in the field by improving their selling to non-selling time ratios, these studies must take place against a given set of working conditions, which may be physically advantageous or otherwise.

The responsibility which is given to salesmen may help to determine sales organization, in that effective communications and the span of control of sales managers may be influenced by it. Where salesmen are required, perhaps to gain a marketing advantage,[28] to make firm statements on delivery dates, production possibilities and even price, then rapid communications to an immediate superior, and from the latter back to the salesman with current information, are vital. Similar efficient communication would be needed through all levels of the organization if the authority given to the salesman was to be used realistically.

The logistics of distribution may determine the suitability of a depot location to serve an area and this may become a contribu-

28. This would affect the calibre of men recruited and the content of training programmes.

tory factor in the establishment of a regional sub-division. Where a production unit has been set up in a territory, this again could help to provide the basis for a territorial sales division.

As with all sales problems, the territorial organization of a sales force calls for continuous appraisal. Population may drift; districts become more or less densely populated; regional potentials may change; competition may stiffen in some areas relative to others; communications may become more or less difficult; the calibre of salesmen may decline, thus requiring closer control; their responsibilities may be increased to meet new competition; and the supply of managerial talent may change, affecting the span of control or size of areas which can be managed efficiently.

6. Budgeting

IN no other field of industrial activity does so little certainty exist as in the determination of budgets for sales activities. This does not imply that they are a useless tool, but it does suggest that considerable caution is needed when handling budget activities or attempting to assess the efficiency of a given outlay on sales activities. Input-output models to simulate the financial outlay and expected consequences of that outlay would involve multiple correlations of a most complex character. The variables are so many and so difficult to estimate, even within a wide tolerance, that the attitude towards budgetary control on the sales side must be different from the more mechanical approach which can be adopted with other budgets.

Difficulties occur because of the non-linear relationships which exist between inputs and outputs and because of the inherent problems of measuring productivity in highly dynamic circumstances. Relationships may be established for one time and place which are not maintained at any other time or place. Nevertheless, to avoid the problem because of these difficulties could well be the ultimate financial folly when sales costs are representing a higher and higher proportion of total delivered-to-customer costs. It is plainly unsatisfactory to engage in minute cost-control systems in production and then hope that all other costs will look after themselves.

THE NEED FOR BUDGETS

Budgets are control devices aimed at setting norms or standards for key activities within an industrial or commercial operation, so that the operational controller will know, to a lesser or greater degree, the achievements expected and, by comparing the actual with the expected performances, be able to take any action needed to bring the situation under control and proceed towards the final objective. On the production side, such norms of achievement for a given outlay are relatively easy to estimate, and likewise the steps required to bring the plan back to its expected path are reasonably obvious; overtime working might be identified as the reason for costs being above expectation, and this can be rectified by better production planning. In purchasing, the input-output aspect of control is perhaps even more simple and more positively accurate and certain. The only contingency likely to arise is an increase in the price of materials, or the cost of borrowed money, or the use of a substitute material. None of these occurrences is likely to affect the budgets by more than a few per cent, and all can be traced and quantified with reasonable accuracy.

A consideration of the budget set aside for research shows a situation very similar to that facing the sales side. Here an investment has no guaranteed return in the form of an innovation or product, its use or method of manufacture, and even if a worthwhile discovery is made, its financial value is dependent on the work done by competitors, which may be a well kept secret. Even if the new device is launched successfully, the true assessment of its profitability can only come after a period of time has elapsed; the copying of the device or innovation by a competitor would quickly reduce its profitability. There is in this example something of the uncertainty and dynamism which is found in sales budgeting.

Research and sales promotion, particularly advertising, are also alike in that there are difficult 'mid-stream' decisions to be taken if the expenditure has not achieved the expected results. An additional outlay might bring the whole, so far disappointing, activity to a successful conclusion; the cost of not proceeding is the sum of the outlays already made without any concrete commercial gains in knowledge or markets. However, in both cases, the extra outlay may merely increase the losses if the expected fruition of effort does not take place.

Certain constituents of the sales budget resemble capital budgets in that the period of output consequential on a given indivisible input may be spread over a long period of time. A large advertising campaign to launch a new brand of cigarettes or washing machine or compressor can rarely, if ever, be considered a viable proposition in the short period. Estimates will be made of the likely time when the launching, advertising-sustenance and other costs will break even with sales revenue, after which true profits will accrue to the product or brand. Estimates of the time when costs and revenue will be equal, or break even, will have to be made as part of the budgeting procedure for the new brand, and these will involve some forecast of prices, the competitive effectiveness of the product and the sales-promotion activities, and the action and reaction of competitors. Obviously, the break-even point may be reached earlier or later than anticipated where forecasts have been unduly pessimistic or optimistic.

The break-even point may occur at a point in time perhaps two or three years or more after the initiation of the new product or brand, and is not therefore related to any conventional budgetary period. The progress towards it would be checked and controlled by means of a budget in terms of costs, revenue and time. Even this protracted budgetary period is inadequate if the full effects of large sales appropriations are to be quantified and perhaps, in some cases, justified.

The full effects of a campaign to launch a new product, brand, or company, or to re-establish a name in a market could well be felt for the full life of the enterprise. The real measure of the effectiveness is the amount of sustaining promotion needed to maintain the established position which was created by the initial campaign; less expenditure may be needed annually to maintain the loyalty needed because of the effectiveness of the original promotion campaign; new products can be launched more cheaply under the umbrella of the established 'name' than would otherwise be the case. All represent, by the extent of the saving involved, the output or effectiveness of the original campaign.[1]

A sales budget must include certain major items if it is to rank as a worthwhile tool of control: an estimate of sales during a given period, with sub-divisions of that period; a stated price policy which will help to generate this sales demand; an estimate of the appropriation required, both in total and in its specialized sub-divisions, to achieve the estimated sales at the price or prices

1. We are assuming here that all other aspects of sales policy and promotion are compatible with such positive returns to advertising outlays.

to be charged; finally, some assessment of the likely profits if the budget standards of cost and revenue are achieved.

A cursory glance at these requirements will suggest that any company could, at any given time, produce an infinite number of such estimates, because obviously one estimate is a function of another. Should a company reduce a price, it will probably sell more, unless there is complete inelasticity of demand for the product. If advertising is reduced or increased, sales would probably also be reduced or increased, although not necessarily in the same proportion. A reduction in price and an increase in advertising should have a double effect on sales, but at a cost per unit of sale. The sales budget should maximize profits when taken in conjunction with the other budgets. This may mean a sales budget which achieves a unit cost of selling which is above the optimum in order to accommodate the requirements of production.

A sales budget is a necessity for three reasons. Firstly, it is a vital part of the synthesis of the overall strategic plan or company objective where it is reconciled with other budgets each representing scales or optima operations. Secondly, it would be contrary to profit maximization if a breakdown of total costs shows a high percentage to be non-production costs and no attempt is made to forecast, plan and control this part. Thirdly, the uncertain conditions under which sales are achieved and the non-deterministic nature of the factors concerned render a control device more vital than it would be if exact forecasts could be made: a planned course is needed in order to know the extent of any deviation caused by unforeseen factors, so that rectifying action can be taken. The very reason why sales budgets are belittled, because they are built on quicksands, justifies their existence.

Despite the obvious difficulties of estimating the output consequences of a given input, sales budgets are essential if any business is to be financially planned and controlled. The plan may turn out to be unrealistic or unattainable because of a change in the economic conditions of the customers or in the face of new and powerful competition which has weakened the company's position, but this does not invalidate budgets as control devices. Without a budget it would be impossible to measure, during a period, the extent of the difference between achievements and standards, and so take the necessary remedial action. Even where the planned outlays and returns are completely awry, the budget provides the signal to indicate the situation and allow the appropriate steps to be taken.

During a period in which a sales budget operates, the various elements making up the budget, such as outlays on sales promotion, distribution costs and expected sales and revenue, will be constantly compared with the standards set in the budget. To the extent that these are incompatible, the final standard, in terms of sales and revenue, may not be met. Action may be needed to change the size of the constituents of the budgets; thus, the relative importance of each one may be altered. The total funds available for sales promotion may have to be changed in the light of changed conditions not foreseen at the time of the budget estimates. A price policy which was considered a tenable one may have to be abandoned, affecting revenue.

If budgets are really to be regarded as control devices, it could well be argued that the more uncertain the estimates made in a budget due to the dynamics of extraneous conditions, the greater the need for budgetary control. Given that the estimate of sales which is included in the budget is based on a figure which reconciles the various optima and is therefore vital to maximization of profits, then the sales revenue and cost situation must be known throughout the period under consideration. It may be necessary to change the sales estimate when economic conditions are at variance with those anticipated. The combined optimum varies with the optima concerned; should the constituent optima change, then so, probably, will the combined one. If market conditions worsen, the selling optimum goes down; if new production possibilities occur, this will put up the production optimum.

If the market becomes an easier one, this may indicate that the estimated sales will be made at a lower cost or, put another way, that the same outlay on sales promotion would result in increased sales. Alternatively, the price could be increased, giving a higher revenue. These conclusions would demand an estimate of the future trend of the market but this is made more easily because it is being made nearer to the point in time than the original one; half the budgetary period may already have passed. A situation such as this, with increasing ease of selling, would raise the sales optimum and would require a decision to be made on the possibility of increasing production facilities, which would move the production optimum to a higher plane as a result of an increased scale of operations, assuming that decreasing costs would operate, perhaps after the introduction of a new indivisible factor of production or control, such as a computer-controlled operation. If it should be impossible to increase production capacity economically in the short period, the budget could indicate an increased revenue from sales, as sales-promotion outlays were reduced or prices increased to restrict sales to the amount which could be most advantageously supplied.

This type of decision-taking is only possible if all the necessary control data are available; and such data should be in the budget. The initiator of the decision-taking process is the budget itself, which highlights the current situation on costs, sales and revenue relative to the estimated situation. The sales budget in this way provides the alarm, and the bases on which the production and distribution budgets were compiled will help to form the correct decision.

Where market conditions have deteriorated since the budget was drawn up, the ability to identify quickly the extent of the adversity is provided by the sales budget. Increased sales costs may be needed to achieve the sales estimate of the budget; lower sales would result if only the budgeted outlays were maintained; a price reduction in keeping with the new conditions in the market would reduce revenue per unit of sale below that which was anticipated.

Decision-taking in mid-period in adverse market conditions would require information about the production and distribution budgets and their optima, which was similar to that needed when sales achievements exceeded the standards of the budget. Thus, any increased sales costs needed to achieve a given figure would have to be set against the effect on the production and distribution budgets of containing their fixed and semi-fixed costs within a smaller total of goods.

If production costs have a high proportion of fixed costs, and if distribution is largely through the company's own depots and vehicles, which represent fixed costs, then it could well occur that the potential diseconomies which could arise in these two divisions would be so great that they might more than offset any extra cost now needed to achieve the budgeted sales. In both conditions of improved and deteriorated market situations, the new circumstances facing the sales activities will create a new optimum for selling, and this in turn will require a new reconciled optimum covering sales, production, and distribution.

If the price policy of an enterprise involved some urgency to recover high fixed costs because of the cost commitment of selling nothing, then the budget, which would be based on the assumption of full recovery of costs, would show the relative cost coverage of various prices and the consequences of accepting or refusing work at the currently available rate; the extent of the bookkeeping loss would be known immediately, as would the loss incurred if work were refused.

Without sales budgets it would be impossible to take rapid, remedial action and so, given the changed marketing conditions, profits would not be maximized or losses minimized. In the favourable situation where production can be advantageously increased, profits are enhanced as the easier selling position is exploited. Where production is fixed in the short period, advantage will be taken to reduce sales costs, or increase price and revenue to contain sales within the requirements of production and distribution; both methods would increase profits.

Budgets in the dynamic conditions found in marketing enable the opportunity-cost of any action to be reduced to a minimum. The cost of missing a favourable outlay-revenue situation is reduced because the budget draws attention to the situation and enables the opportunity to be exploited up to the capacity of the enterprise. When a budget shows an adverse situation, it allows action to be taken to reduce the financial consequences of the new circumstances.

The most perishable item in selling is time. Budgets reduce time lags to a minimum. A good selling situation may not be repeated and therefore must be identified quickly and exploited. A bad one may exist for some time; the longer it is unnoticed, the greater the losses to the enterprise. Thus advertising costs may become too great relative to revenue as shown in the budget, and this would indicate a need to examine immediately other methods of promotion and price policy.

If sales budgeting is judged solely as a device aimed at calculating mechanically the expected sales and revenue which will result from a given outlay on sales promotion, then the dynamic framework in which it operates would make it a questionable managerial activity. As a control device aimed at showing the effects of dynamic conditions on estimates which have been laid down to maximize profits, its use is beyond all doubt.

TOLERANCES

In all sales budgetary control systems there must be an acceptance of some degree of variance from the standard set either by ratios or as sub-goals within the overall budget. This is only to accept the non-deterministic nature of the data used as a basis for the forecast constituents of the budget. Past experience may indicate a degree of variance which can be accepted as normal behaviour in the market situation concerned; this may then be incorporated into control limits above and below the standard set, implying that no exceptional budgeting situation had been achieved unless these control limits had been breached. Without introducing such variance allowances, there would require to be perpetual decision-taking as exceptional or non-standard performances prevail, given the probabilistic nature of the basic data.

BUDGETS AND INFORMATION FLOW

All budgets, to be effective, must be part of an efficient information system. The construction of a budget in the first place must be based on reliable information. This information should be divided into those elements which are considered necessary for the budget objective to be attained: this might be numerate data on functional costs, product and/or brand sales, distribution costs, geographical sub-divisions, breakdown of orders, administrative centres costs, total and segmented revenue, etc. Information is not sought for its own sake but from key result areas which are vital constituents for the achievement of the budget objective.

Information spread over a period of time might show correlations or ratios existing between constituents of the budget: sales to advertising, market share to personal selling costs, sales to distribution costs, etc. Such data might, with caution, be used as the basis for the forecasting element within the budget itself.

The information included in the final budget plan must then be communicated to the people responsible for the key-centre achievements required in the budget: these then become their own objectives.

Finally, the people accountable for these key centres must receive from the information system a prompt supply of data to enable them to establish their actual position relative to the plan and thus allow them to take timely action if this is needed. This aspect of communication is part of the equity framework of any organization: it is clearly inequitable to hold a man responsible for an end-objective and then deny him the control information needed to achieve it.

Other communications outside the sub-system mentioned would be environmental factor changes which affect the validity of the main objective and the key sub-goals expected, and also the communication of achievement to higher co-ordinating management decisions taken outside the sub-system. The latter would be responsible for co-ordinating the sub-goals (market or sales) with other similar status objectives and also with the strategic plan or overall objective of the enterprise.

THE NATURE AND CONTENTS OF THE BUDGET

Sales budgets are a vital part of the scientific management sequence of forecast, plan and control: they embrace all three elements. Estimates must be made of sales at stated prices and the cost of stimulating such sales; the constituent parts of the sales-promotion mix must be stated in the plan in financial terms; distribution and sales-processing costs must be assessed at the levels to be achieved. All these activities, and any other key result area which is significant for the achievement of the overall budget objectives, involve forecasting. Many overall forecasts may be made: the one chosen is that which, when combined with other budgets, e.g. production, finance, will optimize profit (assuming that this is the goal; it may not be when a longer-term objective, e.g. market penetration or survival, is sought).

The elements of the sales budgets are then incorporated into the budget plan, each being chosen because of its key area location in a control system. The only purpose behind the choice of a key result area is that it highlights progress or otherwise towards the end objective. The calibre of control of the plan in operation is determined by the choice of key result areas and the supply of data regarding the actual conditions of the plan at these key points: these control spots would normally be cost or physical achievement centres, but the overall budget will be at a profit centre.

Sales budgets, unlike production budgets, normally incorporate profitability rather than physical objectives: a brand may be considered a sub-profit centre rather than a physical achievement or cost-achievement centre. Sales ratios may also similarly have a profit constituent at higher levels: at lower levels they would be cost- or achievement-based.

An enterprise will make, to the best of its ability, an estimate of the cost of making, distributing, financing and selling a given quantity of goods which at a determined price will produce for the enterprise a given net profit over the period under consideration. This period may be a long one, as when new brands or products are launched at considerable initial expense, or it may be the conventional short period of one year which is used in other departments and activities, and which is reflected in the annual profit and loss situation of the total enterprise.

This comprehensive budget, which would indicate the net financial position of the company, would result from studies of costs in production, distribution, finance and selling, and the gross revenue likely to be achieved. Increasing returns in production and distribution may show a desired scale of sales which look initially uneconomic from a selling point of view, in that to reach the needed sales figure may involve proceeding to parts of the market where the cost of selling is above average and where additional sales give a profit less than the cost of achieving it. However, when selling and non-selling costs are considered jointly[2] the diseconomies of selling may be more than offset by the reduced unit cost of production and distribution which has resulted from the larger-scale operation made possible by increased sales. Some licensed premises may be retained by breweries, even though the profit from them is minimal, because they enable a higher scale of output to be achieved, with consequent economies in production costs which, in turn, increase the profitability of all sales through other outlets, unit cost of production having been reduced, and so increase profits overall.

To arrive at the synthesized figure which reconciles selling and non-selling costs, it is necessary to make some estimate of the relative selling costs of various sales figures and the gross revenues which would accrue. This is really an exercise concerning the constituents of the selling 'mix' and would involve, among other things, estimates of the likely effectiveness of advertising, price reductions, cheap credit and higher incentives to dealers and salesmen. The relative effectiveness of various combinations of selling methods would also have to be studied.

The sales budget may be given as a comprehensive one, covering all sales methods, but this would then need to be broken down into budgets appropriate to each constituent part of selling; in effect, a decision on the best selling 'mix' is needed at the outset. The better the 'mix', the lower the unit cost of selling and the higher the selling optimum. During the operation of the budget, further decisions may be needed in the constituents of the 'mix',

2. As pointed out in the chapter on the Marketing 'Mix', outlays on research and development of new products, design and quality control are all marketing outlays which affect sales achievements. However, it is not intended to include these budget decisions in the present context. Similarly, to avoid confusion, the outlay on sales research activities, which is vital to the whole of budgeting, will be omitted, even though the estimates on which sales budgets are based should be the result of such research, and the effectiveness of promotion outlays will certainly be dependent on it.

as it becomes obvious that discrepancies have arisen between the estimates made and actual achievements. Credit may become more, or less, important; the public more price-conscious and less susceptible to branding and advertising, or vice versa; competitors may have introduced new products, different prices, more advertising or increased credit extensions.

Production budgets need not be so dynamic; they can be made with considerable certainty because the factors influencing physical output are identifiable and, largely, measurable. A given input of machines, labour, power and materials will cost a known amount and will produce a given output; this output can be estimated with reasonable certainty. Any changes in inputs and outputs are obvious and easily accounted for by increased labour, machines, materials, etc. The production activities of competing firms do not have any direct bearing on the physical output of internal production budgets, but the activities of competitors do affect the value and profitability of this output, which is related to the price obtainable in the markets and the cost of obtaining the revenue by sales activities. Thus, the only part of a production budget[3] which is seriously affected by outside forces is that associated with the value of the output, and it is precisely at this point that production and sales budgets come together. This indicates the importance of extraneous factors in the uncertainty of sales budgets.

Although the physical production of a machine or a new extension to a factory is not affected by a similar extension of capacity by a competitor, the effectiveness of a given outlay on advertising, packaging, dealer incentives and increased payment to the sales force will be determined largely by the sales-promotion activities of competing firms. Likewise, any reduction in price which is intended to stimulate sales but which affects the revenue per unit sold will depend for its sales achievements and revenue-raising on the price policies followed by competitors.

All complementary budgets within the sales budget must be balanced to obtain maximum returns per unit of cost; if the budget for the sales force is out of balance with the outlays on

3. Labour and material costs could be, to some extent, affected by the forces of the market, but the consequence is relatively easy to assess.

advertising, the effect of the advertising will be reduced because of the deficiency in personal selling to dealers or industrialists. The distribution budget must not be restricted in such a way as to create inefficiency in this function and so frustrate outlays on sales-promotion activities. Cuts in price which are aimed at increasing turnover, and so maintaining or increasing revenue, can only be fully effective if the necessary advertising informs the market of the price reduction, and production and distribution make the article available in the quantities and locations where it is demanded.

Sales budgets cannot be fixed at a point where the return is greatest per unit of outlay; they may proceed past the point where marginal return is less than the cost of achieving this return. In competitive markets it must be accepted that returns will tend to decrease very quickly, perhaps immediately; an increase in advertising may be needed, a reduction in price, increased incentives to dealers, more distant customers supplied, or more intensive field selling. All these represent either increased cost to get more customers, or reduced revenue for the same purpose; the additional customers are less profitable.

Budgets exist not only to control costs and output within a function, but also to achieve the maximum co-ordination between functions so that profitability of a whole enterprise can be at its highest.

Additional sales created by a campaign may be sufficient to justify the use of more sophisticated methods of production and so reduce the unit cost of all articles; a more complex device may now become economical, shift working may now be viable, and both would affect beneficially the cost of production. It is therefore possible that the cost of obtaining extra customers by advertising, extra salaries and commission for representatives, increased discounts to dealers, or reduced prices, may be more than offset by the reduced cost of production. In a similar manner, distribution diseconomies to reach more distant markets may be cancelled out by production scale economies and perhaps more efficient advertising over a larger area, e.g. one covered by better media.

When budgets are considered jointly, the previously profitable sales may become even more so as the production or distribution cost per unit of output is reduced for the total amount produced, distributed and sold.

Any judgement on the total budgetary situation, including production, distribution, finance and sales, would require some forecast to examine the consequences of, on the one hand, the possible use of a new and more efficient means of production which would be made viable by more sales and, on the other hand, the cost of achieving those sales. Investment decisions taken in this way are really marketing decisions in that the economy associated with the equipment or extension to capacity must be greater than the cost of achieving the extra sales required to utilize the capacity fully. On the sales side there are similar large investment decisions which would involve heavy indivisible outlays, and which immediately increase unit selling cost. It would be hoped that in the long term such heavy outlays would reduce the cost of selling; a large advertising campaign to promote a brand may require, owing to the conditions of the market, a heavy indivisible outlay if it is to be effective; in the long period it would be assumed that such a method is more economical and effective than smaller outlays or a reduced price, or increased dealer incentives.

Large, fixed-cost outlays in sales promotion may create the demand necessary to justify, not only themselves, but also fixed-cost commitments in production. If the decision taken is the correct one and the unit cost of selling is reduced, and also that of production, then quite clearly economies of scale in both functions are in operation and are mutually advantageous. A small enterprise unable to compete at the level of output necessary to achieve these double economies of scale may decide to readjust product policy, e.g. to supply a distinctive segment of the market, or it may change its marketing 'mix' so that it does not depend upon selling techniques in which, because of its size, it cannot achieve real efficiency. Such a company may contract out of large-scale advertising and branding, and depend upon higher dealer incentives or the supply of non-branded goods to multiples.

FIXED AND VARIABLE COSTS IN SELLING

The constituent parts of the selling 'mix' can involve costs of two different types. Some, such as advertising, the establishment of depots and after-sales service points, and the basic pay and organization of sales force and administration, can be indivisible factors and represent fixed costs, particularly in the short period; sometimes they are already committed. Others such as credit, sophisticated packs, premium offers, commission to salesmen, and profit margins to dealers,[4] which reduce the return to the manufacturer, represent costs which vary directly with the sales made; such costs are as divisible as the sales with which they are associated.

The existence of large fixed costs in selling budgets is determined by selling strategy. Much will depend on the entrenched positions of competitors, the normal terms of trade for dealers, the availability of funds needed to finance any large fixed-cost outlays, and the situation in the market regarding the degree of price competition which is possible, desirable or conventional. Where total demand is inelastic, brands are heavily entrenched, dealer discounts are governed by convention, and prices are 'fixed', then promotion through heavy outlays on advertising may be the only means of selling the goods if they are not true speciality goods. The only alternative policy would be one of non-conformity on price, dealer discounts or both; such a policy involves divisible outlays and would therefore be attractive to an enterprise with limited financial resources.

When indivisible outlays with their fixed-cost characteristics are necessary or considered worthwhile, the problem becomes one of reconciling the outlay with the revenue which would become available; this is really an attempt at forecasting the net profitability of an investment. Obviously, such heavy outlays,

4. A reduction in price to the final customer will reduce the profit margin to both manufacturer and dealer if percentage discounts remain the same. Where the discount is increased as a reward to the dealer for assisting in the sale of the product, the end price remains the same but the revenue to the manufacturer is reduced per unit sold – he forgoes some profit for services rendered by the dealer; this is a cost of selling.

like all investment decisions, require a high degree of forecasting skill; whereas, when the costs are, more or less, directly proportional to future sales, no such forecasting ability is needed as the sale immediately justifies the cost to which it has given occasion.

'PUSH' AND 'PULL' POLICIES AND COSTS

Decisions taken on whether to adopt a 'push' or a 'pull' policy are greatly influenced by the different cost and cash-flow consequences of the two methods; compromises, perhaps the most common policy, may be the result of these consequences.

A 'push' policy involves an increased allocation to encourage the dealer to stock the product by increased discounts or some other incentives. Such a policy also would embrace increased personal representation in the field. The advantage here is that the costs are almost totally variable, and, on the assumption of a reasonable sales take-off to cover the fixed element in personal-sales organization, then net profitability should be achieved quickly.[5] Cash-flow problems would hardly arise as funds would become available as sales took off: later the cash flow and sales cost would be simultaneous.

The 'pull' policy, on the other hand, is weighted towards influencing the final customer so that the article is pulled through the distribution system. The desired objective is achieved by undertaking large-scale and often indivisible advertising campaigns. Such a policy clearly has dangerous cost consequences in that the break-even point will not be quickly achieved and in the meantime funds must be available to cover the losses being incurred. In the long run, this policy may be more than justified if the market potential is high, demand is buoyant, and customers are susceptible to branding; the final profit situation may then look healthier than it would if a 'push' policy had been favoured.

Combinations of 'push' and 'pull' are the most common, although policies which are mainly, if not totally, 'push' can be

5. There is a possible tactical advantage here in that competitors might be taken by surprise and profits realized before they become fully aware of the potential.

found in suppliers of dealer-branded goods to large multiples. To maximize the effectiveness of a 'pull' policy, a properly balanced allocation must be made to those activities required to 'push' the products into distribution points; the awareness and attitudinal objectives of the advertising would not otherwise be converted into customer behaviour and sales revenue.

Logically, the use of price policy as an element in 'push' policies should also be considered. Obviously, in an elastic market the lower the price the greater the turnover and the revenue. A reduction in price is an incentive to buy rather than a sales-promotion activity; it does, however, involve a financial sacrifice to achieve the incentive; the sacrifice or cost is exactly variable with the sales to which it gives rise.

SALES BUDGETS AND THE CAPACITY OF THE BUSINESS

Sales budgets provide a means of so controlling costs that they can be contained within the revenue of the business. Any enterprise must aim at making a profit when working at any capacity, and certainly when working at full capacity. Budgets can prevent the embarrassment of full capacity working at a loss.

Although break-even points are thought of mainly in terms of costs, revenue and time, the extension of this technique to capacity working is a useful device. An enterprise can only produce at a given time up to the limit of existing capacity, and it must therefore be able to cover all costs and make a profit out of the revenue which this output can realize. When output is restricted in this way and price is determined by market conditions, the key variable in this situation is the total cost of supplying and selling the product which must be contained within the fixed revenue. The cost structure of such an enterprise could be represented by Figure 2.

This graphical presentation illustrates the danger inherent in having a large fixed-cost element in selling.[6] The ability to carry

6. Certain self-liquidating costs of sales promotion may assume a fixed nature per article sold, however; thus, a reduction in the gross profit margin to retailers may be difficult to enforce in certain conditions. Any reduction

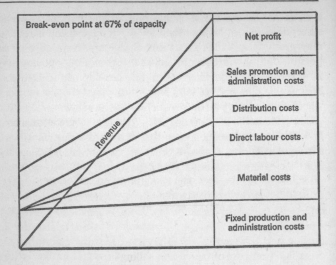

Figure 2. Plant capacity and the break-even point.

this cost is dependent on the price for the product staying at or above a certain level. Should the price fall, it is possible that the total revenue will be unable to hold the production, selling and distribution costs, because of the restricted capacity of the unit preventing any increase in sales to offset the reduced revenue per article sold. The more these costs are fixed ones, the greater the danger.

Fixed-cost elements in selling (which can occur in distribution as well) are usually a result of competition in brand-intensive markets and are encouraged when market conditions are favourable and increased revenues suggest that the costs involved can be sustained out of sales. The crisis arises when these favourable conditions no longer prevail and prices and revenues fall.

The obvious solution, that of reducing sales-promotion out-

in price to the final customer may fall heavily on the manufacturer. Nevertheless, this type of fixed element in costs does not have the potential problems of those costs which are fixed regardless of the number of units sold and which may have become a large part of the sales behaviour of the firm.

lays, is not necessarily a viable one. If the market is brand-susceptible, fear of losing brand loyalty if advertising is reduced may preclude any such reduction. Budgetary knowledge of the possible future consequences of such promotion policies may, however, be the main deterrent to their development. Fixed-cost, heavy-outlay methods of sales promotion might then be replaced, wherever possible, with those which vary with sales.

The application of a 'prices policy' by a central government will have the same consequences in many cases as a deterioration in market conditions. The cost structure, possibly non-selling, will exert increasing pressure until, in the absence of an increase in price, profits cannot be achieved within the capacity of the enterprise. It is conceivable that a company which has obtained the lowest unit cost of production will have to seek economies elsewhere; this action might be frustrated if other costs were inflexible in that they represented heavy commitments in the past or had become part of the organic selling life of the enterprise.

THE POSITION OF DISTRIBUTION

Distribution, like selling, creates value and makes the realization of revenue possible. The more efficient the distribution of a product, the greater the market which can be profitably reached at a given price.

The budget for distribution may be nominal, as when the goods are made to order and collected, or minimal, as when multiples or industrialists are supplied in bulk with little or no need for depots, stockholding, transport or mail orders. As soon as the manufacturer sets up his own distribution network, the budgets for this will have characteristics similar to those for production budgets; physical input and output can be estimated with reasonable exactness; a vehicle or depot, together with a certain labour complement, can be expected to handle a specific quantity of goods; the financial implications of holding stocks are known.

Indivisible factors will also appear; a distant area may be presently supplied at above-average unit cost, but the possibility of reducing this in the long run is presented by opening up a depot to service the area. Initially, unit costs would rise even higher, but the potential sales in the area, perhaps resulting from better service, would lower these costs to below their present level.

In order to remove unprofitable trade, specific costs of distribution must be identified wherever possible; small or distant orders may require more handling than their profit justifies; logically they should be eliminated if profits are to be maximized. This argument, however, can only be maintained with any certainty if the organization is purely a distributive one, e.g. a wholesale organization;[7] it may be more difficult to support such a proposition when other budgets have been considered. The extra cost of handling an apparently unprofitable order may be more than offset by the economies of the scale of manufacturing operations made possible by the total orders. Even the economies of the indivisible factors in distribution may require the support of the small orders which, although not covering their total costs, make a reasonable contribution to these fixed costs such as depots, vehicles and general administration.

When an enterprise takes over the wholesale function or integrates vertically and controls retail stores or licensed premises to help in the distribution and sale of the product, then the distribution costs will become fused with those of selling and production. Thus, an apparently uneconomic activity, in terms of distribution costs, may become worthwhile when selling advantages are considered, as when small orders are dealt with directly in order to maintain a quality standard for branded goods which might suffer if the goods are not distributed correctly; this could happen if goods were perishable, fragile, or were required in specific quantities at certain times and places, e.g. self-service stores and industrial buyers, in order to maintain customer goodwill. Shops and public houses which are not profitable in themselves may make a noticeable difference to production economies and even distribution costs, but they may also involve no extra cost in sales promotion; if a national brand

7. Where two distinct legal entities exist to make and sell respectively, both being part of a large undertaking, a comprehensive view of costs must be taken, rather than one associated with the legal division.

of beer uses extensive advertising in a given region, then closing one public house in this region will in no way affect the cost of this advertising; however, it is possible that the outlet does make some contribution in its revenue to this cost.

Where the distribution system is also an after-sales network, the fusion of distributing and selling the goods is even more complete. In order to maintain maximum goodwill, after-sales service must be available when and where it is needed. If this involves using depots and stores owned and controlled by the manufacturer, the budgeting implications are obvious in that this cost, aimed at maximizing goodwill, is really a selling cost and must be considered part of the sales budget to the extent that it is not self-supporting by service charges and spare-parts revenue.

When independent dealers are used, both wholesalers and retailers, then the extra profit margin to which they are entitled for providing the standard of service needed will reduce the revenue per article received by the manufacturer and is thus, obviously, a selling cost to the manufacturer. Using dealers in this way would remove the need for any large, indivisible outlays for depots; this would reduce initial risk and would substitute a selling cost which varies directly with sales. Nevertheless, it may still be advantageous, where goodwill is vital, to maintain depots which are under the direct control of the manufacturer; the initial cost and risk of doing this would be justified in these conditions.

In many cases, a large indivisible outlay on after-sales service facilities may be needed before any worthwhile sales promotion can even be considered. Where customers give top priority to after-sales service, the existence of the facility is a prerequisite of credible sales promotion. The consequence is that a double initial outlay may be needed for advertising and after-sales service provision. Both parts of the outlay will be in the nature of investments, complementary to each other, with a break-even point in the future beyond the conventional budgetary period, and with after-effects continuing beyond that, if the product becomes an accepted part of the market.

THE ALLOCATION OF SELLING COSTS

The distribution of some costs throughout marketing is so inexact as to require the maximum of judgement. The allocation of costs to particular segments, products, brands, customers, outlets or orders to any exact degree is often difficult, if not impossible; even when apparently valid costing has suggested uneconomic use of resources, judgement often rules out the logical outcome of this finding (e.g. an uneconomic outlet has good potential).

Costs can be more easily identified in a functional context. Thus, the costs of advertising, personal selling, stockholding, credit, after-sales service, administration, and transport can easily be estimated with accuracy. In a similar way, sub-divisions of advertising costs into general and point-of-sale display; personal selling into expenses, salaries and commission; administration into regional and central sales offices; all can be made with relative ease. Even more specific allocations can be made, such as credit costs for particular products or brands; the burden of commission for different products; and advertising which is specifically for one brand, product or segment of a market. The problem basically is one of allocating the fixed costs of selling (and distribution) to particular items which benefit along with others by these fixed outlays.

The allocation of costs to functions can be a useful tool in control and can help towards the achievements of the objective set out in the budget; ratios can be set between any two sets of functional costs, e.g. advertising to distribution, liquidity to sales; but, more important, they can be set between any functional cost and sales, revenue, or profits. Thus, a ratio may be set as a standard for stockholding costs relative to sales; advertising costs to sales and revenue; the expenses of salesmen to revenue; administrative costs to sales and revenue; transport costs to sales. Any ratio can be selected which is likely to improve control of costs relative to sales revenue or profit: it is an exercise in key result areas.

The ratio of advertising cost to revenue would have its basis in the sales budget itself, as would the other main ratios; if they were all maintained, then the budgeted estimates would be achieved.[8] Ratios are means of identifying and controlling trends in inputs and outputs: comparisons can be made between the standard ratio and the one actually achieved between one region and another; between one period of time and another; between various means of promotion and sales; and between the ratios for specific segments, goods, customers, brands, etc.

Ratios are no more sacrosanct than the budget of which they form a part; the dynamics of marketing may make the acceptance of changes in the ratios inevitable. Increased price competition may, if prices are not reduced, mean increased selling costs relative to sales and revenue; if prices are reduced, then sales costs to unit sales ratio might be maintained, but both would grow relative to revenue and profits. This tendency to change does not in any way reduce the value of ratios as control devices, any more than it does the budget.

A changed ratio will suggest the need for an inquiry into the reasons for the change and into methods of rectifying the situation in so far as this is possible. Exceptional ratios outside the tolerances set for regions, periods or individual products within a range can also indicate the need for action.

The allocation of functional costs to an individual product, outlet or order is bedevilled by identification of the incidence of the fixed elements in these costs. It is easy to determine the cost of selling a product where the salesmen receive commission only and are not assisted by advertising; the cost would be the commission on the sale.[9] As soon as brand advertising is introduced, a salary

8. This assumes that one part of the ratio is absolutely anchored to the budget. Thus if advertising to revenue had a 1:10 ratio, this would be meaningless as a control device aimed at achieving a given sales revenue, or profit, unless the sales figure was being achieved in the absolute terms of the budget. Ratios can be maintained and even bettered if only the cream of the market is taken, but this is not enough in budgetary terms, which are absolute totals.

9. There is a widely held fallacy that if payment to salesmen is confined purely to commission, then no costs are incurred on the selling side when nothing is sold; sometimes the situation is camouflaged by calling the representatives 'agents'. However, if there is any profit in the sale of the product, then the true cost of not selling it is the sacrifice of this profit. Where the production costs are mainly fixed, the cost of selling nothing is

is paid to the salesman, common expenses have been incurred, a depot has been set up to hold and distribute the products, and administrative costs associated with selling have occurred, then the allocation of any of these outlays to a specific product, order, outlet or segment of the market is virtually impossible on a rational basis. Where a salesman is visiting a town to sell a range of goods, it is very difficult to estimate accurately the cost of individual calls in that town and the cost of selling particular products. Should brand advertising cover an area, the allocation of the cost of this to particular towns is hardly feasible.

In order to remove unprofitable sales, use can be made of the concept of avoidable and unavoidable costs. If the removal of a product, order, outlet or segment relieves the enterprise of costs in excess of the profits gained from it, then profits will be increased if this part of sales is eliminated. Such action is implied in the maxim that sales expenditure will be continued only up to a point where it equals the profit gained by its outlay. The problem thus becomes one of identifying those costs which can and cannot be avoided if the product or order is eliminated.

Advertising a brand will not always be affected if one product in a range is removed. The sales force will not be materially affected. Depot and transport services are unlikely to be reduced. Sales administration costs will only benefit marginally, if at all. The extent of the effects is a matter of degree; if many orders or products are eliminated, some inroads into the costs of advertising, selling, distribution and administration will be made. Certain costs such as identifiable expenses, commission, and postage or freight charges would be eliminated, and such costs are the avoidable costs. It could be argued that, if the identifiable avoidable costs alone equal the profits obtained from an order, then it should be eliminated.

The elimination of sales which are suspected of being unprofitable might be justified in terms of the opportunity-cost of obtaining and administering them. The expenditure involved in handling such items may be more profitably used on the rest of the range, at other calls, or on new products. The time spent by a

the share of fixed costs which would have been met by the sale which was not made, plus any profit which would have been made.

salesman on an unprofitable call could possibly be spent more effectively elsewhere; the real cost is not the potential loss on the current call but also the potential profit on the alternative one. The elimination of a product cannot be treated in quite the same manner.

Ranges of products may only be attractive to a customer because of their overall content; to remove a product from the range may reduce the attraction of the source of supply and remove the profit on other products in the range. This would be the case where the customer is motivated by convenience when purchasing and does not wish any duplication of buying activity. In such cases the non-profitable line is really fulfilling a sales function, and the importance of this contribution to the sale of the complete range would have to be considered before any decision to eliminate it was taken.

Quantifying future developments is a constant problem in selling, and nowhere is this more noticeable than when a decision is required on the retention or elimination of a retail outlet or a distribution depot. The growth potential of the locality serviced by the outlet or depot may convert the current losses into a form of investment for the future.

Finally, as stated earlier, due consideration must be given to the overall situation when elimination of seemingly unprofitable sales is considered. The scale of operations in production and distribution may only be justified if the total goods now handled continue to be handled; selling-cost diseconomies may be more than offset by economies elsewhere.

PART FIVE

INDUSTRIAL MARKETING

IDEALLY, it could be considered an unnecessary demarcation within marketing to have a separate section dealing with the sale of industrial goods and services. The basic analysis of product and market or potential market is the same, regardless of the category of product or market analysed. This section will contribute nothing of substance to the fundamental maxims of marketing, but will attempt to show the idiosyncrasies of a section of the total market for goods and services.

It is when an attempt is made to identify or define the industrial market that the mistake of considering it as a separate market becomes abundantly clear. The definition becomes a distinction based on an analysis of goods and markets leading to an analysis of motivation; such a definition is merely a repetition of the general marketing principle that any solution of a marketing problem must be based on an investigation of the product to be sold and its market or potential market. On analysis, so-called industrial goods and markets do have certain common characteristics to which we shall turn our attention. These characteristics not only create the distinction of the market but also, as we should expect, form the basis of marketing policy.

The categories of goods and services covered in this market include raw materials, components, supplies (i.e. materials consumed, but not entering into the finished product, e.g. coal, paper, lubricants, etc.), services and capital equipment.[1] Many of the goods used in this market are also to be found in the consumer market, e.g. coal, vehicle equipment, etc., and so, clearly, any worthwhile definition of markets by goods alone is not possible. What then really distinguishes the market and sets it apart from the great consumer market? Motivation behind the purchase of the goods appears to be the most concise and comprehensive answer.

1. For the sake of convenience, real estate is omitted, although logic would suggest its inclusion.

The goods in the industrial market are purchased as a means to an economic end – that of reducing costs or maximizing profits. The industrial unit buying goods and services is obviously selecting a supplier with a view to increasing the profitability of its own activities; a local authority, government department or public body is still motivated by economics, but this time by the desire for cost reduction relative to output. As we shall see later, this does not rule out non-economic motivation or irrational behaviour in this market, but such behaviour tends to be the exception rather than the rule.

Sometimes the basic reason for purchasing an industrial product is social or political, as when governments invest in hospitals, roads, armaments, schools, prestige buildings and overseas aid in kind, or when local authorities buy such things as libraries, schools, sewage works, lighting systems, buses, roads and street furniture. The outlays with political motivation may have an economic purpose in that they improve the infrastructure of an economy, e.g. through education or better communications; or they may help to protect the economy from outsiders, e.g. by military expenditure. Many of the outlays at both central and local levels have a social motivation, probably the furtherance of the welfare state or greater social equality, e.g. money spent on subsidized housing, health and education. Even in the purchase of these goods, the buyer should be thinking in terms of cost-benefits.

In the industrial market, goods are not purchased for themselves but only for the contribution that they can make to the economic, political or social objective of the purchaser. Whereas a member of the public will buy a headlamp for its own worth, the car manufacturer is only concerned with the contribution made by the lamp to his production facility and the vendibility of his assembled car. Industrial goods, then, are goods which are not wanted in themselves, but only as a means to furthering the economic wellbeing of the purchaser.

This approach to the classification of goods has the advantage that it also includes all the buying and the selling in the consumer market which is not done by the final customer. This is logical in that the motives behind the multiple-store buyer, the wholesaler, or even the small retailer are all economic; the goods are needed in order to further the economic wellbeing of the dealer, and not for themselves. The sales manager selling to an industrial complex, local authority, government department, public utility, multiple store, or voluntary wholesale chain would face the same basic economic motivation; priorities of motives may differ, but the ethos would stay the same.

In addition to the fundamental characteristics of the industrial market described above, there are other common features which might justify categorization of these goods, and it is to these we now turn. Again, each distinctive feature is discovered by analysis and plays a part in the formulation of any marketing plan.

IMPORTANT FEATURES OF THE INDUSTRIAL MARKET

The Economic Framework

The demand for industrial equipment components, raw materials and supplies is derived from the demand for the products of which they form a part or are needed to produce. Indirectly, therefore, the demand for industrial goods is dependent upon socio-economic forces in the economy. Governmental buying is derived from social, political and economic pressures.

The demand for capital equipment is also subjected to grand phase trends as the economy moves up to technological maturity and then into the mass-consumption stage. National plans for the use of resources may also have as their objective an increase in the rate of capital expenditure; this can happen in developing countries or those which have been temporarily outpaced, such as the United Kingdom in the mid-1960s. Such national plans may use direct or fiscal means to achieve their aims or be a pragmatic mixture of planning and free enterprise. The effect on the market for capital equipment is obvious.[2]

Within national and/or cyclical investment trends, there are more direct influences which help to determine the attitude of

2. National capital investment extends outside industry to cover public services, roads, hospitals, schools, docks, military outlays, etc. All represent market potential. Infrastructure investment represents mammoth market opportunities.

entrepreneurs towards investment. Investment and depreciation allowances may be a stimulus or otherwise; they may be general, or favour some areas or industries as compared with others. State-sponsored or -guaranteed credit schemes might also have a general or discriminatory effect on capital-equipment sales. The attitude, as shown in the taxation system, to distributed and undistributed profits could affect willingness to invest and also introduce some rigidity in its direction, in that capital flow to newer expanding industries may be reduced as the differential tax encourages the ploughing-back of profits into the same industry. Large diversified units could reduce this rigidity by syphoning off profits from stagnant to growth segments. Labour unrest and its effect on costs and delivery promises to customers is a more specific type of reason for introducing equipment to replace labour. Payroll taxes and the levy of any tax on emoluments is a further incentive to replace labour to the advantage of equipment sales.

The relative costs of labour, land and capital could be a dominant motive in investment decisions. Where labour is costly relative to capital, then sales of labour-saving equipment become easier, and vice versa, the whole being dependent on the availability and economic value of the equipment in terms of labour. The marginal saving in cheap-labour areas could be an attractive proposition in others where labour is more expensive. The cost of land might result in more sophisticated use of it; the building and construction industries may be required to make the greatest use of an expensive asset; ventilation and elevator equipment would be in greater demand.

Political direction may affect the nature of an economy's capital investment by increasing the amount used for social capital schemes. Welfare-state economies would tend to develop the educational, health and general amenity aspects of life such as libraries and housing. This interest in the welfare of the community might also extend into overseas commitments, leading to an increased rate of aid programmes to less-developed countries. Military expenditure has considerable interest for many industrial marketeers.

The decision to replace capital equipment will be determined, taxation and other incentives being equal, by the economic urgency of such replacement. When demand is increasing, replacement and extension of existing capacity might take place simply in order to permit participation in the rising market; there would be little or no need for the new equipment to be economically superior to that which was replaced; the economic urgency would be derived from the possible perishability of the increased and profitable market for the end-product. Should a more economically efficient machine or device become available, the urgency to replace is increased to the extent that the use of the machine will enable the end-market to be supplied more cheaply than the use of the existing one, and that the possibility of this comparative cost advantage is available to others. The sales of industrial equipment, normally dependent on a rising end-market, can be maintained even in periods of stationary end-demand if the comparative economic advantage of the new machine being offered is great enough. The state of competition for a fixed end-market might even be such as to encourage this type of replacement.

The economic background to industrial purchasing, and therefore marketing, is really the foreground also. The immediate purchasing decision is based on an objective analysis of all the economic factors generally and intimately concerned with the purchase. It is not a matter of mechanical calculation, because the economic forces involved are difficult to quantify in mathematical terms; neither is it devoid of irrational behaviour; but the degree of scientific appraisal of the consequences of purchase relative to its cost is very high, being based throughout on the most objective purchasing drive, that of cost-benefit or economic wellbeing. In one important case the objective and professional nature of industrial buying may even override the obvious outcome of economic factors, that is in the effect of changes in interest rates. The assumption that an upward movement in interest rates will result in a reduction in stockholding because of the increased cost of inventories may be invalid.[3] Inventories of

3. A survey by the writer in the West of Scotland showed that only one out of 27 firms was in any way immediately affected by changes in interest charges – all admitted the *eventual* possibility of effects.

raw materials, supplies, spares and components are geared scientifically to production schedules (although it is possible to have commercial or even speculative stocking). The inventories held will only be affected if the changed rate of interest affects the demand for the end-product, which will then affect production schedules and so the demand for materials. The more professional the materials controller, the less likely the immediate impact of a change in interest on stocks, because these are fixed to suit production with little or no tolerance or slack.

The Demand Is a Derived One

The demand for industrial goods and services is derived from the demand for the product or service to which they contribute. This may be an end-product, e.g. a motor-car, or any of the components from which the car is assembled. The demand for oil tubes for refineries depends on the demand for transport affecting the demand for petrol and oil, which influences the need for extra refinery capacity; a trend towards more economical vehicles, or a restriction on road users would affect the demand for tubes. This demand for tubes would affect the entrepreneur's expectation of profit in this industry and might prejudice investment in tube-making mills, which would in turn affect the engineering firms who supply these mills. Obviously, the end-market demand from which the industrial demand is derived may be many stages away. It may also be many-sided and not confined to any one market; thus tubes are used for boilers, sewers, lighting standards, water, ships' masts and derricks, construction, bridge building, etc.

The secondary nature of the markets for industrial goods makes forecasting the demand more difficult. The manufacturer has no direct influence over the final market, which, to the extent that it is controlled at all, is in the hands of others. Consumer-goods sales can be boosted by sales-promotion devices; industrial buyers are not so malleable. This does not preclude any type of stimulus to the final market coming from the industrial goods supplier; thus, direct advertising to the final customer may be used, e.g. 'Insist on leather', 'Ask your builder to specify'; similarly, the development of a better component, machine, or finish to a product may influence the attitude of the final customer towards the end-product. If the demand for laundering services is affected by the widespread use of home laundries, the makers of laundry equipment can help themselves to sustain their market by helping laundries to reduce costs and so remain competitive; this they can do by designing more efficient machines. Nevertheless the nature of the demand for industrial products does introduce an additional risk in that the ultimate market is beyond the control of the marketeers and in the hands of others.

The demand created by governmental buying may be influenced to some extent by the manufacturers forming pressure groups or lobbies, e.g. civil-engineering companies may bring pressure to bear on road-building programmes. Nevertheless the basic causes for governmental buying, such as the need for an improved national infrastructure, social inequality, the desirability of the welfare state, international tension, etc., are all beyond the control of the marketeers; they cannot materially affect them.

A high and stable level of demand for the end-product is not in itself enough to maintain the demand for certain types of in-dustrial goods, e.g. machinery, plant, vehicles, etc., although it would obviously keep up the need for raw materials, supplies and some services. The maintenance of the demand for capital equipment is dependent on a complex group of factors including the supply of funds and governmental policy, but more important are likely to be the economic influences on the investment decision. The decision to invest in replacement of equipment or to increase the capacity of the firm is taken in the light of the estimates of future demand for the end-product and the economic urgency of replacement: the supplier of industrial equipment can only influence the economic urgency for replacing the equipment and the opportunity-cost of retaining the present equipment by increasing the latter's diseconomies relative to newer machines. The product is the sole source of customer patronage in these cases – a factor which must show itself in the marketing 'mix' by an increased allocation of funds to product development.

Finally, it should be noted that apparently proven correlations between the final and the derived demand may require careful handling. Thus there may be an obvious connection between changes in G.N.P., the consumption of electricity and the consequent demand for power stations and their many components. Unfortunately, advances in the technology of electricity generation may render an obvious correlation invalid; power stations may become more efficient and so the derived demand for their components, e.g. boilers, may be less than past experience had shown. When world shipping tonnage increases because of an increase in trade, it is wrong to assume any automatic correlation between this and the demand for ship's gear and equipment; the extra tonnage may consist of much larger ships, thus reducing the number of sets of gear. Container ships, because of a more speedy turn-round, can cope with any increase in trade without the old-established increase in ship tonnage; again the effect on shipbuilders and auxiliary suppliers is obvious. Technology may thus be reducing derived markets in some cases.

Product Policy Is More Complex

In the consumer market it is possible to envisage a company's image being sufficient, up to a point, to carry that company over a period when its products were momentarily behind those of its competitors. There have even been instances where brand loyalists have waited for a product. In the more rational industrial market, the more professional assessment of products largely eliminates extensions through imagery: although again an image based on a substantial favourable past experience, particularly one based on services rendered, may create considerable bias even in the professional approach. Nevertheless, despite these qualifications, it is essential that there be as little slack as possible in the schedule and introduction of new products in industrial markets – a situation which is made more urgent by the derived nature of the demand, which prevents the sustenance of sales by promotion.

The execution of product policy is also likely to be a more complex matter than in those markets catering for 'mass affluence' consumers. The basic need of all product policy is to maintain maximum compatibility between the assets of an enterprise and the market or potential market: the achievement of compatibility is more difficult in the industrial market because of the greater complexity of assets which may be present.

The industrial-goods supplier can have strength (assets) in pre-production, production, post-production or any of the support services. Thus a company may have made a name as being capable, because of its design and drawing office capabilities, of responding efficiently to customer requirements in a sophisticated equipment field. Such a spectrum of capability might preclude all products which do not demand this source of a comparative advantage: 'standard' package units may be ruled out even though the market looks promising.

Companies with a big competitive advantage based on after-sales service might have to bear this in mind when new products are being evaluated. It is not merely balancing the need for foundries and machine shops with new products and markets but also estimating, design, and drawing office capability, quality engineering and control, production management, after-sales service, perhaps even installation and construction facility. Any new product or new market must ideally be compatible with this very extensive range of sources of patronage (assets to the patronized company) or, where balance of asset use has been lost, then the new product should redress the balance. The problem of product change and cash flow – the receipt of money relative to inputs – is likely to be more intense than in the consumer field. The lumpiness of the orders contrasts with the atomistic nature of most consumer markets. The cash flow associated with a product costing £4 million paid at various agreed points in its production/construction life is not likely to coincide with a previous range of products individually averaging £50,000 and sold to separate customers: new product policy in the industrial field thus has an additional financial hazard.

The complexity and size of many newer industrial products presents similar cash-flow dangers; a more sophisticated, computer-controlled ship costing £10 million differs in its working capital characteristics from a smaller simpler one costing £1 million and produced in much less time. Making profit on such complex items, as distinct from getting a sale, involves an acute analysis of the cash-flow implications in cost terms and even in terms of liquidity and ability to complete the job. Consumer goods do not face such new product policy problems.

The Market Is More Clearly Demarcated

The supplier of coal-cutting machinery can state with much more conviction and certainty than his counterpart in the consumer field the extent of his market; it is not unusual to find industrial markets where every potential buyer is known. Similarly, the extent of each customer's demand is limited. Whereas in the consumer field additional sales pressure may create a real increase in the overall market for a product, this is more difficult on the industrial side. The motivation for the industrial purchase is rational and the size of a purchase is dependent on certain given factors; to buy beyond this economic need because of sales pressure would be the antithesis of industrial purchasing.

This apparently severe limitation on the extent of an industrial market must not be overplayed. The demand for a machine is not solely dependent on the physical obsolescence of the existing one but, as stated earlier, on its diseconomies as compared with the one now offered for sale. Technological obsolescence, or more precisely economic obsolescence, is the key to industrial-equipment sales in any economy where the end-markets are competitive.

Similarly markets can be increased by discovering new uses for products outside their conventional application. The development of the uses of cold aluminium extrusions, nylon and laminated plastics would well illustrate this point. The product development policy of the company should be such as to utilize the amalgam of skill and mechanical capacity to the best of its ability; this may mean changes in end-product in order to achieve maximum sales; firms making ventilator equipment for liners can turn to the land use of this equipment as buildings go higher and deeper. As a general rule, the manufacturer of industrial equipment has an advantage over his consumer-goods counterpart in that his human and mechanical assets are more flexible in their output capabilities.

The ability to see clearly the extent of a market does give an advantage in the deployment of sales-promotion forces; advertising can be located exactly and sales forces organized to perfection. All aspects of marketing research are also simplified; the product idiosyncrasies of all customers can be known; total demand more accurately estimated; customer reactions and motivations intimately observed and exploited.

The marketing implication of a fixed market is seen in the need to increase market share, obviously at the expense of competing suppliers. The more rigid the market size, the more this is so. Increasing market share means achieving a greater compatibility with the needs of customers, in a rational market, than any competitor. This characteristic may also create the need for selling, in the strict sense, in this field as competitors struggle with each other, particularly if none of them has a real product or company advantage to offer the customer. We shall return to this in the next section, as the intensity of the competitive struggle is clearly a result of the increased importance of individual orders.

The Special Problem of the Balance of Orders in the Capital Equipment Industry

The different demands made by orders on the range or 'mix' of company capabilities and resources can have serious unbalancing consequences. These differing demands might affect the ability of the current resources to meet new orders, e.g. there may be too large a design element in them so that, although the production side is capable of handling the demands made upon it, there would be a bottleneck in the drawing office or engineering stage. Clearly such potential overloading of one section could have serious repercussions when new orders were being considered as an addition to the existing load unless, by chance, these redressed the balance of resources needed in that only a minimal demand on drawing office work was required.

It is vital that there should be a continuing total compatibility between resources and order content. Where this is impossible, then sub-contracting of certain sections of the work involved may be required, e.g. site construction work when the company's capability in this direction has been fully utilized.

The problem of balance should be part of the evaluation of inquiries and responses to them; an order which badly affected resource utilization might, as a consequence of this, be less attractive.

The lack of balance in the demands made on human resources by an order intake may have even more serious repercussions where there is high mobility of labour. Thus, if there is a temporary shortage of work for drawing office staff because the contents or types of orders taken do not need so much of this particular capability, then the staff concerned may be lost and difficult to recruit when a new order contents balance is different and requires these specialized techniques. Short-term manpower planning policies are vital in such circumstances.

Some types of capital goods work, e.g. shipbuilding, civil engineering, large-scale engineering etc., may take so long to evolve from the order being taken to its final execution that the demand for different types of company capability may be very uneven unless some attempt is made to maintain a flow of orders to strike a balance. Thus it would be unrealistic to employ staff and facilities at the design stage and then unload these as the emphasis moved to production until they were needed again: similarly with the production capability, men and machines, which was lying idle at the design stage. When orders are scarce the problem takes on a new aspect because the balance of contents and/or the timing of orders cannot be so easily achieved. Thus when a company is short of work it may have to take an order, perhaps with considerable press publicity, only to follow this with redundancy notices to the production staff because of the time needed to convert the new order from drawing board to shop floor; in some cases, e.g. power stations, this process may take months.

To deal with the problem involves a much more sophisticated approach to the loading and programming of individual key centres of resources and capabilities, both physical and human, so that an order can be judged as to its effect on the balanced use of these limited resources. A vital aspect of all such decision-taking is the flow of information from production programming and its confluence with information on the contents of current and potential future orders. In some cases a perpetual limitation in one centre, e.g. the drawing office, may result in radical changes at that centre; there could be changes in recruitment, training and manning, or attempts may be made to replace or complement limited manpower by mechanical or electronic aids.

In addition, the mix of orders, their joint work (cost) content, and the times and method of payment during contracts may present special and changing problems of cash flow and could, if not controlled by efficient financial management, lead to acute financial embarrassments.

Individual Orders Are More Important

Whereas the consumer market is atomistic in the extreme on the demand side, this state of affairs is much less common with industrial goods. In fact a degree of monopsony can easily become established where take-over bids and technological developments are creating and demanding larger integrated units.[4] Centralized control of purchasing is now widespread, and in many cases local autonomy may be restricted to a very low level of expenditure. Nationalized industries represent a similar monopsonistic threat to industrial marketeers. The marketing consequence of such a buyer-seller relationship is that each buyer must be treated with much more respect and this may involve sales promotion at the highest or director level. More basically, the whole of marketing will be geared to the important customer; research and development, design, quality policy, the maintenance and credibility of delivery dates, price and after-sales service may all be influenced by the fear of losing one customer or order.

4. The tendency towards take-overs, larger complexes and centralized control of industrial purchasing has increased, and so further enhanced the importance of individual orders. This movement should have been matched by a sympathetic change on the part of the marketing policies of suppliers.

As with the need to increase market share, so the importance of each customer or order generates the necessity for maximum compatibility between what the customer wants or needs and what the company can offer. Patronage motives by the customer must be identified and their relative strengths measured. The marketing 'mix' of the supplying firm must be analysed to discover its relationship to the customer's motivation 'mix'; if product patronage is a dominant motivation, attention might need to be given to greater product research and development; if patronage is impossible from the product source, it must arise from other aspects of the company's activities, such as its ability to supply at a given price, reliable delivery, consistent quality, and efficient service both before and after sales; again the company may require to increase the attention it gives to any or all of these customer motives by the necessary adjustment to its activities. Also, as with attempts to increase market share, some pure selling may be involved; perhaps to retain a customer when competitive pressure has increased, or to introduce a new buyer to the product or service which the company can offer.

When the loss of one or a few orders is so significant to the viability of an enterprise, this can lead to the taking of orders at a price well below total cost (but not below direct cost). The alternative to taking such orders is the allocation of all the fixed costs to the few remaining orders which it is hoped to achieve; this in turn would increase their price and possibly lose these other orders.

The industrial buyer is fully aware of his strength in the bargaining situation, so that he is not only economically stronger than the buyer in the consumer market, but he is more aware of his strength. This tendency towards equality in bargaining power is now apparent even in the supply of goods to multiples and large wholesale groups, and again the professional knowledge on both sides is considerable. The good buyer will know the degree of indispensability associated with his potential purchasing power; the industrial marketeer will be familiar with the buyer's ability to substitute other sources of supply and the importance of the order to the successful running of his own firm.

A dominating buyer may deliberately maintain duplicate

production capacity in two supply plants, each of which is adequate to meet his orders, by splitting his purchases. This would create competition in the service aspect of each supplier, which, in turn, would improve the standard of service received by the buyer, e.g. better delivery, more consistent quality, perhaps a lower price. On the other hand, mass-production units may not wish to concentrate their component orders in such a way that they dominate a supplier for fear of a breakdown in his organization, e.g. because of strike action. Such units might split their orders and in so doing retain in the market supply firms which are not of the optimum production size – a commercial advantage offsetting a production or cost disadvantage.

The industrial buyer should always know the extent to which his order is needed to maintain the viability of specialized production capacity in the supply plant; such knowledge will naturally be used in bargaining. The tendency would appear to be to use any excessive bargaining power to take up a position just short of the keenest price situation in order that there still exists a fund of goodwill between buyer and seller to the extent of this short-fall on the lowest price possible.

The size and importance of orders also has a serious effect on the planning and use of company resources at the production stage. Thus where a company has only a limited estimating and design capability (in terms of size) then it is desirable to establish some means of evaluating invitations to tender where these involve any committal of these limited resources. The result of not doing this could well be indiscriminate use of staff on tenders which were very unlikely to be productive, coupled with the risk that not enough capability remained to handle the more likely jobs. Where orders are so big and important then scientific analysis of impact in relation to pre-production resources is vital; but it must extend beyond this.

It is absolutely essential in such 'lumpy' order markets to have some research intelligence of the possible forward situation of order placing. If it is known that an inquiry is expected in the near future with a greater possibility of patronage and also of profit but dependent on a good firm delivery date, then it is obviously bad marketing management to throw in resources prematurely to obtain lesser orders which prevent the quotation of the desired delivery promise on the more attractive inquiry.

The lumpiness of the market and the increasing tendency for a few big orders to dominate also seriously affect certain conventional techniques. Past correlations between total markets and market shares may be totally invalidated if the larger orders begin to dominate, making coefficients meaningless. Sampling techniques which may suffice in accuracy in atomistic consumer markets may give dangerous results if taken too literally in a market with only a handful of potential customers; your customer may be the deviant. An expected response or tender strike rate of 1 in 10 may be a reasonable basis for forecasting (probably based on past experience) when there are 300 inquiries for steam-raising plant per year; it is a meaningless guide if there are only 10 very big orders per annum from public power suppliers and giant private undertakings. It is reasonable to conclude that the only scientific method is to concentrate more on micro marketing analysis to discover the idiosyncrasies of such vital individual customers; it would seem that we have here a more exact form of customer orientation than is to be found in the consumer markets.

Customer orientation is more necessary in this market than is normally alleged; it involves a detailed study of every source of motivation and of patronage source, both rational and emotional. The very large customer may not only demand a given quality with no tolerances but he may also insist on indicating how quality engineering and control be executed in the supply company. In some cases, the size and importance of an order may show itself in fear on the part of the customer himself, who may wish to protect himself by either placing an employee within the supply organization, or having a senior man within that organization with special responsibility for his project, or both; customers' motivation here is obvious and supply firms might do well to respond; organization structures may thus be reorientated to reflect customers' motivations and fears.

Sales Policy Is More Important Than Sales Promotion Planning

The function of selling is to change the nature of the demand to suit the product or service being offered for sale; it assumes that the producer's output is already determined in nature and perhaps even in quantity, but that the customer is malleable. In the industrial field this is not, by any means, the case. Each industrial buyer knows exactly what he wants and the needs of his requirements to within a very narrow tolerance on physical specification, quality, price, credit, terms, pre-installation and after-sales service, and any other detail with economic significance which might affect the wellbeing of his enterprise. This near-dogmatic approach on product needs does rule out the type of sales-promotion activity which prevails in the consumer field and is aimed at inflated valuations of products, leading to increased purchasing based on non-rational motivation which exists largely because of the lack of knowledge and appreciation in the customer. To imagine an industrial buyer for emotional reasons ordering more than is needed is the antithesis of the cost-benefit motivation which forms the basis of professional buying.

The ability to meet a specification is largely a sales policy matter. Production planning and control, product development, price, quality consistency, reliability of delivery dates, and the standard of service are more important than advertising, branding and personal selling. Where a need rather than a product is specified, then product research and development and design would be top-priority activities in the company's attempt to meet the specified need. The need of a customer to achieve the maximum output per unit of stock or to adhere strictly to a schedule of operations would have to be met by a sympathetic response from the supply firm to meet these needs. All these aspects of customer motivation are met by sales policy (including production planning and control) decisions.

Where an outside body, such as the American Petroleum Institute or the British Standards Institution, introduces a specification or when public safety demands the maintenance of a standard, as with the British Pharmacopoeia, then the supply firm is judged on its ability to meet these standards at a given price.

In the sales of equipment, the factual assessment of the economic or ergonomic capabilities of the machine is the dominant factor. Ease of maintenance, commonization of spare parts and components, and training facility, all of which are associated with research and design, will be the next basis of choice after fundamental economic assessments have been made.

If the main reason for change on the part of an industrial customer is dissatisfaction with the existing source of supply, then the importance of sales policy is very obvious if companies wish to maximize sales. Dissatisfaction with a current supplier normally stems from a sales policy activity such as inconsistent quality, unreliable delivery, bad after-sales service or unsuitable trends in price. With the exception of price, which could be outside the complete control of the company, all other possible causes of dissatisfaction are under the direct authority of the firm.[5]

Although it would appear that the sales policy aspects of marketing are largely responsible for the retention of customers in the industrial market by enabling customer needs to be met satisfactorily, and that the ability to meet a specification of need or product is fundamental before any sales can be made, the customer being fixed in his requirements, selling might still play an important part in industrial marketing in certain conditions. It is impossible to imagine sustained sales based on selling only, sales policy being lacking, but selling must be given its proper place in industrial marketing. Even complete customer orientation has to be communicated to potential customers; many units seem to believe that everyone will know of the change. Where competing units have all reached a similar level of customer orientation, then persuasion is needed.

Where a company is trying to break into a market for the first time, there is the need to persuade the potential buyer that the newcomer is capable of achieving the desired end. This is a selling activity. If the market is one which is sophisticated and the buying firms have evolved vendor-rating systems, then gaining entry may be even more difficult as a selling job; the existing

5. A survey carried out in the West of Scotland by the writer showed that dissatisfaction was the major cause for changing supplier, and not the discovery of a new source.

suppliers are known and rated as to their ability to meet the needs of the customer; the new entrant is unknown.[6] Should the industry concerned be based on progressive-assembly methods or be a processing industry with the resulting fear of a breakdown in machines or supplies, then the problem of persuading the customer to give an unknown or unproven supplier a chance against the proven ones suggests that an even greater act of selling is needed.

Neither must it be forgotten that where sales policies are equal, the selling activity may make the marginal difference. If a product is specified by a large firm, the price is known within narrow limits, and the general efficiency of the competing firms is equal, then the choice of supplier could be due to persuasion. Similarly when a company becomes dissatisfied with an existing supplier and seeks a changed source of materials, service, components or supplies, the final choice of the new supplier could well be due to the selling ability of competing firms in the recent past.

In the case of selling replacement equipment, the marginal advantage of the new machine relative to outlay and the disturbance during installation may be so small as to require the most positive and persuasive form of selling – although the latter will be technically and cost-benefit biased. In such a highly competitive situation, any activity which in any way, emotionally or rationally, disturbs the customer must be avoided; this maxim would cover any 'unselling' behaviour by servants of the company, particularly those connected with a strong source of customer patronage, e.g. after-sales service. All employees must be made conscious of the marketing implications of their efficiency and, perhaps more important, their inefficiency. Even the sales force must be made aware of potential 'unselling' behaviour, such as bad briefing of customer needs, slights to managerial

6. There may be something in the contention that vendor-rating systems could result in rigidity in markets as buyers become obsessed with established ratings which indicate proven ability on the part of suppliers. In the progressive-assembly or flow-production industries, particularly if there is no obvious source of dissatisfaction with existing suppliers, fear of breakdown might preclude the entry of a new and perhaps more efficient supplier. Certainly industrial selling could be as intensive as other forms of selling in this type of situation.

authority within the buyer's organization, and poor face-to-face conduct.

Finally, in assessing the relative importance of sales policy and sales promotion in the industrial market, it is essential that we do not over-estimate the ability of the industrial buyer to be immune from emotional activity, enabling him to achieve completely objective assessments of suppliers and their products and services. The continued co-existence of many different firms in certain markets where the buyers are assumed to have common cost-benefit motivations tends to suggest that assessments do vary, and perhaps even implies emotional behaviour in the choice of supply firms.[7]

Before leaving this analysis of selling industrial goods, attention must be drawn again to the similarity between buying for an industrial unit and buying for a multiple retail store or large wholesale group. The tendency is for these large buyers to try to maintain the image of the multiple organization which has been laid down in the general policy. The most successful multiples are those which have achieved a common and obvious price-quality relationship going throughout their whole organizations and thus creating for them a national image. Clearly, when a company is contemplating sales to such a customer, the tolerance or specification is as close as it will be with the industrial customer; design, quality and price will allow little, if any, discretion on the part of the supplier. The product supplied is really a component part in the image and trading of the retail store; it must, like a component, add to the vendibility of the store.

Inertia between Buyer and Supplier

The industrial market has a built-in danger of inertia which will render the market less perfect than is sometimes imagined,

7. A good exercise to measure the rational and emotional content of industrial markets is to carry out a vendor-rating programme of the company's own suppliers and then to determine the extent of non-professional or emotional buying which exists. Naturally the implication would be that some suppliers were benefiting and others suffering from this. Then the firm should examine its own sales and customer relationships to discover if this experience or these findings are repeated.

though without approaching some of the more flagrant inertia situations found in heavily branded consumer markets.

The inertia, when it exists, can be exploited by the current supplier even though it may present insuperable problems to firms wishing to break into an account. What are the causes of such apparently irrational behaviour in this professional market? Is it really irrational?

Basically the weight of reasoning behind the choice of a supplier may be non-product in nature; a company may be chosen because of price, quality consistency, delivery reliability, good past service, past co-operation, meeting emergencies, etc. Only one of these, price, is capable of being proven at point of sale. The risk of the buyers being wrong in capital-intensive progressive-assembly industries will favour the existing proven supplier, even when the new supplier has a price advantage. Where a sub-contractor has met delivery needs punctually, a main contractor is unlikely to trade this degree of security for a minor price advantage. Bad-quality components may only show themselves later; a proven supplier is a company asset. The list is endless and it all points to potential inertia in favour of existing suppliers.

Vendor rating may even worsen the situation for the new entrant. Vendor-assessment systems, by introducing a mathematical measure of proven service capabilities, could totally confirm the inertia in an apparently scientific way; we do not *think* they are good, they *are* good.

Over and above the potentially irrational behaviour sources mentioned so far there are some rational ones (this is assuming that the foregoing were irrational, which could be disputed). With complex contracts, e.g. large sub-assemblies for major contracts perhaps specially designed for each and every order, the desire to retain the existing multiple inter-face between a buyer and a supplier must be very strong, if it has proved in any way successful.[8] Apart from the flow of technical liaison there will have developed personal links between people who have worked together, possibly for months. To re-establish all such contacts each time a new contract was placed would clearly be

8. If it has not, there may even be a tendency to learn by past mistakes, rather than start again with another supplier.

undesirable. It suggests that the buyer should choose correctly in the first instance. Inertia between supplier and buyer may be said to be a function of the number and depths of inter-faces.

The marketing lessons of inertia are clear. If it has been established in your favour, then you must maintain it to your obvious advantage. Marketing must become an appraisal function; identifying the profile of the buyer and advising his own supplier unit so that the buyer-supplier compatibility is total. As a measure of efficiency, it might be tentatively suggested that to lose a customer in a potentially inert situation is a good measure of company inadequacy. That there is not universal adequacy gives hope to the new entrant, who must fertilize an apparently barren field until inefficiency on the part of the current supplier manifests itself.[9]

Reciprocal Pressures Can Exist

The customer buying consumer goods is untrammelled by the fear of reciprocal action if he does not favour certain suppliers; the purchase is made in a context where reciprocity would be difficult even to imagine. In the industrial market the situation is one where the buyer may be circumscribed as to his complete freedom of choice, and the seller may have at his disposal strong forces which he can bring to bear on his potential customer.

Reciprocity forces its way into the industrial market in many ways, ranging from the relatively innocuous, through to organized systems which greatly reduce the alleged perfection of this market. If a company is making a product which has a fairly universal market in industry, e.g. a typewriter, then the way is open for numerous variations of reciprocal trading. The manufacturer may spread his purchases of fuel oil, a type of industrial convenience goods with close substitutes, in such a way that no potential customer for typewriters is commercially offended. This is a negative policy, as all other similar manufacturers will perhaps do the same thing, but this makes it more important for each

9. Even then the inertia may show itself in the buyer pointing out the inadequacy and giving a period of grace to rectify the situation, e.g. lower price, better quality.

one to conform rather than risk offence to any particular supplier and potential customer. Such a policy of spreading orders, which may be incorrect from a purchasing-economy viewpoint, is more likely to occur where the number of potential customers is small and/or where each represents a large order, or possible loss of such an order.

Companies may introduce formal systems for the communication of information between the purchasing and sales departments. Purchasing officers may be asked by the sales department to show a special disposition towards a company which has favoured the company with a large order, or to display an amenable attitude prior to the sales department making a sale. Purchasing departments may inform the sales departments of current orders which have been placed, in order that the sales potential of such information can be exploited. Sometimes these formal communication systems aimed at using potential goodwill to the utmost, may be supplemented by less formal arrangements involving personal appeals by senior managers or directors for the patronage of a particular supplier if possible.[10]

The extent to which reciprocal arrangements limit the freedom of customers in the industrial market is difficult to quantify, but certain factors are basic influences on it. Clearly, if the products of the companies do not represent a double coincidence of wants, reciprocal trading is impossible between them; this occurs where a product is made for the government, e.g. armaments. Similarly, when supplying a shipyard with components, e.g. refrigerator equipment, it is difficult to conceive of any reciprocal arrangements because the supplier is unlikely to have any interest in buying ships. Unfortunately we must often look beyond the immediate companies; the make-up of industrial units in modern society is not always so simple as to produce completely autonomous buying and selling units unaffected by associated ones.

10. A slightly different type of reciprocal pressure can show itself where a customer for a large complex item prescribes the supplier of one section of the total complex regardless of the buying opinion of the main contract suppliers. The freedom of choice of the supplier to purchase as he thinks fit is thus limited. Although this practice could have a base in reciprocity or counter-trading, it may simply be a choice based on past experience which has given satisfaction.

Take-over bids and the potential economies of larger organizations and complexes have within them a much greater threat to freedom of choice on the part of the industrial buyer, in that although neither firm, i.e. potential buyer or potential seller, can or does have any direct interest in reciprocal pressures, each or both may be part of industrial complexes, parts of which do have such an interest. The industrial units may not be potential reciprocal traders, but the groups to which they belong could be. A purchasing officer may buy paint from a subsidiary of a company with which his own company has had, or hopes to have, selling transactions; a sales department will be furnished with the purchases made from other companies by all associated companies or members of the complex. Clearly, the growth of diversified large-scale industrial organizations represents a possible reduction in the commercial freedom of industrial buyers and also increases the reciprocal forces supporting industrial sales departments.

The industrial buyer, unlike his consumer-market counterpart, may also be the victim of a further reduction in freedom in his lack of autonomy and his degree of accountability to superior authority. This is related to the restrictive nature of reciprocal arrangements, and when centralization of buying authority, as seen in large organizations, is linked to diversified large industrial complexes, then the inroads into the perfect competition of the industrial market are considerable. It has always been accepted that in a diversified group the ability of the group to meet an order from a member should always be sounded first; but this practice might be extended to cover the ability to meet the order of any firm which has dealings with or could have such dealings with any member of the group, the whole process being centred on centralized control or group buying.

The practice of centralized control proscribing local buying power is not confined to the purely industrial sector. Vertically integrated retail manufacturing groups frequently restrict the goods to be sold through their retail points to those produced by the groups. This, as with the industrial goods decision, calls for a precise judgement of the net advantage to be gained; the greater certainty of sales through controlled outlets and therefore the better spread of on-costs at manufacturing points must be offset against the possible deterrent effect on customers of a restriction in choice.[11] Similarly, buying components from within a group at a price above that which could be obtained elsewhere may or may not reduce the overall profitability of the group depending on the relative prices, the elasticity of the end-market, and the potential idle-capacity on-cost losses if the product is bought outside the group.[12]

If the oligopsonistic nature of some markets is considered along with the tendency to diversified larger industrial complexes and the drive to centralized control of buying and even selling, then the traditional viewpoint that these markets are more perfect must be in some doubt. Perhaps an overriding factor which allows or limits the extent of reciprocal trading, where this type of trading is feasible, is the pressure of profit margins in the final market; this would be projected back to the purchasing budgets and would reduce the monetary tolerance which might be needed for reciprocal pressures to be effective.

The practising marketeer must react to reciprocal pressures on the ground. He requires complete knowledge of all the existing and potential reciprocal arrangements when planning his marketing strategy. This will indicate customers on whom pressures can be brought to bear and those subjected to similar pressures from competitors. The situation is dynamic, as companies are taken over and industrial complexes become larger and more diverse. The possible consequences of such developments should be foreseen wherever possible, so that the necessary hedging can take place. The marketeer should be aware of future possible

---

11. There may also be other advantages, such as a more accurate control of distribution stocks at all levels, and better knowledge of retail turnovers, which can be the basis of production planning. On the managerial side, it can be argued that the managerial function at retail level has been so commercially restricted as to create the need for a different type of manager who can carry out his function with very restricted terms of reference, e.g. on the goods he buys and sells.

12. Marginal analysis and its application to costing could well work here if there were no possibility of outside work for the capacity which would become idle within the group. If direct costs were met, plus any contribution to overheads, the practice of in-group trading would be justified.

groupings and the effect of these on the freedom of choice of his existing customers. If this freedom is in danger of being restricted, emphasis may have to be placed on other customers to maximize goodwill, and on the discovery of new ones to replace those likely to be lost.

The Customer Is Knowledgeable and Rationally Motivated

The buyer is a professional: he might be a purchasing officer, machine-shop superintendent, plant manager, transport chief, accountant, multiple buyer, civil servant, personnel manager, etc. Sometimes the knowledge of many will be grouped to achieve the best buy in the known circumstances. Whatever the form of the purchasing activity, individual or group, it will be informed both commercially and technically, and motivated almost entirely by economics, i.e. the need to maintain and improve the wellbeing of the enterprise. (We shall question the complete validity of this statement later, but it provides a reasonable statement of the general industrial marketing situation and it would be folly to assume otherwise; any irrational motivation is superimposed on this.)

The sources of economic motivation can come from within the product itself or the company which supplies it; these are termed product patronage motives and company patronage motives respectively. Among the motives associated with the product in the purchase of capital equipment are economy, productivity, dependability, labour-saving and durability. In raw-material and component markets we find correct quality, uniformity of quality, purity, dependability and the ability to enhance the vendibility of the end-product, as dominant product motives. In the market for supplies (consumed items not entering into the final product) we find motives similar to those for raw materials.

Company patronage motives, like product motives, result from the cost-benefit drives of the three types of industrial goods. Reliability of seller, technical co-operation, price policy, good after-sales service, and past experience of the firm are dominant with capital equipment; continual supply under all conditions, quality and delivery reliability of the seller, ease of access to seller (physical and communications), prices and ability to meet emergency needs, are crucial company patronage motives for raw materials, components and supplies. Credit is always a potential company patronage motive, particularly if the sale is of expensive capital equipment or there is pressure on the working-capital resources of the customer.

Where the specification is given,[13] either by the customer, as in the case of large progressive-assembly manufacturers, or by a third party, e.g. the B.S.I., A.P.I. or B.P., then product patronage does not exist, as no product advantage can be obtained by any company. Company patronage motives will then fully occupy the customer's choice of supplier. Suppliers will be chosen on their ability to meet the specification in terms of technical ability, quality standards, consistency and reliability, price, delivery, performance, etc.

If the article is a speciality good without competition, then product patronage dominates. Where the customer need is met by the evolution of a better component or substitute raw material, or more effective machines, then again product patronage motivation is the one which has appealed to the purchaser.

To the extent that the product is specified, company patronage tends to dominate; whereas if the product to be sold is unique in any way or has economic advantages, the motivation will derive from this source.

Companies should analyse customer motivation and its breakdown into product and company patronage in order to ascertain the aspects of their organizations which should receive emphasis to enable them to meet customer motivation. Supplying a specified product to a main public contractor who is using network analysis will become a matter of price, quality control and, in particular, production planning and delivery – all company patronage motives. Meeting the needs of a customer faced with reduced profit margins for his end-product may involve both product patronage motives through value analysis and the provision of a cheaper component, and also company patronage motives through price, reduced inventories, cheaper credit, etc.

13. The greater the occurrence of horizontal disintegration and progressive assembly at centralized locations, the more likely it is that suppliers will make to customer specification.

Although there are more obvious motives which must be exploited in the industrial market, the scientific marketeer must recognize and identify the dynamics of the buying situation which result in different priorities being given to these motives. The industrial marketing 'mix' must respond to the motivation 'mix' of the customer in the same way as in the consumer field but, whereas in the latter case the consumer can be modified to a large extent by persuasion, in the industrial field the motivation is relatively fixed as it is the result of external economic forces which cannot be rebuffed.

The sales-promotion policy of the industrial marketeer must respond to the rational behaviour of the customer by presenting in its content a pronounced economic bias. Advertising will be informative in a manner which appeals to the potential buyer; this may show a purely technical emphasis, but is more likely to appeal to the hybrid technical and cost-effectiveness motivation of the reader.

The recruitment and training of sales representatives will be based on the need to sell on economic information rather than on emotion. Representatives will be required to develop a controlled sympathy and understanding, i.e. empathy, for the technical and cost problems of the firms on whom they call. Motives are identified and exploited by the industrial representative as much as they are by his counterpart in the consumer field; only the nature of the motives is changed.

Nevertheless, sales-promotion devices may contain within them emotional elements to help achieve their objective even in this allegedly rational market. Sex, curiosity and humour are among the emotions which can be used to attract attention in advertisements or at exhibitions. Salesmen will be seen to be equipped in clothes and transport to perform their jobs on behalf of an obviously successful company; to be otherwise may be considered an 'unselling' activity which would be serious in a marginal or difficult market.

The ability to attract or to retain the confidence of the customer in the industrial market can only serve as an introduction to the product or service which is for sale. The rational, mainly economic motivation will take over control of the customer once the introduction has been successfully made; nevertheless, the importance of such introductions, even to the best products and companies, must not be underestimated.

We must now examine the more dynamic motives in the complex of the purchasing 'mix' of the industrial buyer; the total sales policy and sales promotion plan should always be in harmony with the current priorities and this may require research beyond the immediate transaction.

The Quality Standard

Where a quality standard is enforced by an outside body, then this is 'given' in the specification and is dominant in the motivation; it must be met.[14] The same applies where a large assembler has laid down his material or component requirement; it is beyond argument and has to be technically met; it may be of high or low quality, however.

Where a component forms an important part of an end-product and is a potential cause of dissatisfaction, economic or emotional, on the part of the final customer, then the necessary priority quality rating will have to be given to it by the supplier. Any failure by the component or industrial finish would react unfavourably on the end-product brand-owner, who would then project this on to the real source of the loss of customer goodwill, i.e. the supplier of the component or finish.

Where a company enters a new quality segment in the end-market, the potential supplier of industrial goods must re-orientate to meet the new customer needs. If rapid obsolescence is becoming more common in a market, then the lower intrinsic quality standard which may be associated with customer motivation in such a market will make itself felt in the specification of industrial buyers.

14. Quality standards may vary as between markets. Sometimes a country may be more tolerant on quality standards than others, e.g. one country may be more tolerant on certain safety or equipment standards than another. The marketeer must expect a different quality-price relationship to exist in such markets. Quality priority to an industrial customer does not always imply top quality, but only the specified quality, which could be high or low.

Clearly, all quality motivations are dynamic as markets and segments change; price and quality are linked motives but do not necessarily move in unison. The priority given to each one by the customer and their relationship to each other must be appreciated by the marketeer, who must respond accordingly.

Vendor-rating systems are often dominated by quality control – they may even be run by quality-control departments. This is a manifestation of the weighted importance given to it by the potential customer. Many industrial orders are prefaced by visits to potential suppliers to investigate quality-control capability in practice. As stated earlier, very important customers may request changes in the management structure to enable them to feel more confident in quality capability and assurance. Thus the quality-control department may be made directly responsible to the General Manager, rather than to the Production Manager.

The State of the Final Market – Price Motivation

There should be complete commercial compatibility between the seller of industrial goods and the final market of his customer. Where profit margins in an end-market are under pressure, or where a new type of competition has shown itself, or the final customer has become more price-conscious in a saturated market, then the dominant motivation of the industrial buyer will move towards price. The supplier might meet this new situation by increased efficiency, by suggesting greater quality tolerance where this is possible to allow for a lower price, or by introducing value-analysis techniques in order to supply the customers with a cheaper but suitable product. There is a continuing need for the industrial supplier and his customer to be compatible in their expectation of profit margins; if end-product margins are reduced, high ones cannot be expected by component suppliers.

The supply of raw materials and components must always be made with an awareness of the possible consequences on the end-market of price changes in these products. If the component makes up only a small part of the total cost of the end-product, the market for which is inelastic, then price changes in the component are not significant, e.g. a £200 component for a power station; when the component is an important part of the cost of the end-product and the market is elastic, then the situation is totally different, e.g. a small component used many times in the manufacture of a car.

Price-consciousness might show itself in high fixed-cost industries faced with a declining market. These circumstances may lead to orders being taken at a price below total cost but covering direct costs and making some contribution to fixed costs. Clearly, in this type of situation the buyer will make a greater contribution to fixed costs the more he can cut down the cost of bought-out components, supplies, raw materials, etc. The marketeer selling to a firm in this situation would identify price as the prime purchasing motive.

Where material or component costs are high because of their intrinsic value or the quantities needed, then in price-conscious markets a cost-benefit motivation could be a reduction in the working capital needed by the buyer to sustain his production schedule. Tighter control of delivery by the supplier could reduce the buffer-stocks needs of the customer, thus reducing his working-capital budget. A similar economy might be achieved if inspection of incoming goods could be reduced or eliminated because of the proven consistency of quality of the supplier.

If the end-market is increasingly competitive, the supplier of equipment should develop more economical machines to help the potential customer meet the challenge. Suppliers of components and industrial finishes might aim at increasing the vendability of the end-product by improving their product or reducing its price.

The demand for industrial goods is a derived demand and cannot escape the conditions of the final market. A washing-machine manufacturer will respond to cost benefits from his component suppliers if his own market becomes more difficult; a cheaper 'standard' electric motor may be viewed with distinct pleasure as a means of reducing the costs of production, spare-parts inventories and after-sales service.

Naturally any attempts at price reduction or containment do require a caveat to cover quality standards. Tolerance on quality specification makes price concessions easier to achieve.

The Degree of Control of Buying

Tighter profit margins can result in a much closer control of costs and lead to a wider use of budgetary control, but an enlightened firm will use such a system regardless of the state of the end-market as a means of maximizing profits. Wherever a customer introduces budgetary control, including strict material budgets, then the range of prices which can be considered by the customer is, by definition, within the confines of the budget. Where it is known that a company is seeking or has obtained a contract by competitive tender, then this would appear to presuppose the existence of an estimate for materials, sub-assemblies or even pieces of equipment; the seller of any of these commodities must then operate within this strict term of reference relating to price.

When an autonomous unit has been taken over by a larger undertaking, it might become subjected to a centralized control which extends over the purchasing function; the consequences of this are many. The various units may be required to obtain approval for purchases made locally; group buying may be a source of economies which cannot be ignored; comparative costing or auditing might be introduced between units buying and/or making similar articles. One outcome of such practices is the removal of any scope for regional sentiment on the part of the local buyer; his scientific controllers are not involved in these human relationships; the very rational type of buying always assumed to exist in industrial markets will now become even more so.

Industrial marketeers would require to react to the new centralized situation sympathetically. Power and authority in purchasing would have to be identified and sales methods changed to comply. Negotiations with more senior people over potentially larger orders might replace local unit selling; the use of agents might be examined and rejected as being unsuitable for the new type of market situation. Complete scientific objectivity and cost-consciousness on the part of the purchasing function would be met on the supply side by discounting any emotional content and placing increased emphasis on cost benefits.

At the same time, centralized control of purchasing might open up new opportunities for suppliers who had previously only enjoyed a local market. The natural corollary to centralized purchasing is that the local supplier becomes known throughout the larger buying organization, to his benefit or otherwise. If the local supply price is acceptable, the larger organization, in effect, becomes a marketing organization for the local supplier; the central organization buying and helping in the distribution of a much larger order.

The tendency towards larger industrial complexes and the wider use of budgetary control of all aspects of production could lead to a continuing reduction of local purchasing authority and its replacements by centralized agencies. The total development would diminish any emotional content associated with regional sentiment. Extra-regional purchasing will be increased as units become larger and less parochial in knowledge and sympathy. The local supplier must then compete in his selling with a much wider range of potential suppliers.[15]

Fear of Breakdown

Throughout any discussion of motivation in the industrial market, cost benefits or economic wellbeing must be the recurring theme; any slight variation in detail, e.g. increased price-consciousness or greater quality tolerances, is based on this basic motivation or drive. The organization of many modern industrial units is of the progressive-assembly or flow-production type. This method of production normally entails heavy fixed costs in equipment and the implication that a breakdown in any part of the production process can halt the whole activity; heavy on-cost losses can thus be incurred if, through any fault, the plant is reduced to less than top efficiency. A breakdown by machines or in the provision of components, raw materials or supplies from outside are clearly among the more obvious causes of economic

15. The knowledge of extra-regional suppliers and the ability and willingness to engage in commercial dialogues with overseas buyers have perhaps been affected by the increasing professionalism of industrial purchasing, the liberalization of trade, the widespread discussion of overseas and 'common market' arrangements, etc.

frustration in modern industry. Whenever a firm is so organized that fear of a breakdown is a dominant economic motive, the marketing mix of the potential supplier must match this motivation.

Machines will be sold on their dependability, which will be linked with the design of the equipment. Maintenance and repair facilities demanded by the equipment will be geared to the standard of labour available within the buyer's plant; if maintenance labour is of poor quality, the machine will be designed to allow for this; replacement of parts may replace repairs; the need for maintenance will be reduced or the job will be made easier. After-sales service will be of the calibre necessary to reduce to a minimum the economic consequences of a breakdown.[16]

Raw materials and other supplies will also be sold on consistency of quality and availability of supply under all conditions. If the supplies are intended to dovetail into a large schedule of operations, perhaps governed by network analysis, then the onus of correct and timely delivery is even more important. Even where penalty clauses do not make obvious the loss to the customer of a breakdown in supplies on such work, e.g. shipbuilding and construction work, the loss of customer goodwill in a market with a high degree of awareness and inter-customer communications could have serious repercussions on future sales.

Labour unrest, or a threat of it, in the supply unit might show dramatically the fear of breakdown in the motivation of the customer, in that orders may be split between suppliers when purchasing economies might suggest otherwise. Personnel policy thus has clear marketing effects.

The fear of a breakdown in supplies militates against a continued use of intermediaries in industrial selling. The natural desire is to make direct contact with those responsible for a breakdown in supplies or machines; the introduction of an agent

16. Tentatively, the writer suggests that his findings show that engineers and buyers always assume that a machine will break down; the worth of a supplier is seen in the speed of after-sales service. There is even a suggestion that a firm which has diligently attended a breakdown or meets an emergency is rated at least as high as the firm whose machine has not broken down. An 'unselling' event, a breakdown, can thus be made into a sales aid: another quality of the supply firm has been proven.

prevents this and might even add to the sense of frustration caused by the breakdown.

Again the buying situation is dynamic. The method of production may move from job to batch and then to mass production, the motivation changing accordingly. Machines may become more expensive, and so fear of their being idle increases. Labour may begin to assume the character of fixed costs because of wage awards, thus increasing the cost of producing nothing when production is interrupted. The machines themselves may have to be more complex to be economically desirable in production terms; if this is incompatible with the standard of labour available for servicing, then steps must be taken to remedy this either by training customers' employees or by setting up the necessary after-sales service.

The consequences of a breakdown caused by any aspect of the supply company's activities should be determined and should play a major part in the marketing strategy. The breakdown could be in the product or in its supply or after-sales servicing. The article may only be a very minor part of an installation, e.g. an electric motor, a compressor, or even a lubricant, but the consequences of its failure could be economically serious. The resultant loss of goodwill between the customer and the supplier is a function of the extent of the economic dislocation caused by the disruption; further orders will be influenced by this and the availability of substitutes. In addition, the speed of communications between customers in this market may increase the penalty consequences of the breakdown so far as further orders from other customers are concerned.

Other Factors

CREDIT

The importance of credit could vary with the financial size of the buyer; the larger and increasingly dominant industrial unit could well reject credit as a purchasing motivation affecting selection of supplier. This would be logical in that the financial resources at the disposal of the larger unit would render trade credit facilities less necessary. Nevertheless there could be specific cases where there is an increased pressure on working capital which might increase the motivation rating given to credit. Studies of cash flow may show the extent of credit already given to customers, quite apart from the longer-term conventional credit. An analysis should be made of the working-capital costs of the current method of instalment payments during a contract, particularly during periods of high interest rates. The marketing advantages of such methods of payment and the consequences of changing them must be measured against their financial implication. Where credit is standard practice, to refuse it on the normal terms may create a comparative disadvantage, dangerous if other things are equal.

The Independent Dealer and the Agent

The high value of the unit of sale will often preclude indirect dealing in the industrial market, because of the desire to have complete control of the selling operation. This is largely rational and is based on the size and importance of the order, but clearly it could have a basis in the fear of losing the order through the default of an outsider. Reciprocity is clearly difficult, if not impossible, when dealers intervene between the two sides.

The complexity of the product or the range may also militate against the use of independent dealers, particularly if the dealers with the necessary technical 'know-how' are already under a restrictive contract to other competing manufacturers. The new entrant to a market may then have to choose between direct dealing, perhaps even for small orders, and the alternative of using below-standard dealers with possible serious long-term effects on the reputation of his goods and the service provided with them.

On the other hand, exclusive concessions to dealers of the required calibre would be an advantageous arrangement if it was necessary to combine maximum economy in distribution with loyalty and efficiency in selling and service. A by-product of such a policy is the restricting effect that it would have on the entry of later competitors if the concessional agreement had restrictive clauses.

The use of independent dealers or agents for components, supplies, raw materials, or equipment suffers in that it prevents the customer from making the direct contact with the manu-facturer which he may rationally and emotionally desire. The introduction of an intermediary in the communication system to the manufacturer might be thought to delay complaints regarding service, delivery, etc. This fear by the customer will be enlarged with increases in the fear of breakdowns which, in turn, is deter-mined largely by the method of production of the customer; progressive-assembly or flow-production units may well prefer direct dealing.

Difficulties in communication, created by intermediaries, can reduce the effectiveness of field marketing research. The face-to-face contact of the industrial sales representative can be a most useful source of consumer reaction and make a constructive contribution to product research and changes in the range and services of the company.

THE POSITION OF THE PURCHASING AUTHORITY

It is vital in industrial marketing to identify in each firm the source of authority for purchase of each type of product or service. This information can influence the whole sales-promotion activity from advertising and exhibitions to personal selling.

The industrial purchasing officer does not enjoy a consistent level of authority and responsibility throughout industry: some-times the function may be comprehensive and cover the com-mercial aspect of all purchasing, including equipment; at other times, the holder of the position may resemble more closely an order-clerk, as the work-flow through the department does not allow for any initiation of work. The order-processing aspect might completely dominate, to the exclusion of the research function which is vital if any really comprehensive view is to be taken of purchasing. The status of the professional purchasing officer may be enhanced where progressive assembly has been introduced and fear of breakdown of supplies is great; value analysis may also benefit from the contribution of a purchasing officer with full knowledge of potential suppliers, costs and sub-stitute materials; pressure on profit margins in high-material-cost industries could help boost the position of purchasing in the management team.

The more important the purchasing function in any buying activity, the greater the need to orientate all selling towards the professional industrial buyer. This could involve a reappraisal of personal attitudes on the part of salesmen and their management; similarly, other sales-promotion activities would be re-orientated towards the attention and needs of the purchasing officer; advertising may need to be realigned as to media and copy to meet the needs of a possibly less technical mind; invitations for him to visit supply plants will be increased; the commercial and economic aspect of the selling activity may be emphasized rather than the technical.[17]

The decision to purchase may be in the hands of other executives, all of whom must be identified and appraised. Formal or informal committee decisions may be the basis of a choice of industrial supplier, and this could require a much broader-based sales-promotion activity. Advertising may have to be aimed at all members of such committees who in any way contribute towards the purchasing decision; this could involve media and copy covering the whole spectrum from the informative to the prestigious. The formal and informal committee decision is an open manifestation of group dynamics in buying; but this could be more covert. Dominant personalities within a decision-taking group might have to be identified and exploited by the marketeer; clearly, this could be a situation calling for the maximum detection effort by the sales organization in order to maintain contact with a possibly changing balance of power and personalities within the buying unit. The group dynamics associated with buying decisions could clearly lend themselves to emotional exploitation, contrary to the widely held belief that this type of marketing is completely rational.

All buyers, including those buying industrial goods, are human. The purchasers of components, materials, machine tools

17. It is probable that sheer technical ability is not enough to equip an industrial salesman; cost-benefit knowledge is a better means of meeting the motivation of the customer. Selection, training and sales planning would be organized to meet this need.

and office equipment, all possess to some extent the normal instinctive complexes which will respond to a lesser or greater degree to emotional sales techniques. Where industrial goods or services are equal in calibre, or where the sale of these goods through rational motives has reached a stalemate, emotions could well take over to make the marginal distinction.

To meet such situations, the private likes and dislikes of industrial customers should be identified and exploited; both are potential sources of selling and 'unselling' behaviour. Health, families, sport, religion, education, holidays and hobbies are some of the social bridges over which the qualities of the products can be conveyed. Promotion and managerial politics often dominate industrial buyers and it would be folly to ignore these strong interests. The marginally better product may be reduced to the level of the average by an 'unselling' remark; the average one taken above the margin by good emotional exploitation.

INDUSTRIAL MARKETING RESEARCH

The use of the term 'marketing research' rather than 'market research' is not due to a semantic quibble. The importance of each customer in most industrial markets demands a micro-approach to be superimposed on the research into the markets or total political economy, i.e. the macro-approach. A complete and objective analysis of the comparative compatibility of asset utilization or activities of all the suppliers to a market and the current motivation of customers would require to be made. This would involve a scientific auditing of comparative strengths of competitors in a market and the current and/or potential motivation priorities of customers. This audit would then be followed by recommendations on asset usage or activities to improve the current or future competitive position of the company. The steps in the process might be as follows:

1. A complete appraisal of the current and/or potential patronage motives of the customers. This would cover product and company patronage with their sub-divisions.

2. An attempt to list these motives in order of customer priority. In some cases, product patronage motives may rate very low, motivation being dominated by the expected service from the supplier, e.g. prompt delivery, price, etc. In other cases, patronage may be entirely a creation of the product, as when speciality equipment is supplied. Broadly, where products are equal and available from many sources, then motivation will stem from company service, the product being neutral; and vice versa.

3. An impartial self-analysis of the strengths and weaknesses of the company, i.e. its marketing 'mix'. This would be extended in appropriate cases to the sales-promotion activities, i.e. the selling 'mix'. Where marketing 'mixes' are equal, selling may create a comparative advantage. However, selling ability is less likely in this market to make up for inadequacy in other aspects of the company's activities. Thus if reliability of delivery or quality is defective, selling could not compensate for these shortcomings.

4. A comparison of the marketing 'mix' and the priority ratings of customers. This is an exercise in measuring compatibility between the company's activities or asset usage and the needs of customers.

5. An objective study of the marketing 'mixes' or strategies of competitors and their compatibility with customer motivation.

6. An estimate of the comparative or relative standing of the company in the market.

7. A decision on the need to, or feasibility of, changing the marketing 'mix' to create or enhance a comparative advantage over competitors. This could concern redeployment of assets, e.g. an increased allocation to production planning and control to ensure better delivery in response to customer rating.

This type of investigation is mainly concerned with achieving economic advantages over competitors in a rational market. Where these advantages are equal, others may be sought on the emotional side. In particular, any company enjoying an emotional advantage with a customer should identify the extent of this and the consequences of disturbing it by bad marketing behaviour;

this would be measured not only in any profits lost on those orders, but also the fixed cost no longer covered by the orders; this cost may be considerable and could affect price policy towards other customers.

Marketing research must identify changes in the motivation 'mix' of each customer; perhaps less attention to quality, more to price, greater need to save labour through equipment, more urgency about prompt delivery. The importance of each customer justifies this detail. His motivation is 'given', it must be discovered and reacted to sympathetically and quickly. Good communications to the various important activities likely to influence the competitive position of a company are vital.

The research must attempt some assessment of the importance of customers both at present and, particularly, in the future. This may influence the desirability of a change in activities or asset usage. Similarly, the investigation must cover the nature of reciprocal pressures within the market so that strategy can be adjusted accordingly; once again, the future situation is vital. Trends towards a monopsonistic market must also be tracked and their implications studied. The influence of increased centralized control of the buying of subsidiaries would require attention, particularly if the tendency in a market was towards bigger groupings.

Marketing research should mean what it says – research which maintains the marketing position of the company at the most profitable level. It helps to achieve the maximum compatibility between customer attitudes and assets and their utilization. This also involves forecasting the trend of the present usage of assets and the need to change either the assets or their uses, i.e. the markets they supply. In the industrial market, the time needed to introduce a new plant, develop a new product, or improve a process may be very long indeed. The need to have the plant, product, or process available and proven when the new market is ready requires a forecast in time for all the necessary development work to be done, plant to be built, prototypes tested etc. Good marketing research would enable the necessary synchronization of availability and market impact; in the industrial market with its increasingly complex items and the time needed to develop them, this aspect of marketing research is more difficult but even more vital if profit maximization is to be maintained at all times.

A POSSIBLE SOURCE OF IRRATIONAL BEHAVIOUR BY PURCHASING OFFICERS[18]

It is not suggested that attention to the emotional aspect of industrial buying will succeed or offset any economic disadvantages that a product or service possesses. All marketing is concerned with seeking comparative advantages; where these cannot, or do not, exist on an economic or rational level, then they must be sought in other ways, i.e. by appealing to emotions. In addition, the power of emotions in the industrial market may be more evident in that they result in a lack of the expected complete objectivity on the part of the buyer, who might have his judgement impaired if he is emotionally disturbed. This could be caused by an unconscious 'unselling' act on the part of the industrial sales representative or his supporting organization. It is often the 'unselling' consequence of emotional disturbance which might create a comparative disadvantage which we are considering, rather than the positive contribution to industrial selling which could be achieved by appealing to the emotions. Also we must not underestimate the importance of emotional relationships in the rectification of a selling situation between customer and supplier, e.g. when past inadequacies must be explained to regain the old standing of the supply firm.

For too long it has been assumed that motivation research techniques are restricted to the markets for consumer goods; certainly the esoteric nature of some of the work in this field seems more appropriate to the sale of cosmetics, cars and refrigerators, rather than nuts, bolts and gaskets. An analysis of the function of industrial purchasing, however, suggests that there are possible sources of irrational behaviour in the industrial market and that basically these have the same roots as those giving rise to emotional buying by the general public.

18, Largely extracted from an article by the author in *Scientific Business*, Spring 1966.

The purchasing officer is in a unique position in the formal organization of most firms; the function, and therefore the office-holder, is generally completely cut off from any vertical or line relationships within the organization structure and both formally and informally all relationships and communications are lateral. He enjoys a staff status advising line managers in engineering, scheduling, design, estimating and costing, sales, etc. Even his line authority within his own department is usually limited in terms of staff employed and under his control. He does not, as a rule, initiate any work in the same way as his managerial associates instead he works to specifications given by others who are in a lateral relationship to him. This order-clerk aspect of his function could soon lead to a feeling of subordination and frustration due to the nature of the job and the direction of normal work flow; such a situation completely lacks any source of authority.

Lateral relationships, with their suggestion of formal equality, are an obvious source of political pressures and 'bureaucratic gamesmanship', and investigations have shown that the purchasing officer, in order to boost his position in the group, will resort to many devices;[19] clearly, in this particular case the practice is further encouraged by the lack of formal authority. The measures taken to increase status are intended to compensate for the lack of initiative within the job of buying, and would cover such devices as questioning a specification, suggesting substitute materials, demanding more time to place an order, querying the costs, modifying quantities in the light of inventories and price changes, etc. All these activities show a desire to initiate rather than merely receive an order. They could be based on genuine appraisal; but they could contain some degree of emotion. The nature of the job and its position in the organization structure will engender a greater desire to enhance authority than might be the case with other members of the management group. It is part of a striving for indispensability, acceptance and security.

The overall true function of a purchasing officer does not, however, merely cover the order-processing activity; in addition, there is the active research into markets, prices, materials, suppliers,

19. See Strauss, *Administrative Science Quarterly*, Vol. 7, 161, on 'Practice of Lateral Relationship: the Purchasing Agent'.

terms, etc. This is the side of his function which could be a good source of authority and might lead to irrational behaviour which is of special interest to industrial marketeers.

The environment in which the modern purchasing officer works is world-wide; communications and the increased liberalization of trade over recent years have put distant suppliers within his reach. Discussions on E.F.T.A., E.E.C., etc. in professional journals and in newspapers help this widening of his horizon, and make him much more at home with distant suppliers. The purchasing officer, when looking for increased managerial status, could seek this by emphasizing the market research function of his job. There could be a possible source of authority in an ability to deal with consummate ease with suppliers from afar; the more distant in miles, customs, language, political ideology and finance, the greater the esteem created by the dialogue. Buying outside the region might be expected to increase the mystique of the activity, whereas buying locally could have the opposite effect; to show their professional approach it may become necessary to deliberately fight against local sentiment.

There could be a conscious attempt to gain authority from within this research aspect of the job and, from a marketing view-point, this is of some importance. It could lead to the reframing of advertisements which stress local sentiment rather than the product; sales forces could be redeployed; point-of-sales techniques altered; invitations to purchasing officers to visit distant plants could be stepped up, etc. At the least this desire to boost the standing of the function by dealing with extra-regional suppliers could remove the assumed strength of local suppliers; at the most, it might even be an advantage to be from afar. (N.B. There is obviously a basic assumption that all other things are equal, e.g. price, quality, delivery, etc.) The distant supplier is identified with the subconscious desire for acceptance within the group – a motivation force very similar to the ones used in consumer goods selling. This similarity between the two markets, consumer and industrial goods, can also be seen elsewhere in the industrial seller-buyer situation and can be similarly exploited.

Although value-analysis and vendor-rating activities are obvious ways for work initiation, discussion and the advancement of status by the purchasing officer, any desire to obtain as much technical information as possible, regardless of the existence of formal value analysis or assessment activities, might show a belief that security and acceptability are linked with technical and economic contributions to management discussions. Non-informative advertising should therefore perhaps be avoided in journals and brochures, because such advertising may be a reminder of ignorance and may even increase awareness of it; it in no way helps the purchasing officer to achieve the desired status. This is the antithesis of good advertising, which tries to identify itself with the wants of the reader. Informative copy is required to help the reader, the industrial buyer, in his attempt to achieve authority and security in his working group; lack of information in an advertisement could alienate the potential customer.

The purchasing officer wishes to initiate discussion with other managers based on newly acquired technical and commercial information or, less positively, to be able to question their specification, etc. In those situations where many suppliers are equal – common enough today – and where the search element in the purchasing function is greatest (specification and brand ordering being limited), then the effects of bad communications through advertisements, etc., could seriously jeopardize sales. In these conditions, all sales literature and every sales representative should obviously do all that is possible to help the industrial buyer to make the maximum contribution to inter-departmental discussion. Advertising which stresses branded goods, to the exclusion of other matters, accentuates the order-processing aspect of the purchasing function; where a departmental initiation specifies brand, supplier, etc., giving the buyer no chance to show his professional ability, so this could tend to alienate him.

The external relationships of the purchasing function, unlike the internal ones, are good sources of authority. The purchasing officer, through a commercial sanction, has more power and authority over people outside the organization; he has a type of external vertical line relationship given authority by commerce. The implication of this from a marketing viewpoint can easily be deduced. It is important to avoid, on the part of representatives or sales officers, any action which reduces this feeling of power and authority which is needed to compensate for the lack of internal status. The professional purchasing officer will dislike representatives who are late; those who are badly briefed, technically and financially; those who are inadequate in the knowledge of their firm's requirements; the speculative caller who thus tends to assume that the officer could always find time (belittling of the importance of his work); those who call with nothing new to offer, again with the assumption that time is plentiful. In a marketing situation where so many potential suppliers are equal, this slighting of the buyer could be the marginal 'unselling' activity. The officer's professional objectivity and impartiality could be affected by such incidences, to the detriment of the offending firm.

Purchasing officers may also dislike dealing with agents and agents' representatives; they may prefer direct dealing with the manufacturer. The reasons given may be rational: the need to be near to the cause of any breakdown and not have to deal through an intermediary; or the lack of technical know-how on the part of representatives. Is there a chance that behind this rationalism there is an emotional protest against dealing with the second-best? Could it be that the contact with the industrial heart of things gives rise to more satisfaction than dealing through a local commercial intermediary? Does it not give the sense of authority which is lacking elsewhere?

Any analysis of purchasing motives which investigates progressive-assembly firms must draw attention to the top motivation fear of breakdown, either of machines, services or supplies. Purchasing officers might enthuse about the speed with which a defaulting firm rectifies a situation; this is remembered perhaps more than the breakdown itself. Is there, perhaps, some subconscious desire to be proved correct in the choice of supplier? It would be somewhat naïve to suggest that the defaulter who remedied the breakdown quickly is more respected than the one who never defaulted; but, as the main reason for change of supplier might be the negative one of dissatisfaction with the existing supplier, sales people might note that what is an 'unselling' activity (the breakdown) can be converted into a sales aid.

Reciprocity often concerns pressure from the sales manager or a director on the buyer to be less objective in choosing his source of supplies. With tight budgets, the practice would be restricted if not eliminated, but slack budgets could help to foster it. Unwillingness to upset a fellow manager or director could also play a part and, in certain economic circumstances, the buyer's acquiescence in reciprocal dealing may result. However, it is perhaps just as logical to suggest that such a situation might enable the buyer to demonstrate to other managers the professional content of the job; this would result in an 'anti' attitude towards the unprofessional practice of reciprocity.

Another possible source of emotional alienation between supplier and buyer occurs where the price quoted is suddenly drastically reduced in the face of new competition; such a happening tends to deflate the professional ego of the buyer who has failed in the research side of his job. Firms which charge 'what the traffic will bear' might well be advised to be fully informed on potential competition so that the price can be voluntarily reduced, if possible, in stages. In this way the maximum amount of goodwill could be built up.

As with all motivation analysis, this topic is open-ended; deductions and conclusions, some tenuous and some reasonable, could continue to be drawn from the basic analysis. The aim of this section has been to draw attention to the possible existence of irrational behaviour in a field which has been considered largely free from emotions, and to suggest a possible cause in the nature of the work done and its place in an organization. From the analysis follow a number of tactical moves which should be made by sales planners. Perhaps the conclusion is that motivation research, by going into the emotional aspect, can discover sources of irrational behaviour in most types of purchasing and not just in the consumer-goods markets – 'Jonesmanship' in office furniture and equipment has long been suspected. Selling industrial supplies, raw materials, components, services and perhaps even equipment might utilize the desire of industrial buyers to be accepted by the group and to achieve increased security.

PART SIX

WHITHER MARKETING?

All professions are a conspiracy against the laity.

G. B. S.

IF marketing is regarded as the means to the perpetuation of optimum profit, then, given a competitive system, there can be no reason to consider any reduction in its importance; and certainly any consideration of its demise would be so premature as to seem improper.

The future position and content of marketing, both functionally and conceptually, depend almost entirely on the position taken up on the content of marketing. Marketing has often fallen into disrepute, within firms and sometimes over a wider field, because it has appeared to be doing as a specialized function what was already being done by the existing functions. This is often true and is not peculiar to marketing: personnel specialists are only doing what was done previously by line management; so are accountants and production engineers. Marketing is only performing the tasks of the entrepreneur by finding markets, matching these with capabilities, finding new markets to take up existing capability, studying customers, analysing competitive standing, presenting possible new sources of comparative advantage, and recommending and executing policies and plans to optimize supplier–customer relationships.

Should a business fail to do well or if it does no better than before marketing was functionally specialized, then it is a natural reaction when cutting overheads to remove an obvious candidate. In practice, advertising is often a function of profits, rather than vice versa; it may well be that the unquestioning establishment and acceptance of marketing departments are, in many instances, the consequence of easy market conditions and profits, rather than that marketing departments are seen as the basis for profits when these are under strain. Why has marketing not received the same degree of acceptability as a functional specialization as personnel management or accountancy? Are there any reasons other than the one already outlined, i.e. that it is a worthy specialized activity which we can only afford when costs do not matter?

Often the practitioners are to blame for its non-acceptance; this statement can be aimed at the general practitioner (marketing managers) as well as towards the many subdivisions of the practice (e.g. advertising managers). Rarely are positive efforts made by these specialists to demonstrate their contribution to the common weal of an enterprise; yet the very intangible nature of their output makes it even more important that acceptability should be worked for, rather than deemed to be natural. The setting of agreed and definable objectives and their subsequent achievement would undoubtedly accelerate acceptance. But perhaps the greatest threat to the separate existence of marketing as a function (as distinct from, but comprehending, selling, which usually has little to fear in most cases for its recognition) is in the static view of the nature of marketing from the functional viewpoint.

If marketing is viewed as merely the research and forecasting element in scientific management, then its future as an important specialist activity could well be limited, particularly when such work is restricted to general information such as market potential, trends, shares.

The use of such information as a source of comparative advantage was only possible when the practice of market research was rare; advantage can be gained from statistical forecasting and analysis of this type only in so far as one's immediate or potential competitors desist from the practice. The refinement of the research technique may be relied upon to give further possible comparative leads; but these refinements themselves tend to shorten the period of such leads by involving more scientific and mathematical methods which remove intuition and so replace chance distribution of knowledge and capability by a plateau of market awareness achieved through common methods and information sources.

Furthermore, the investigation of customers themselves has become a transferable and largely common technique. The discovery of a segment and the design of a consensus model for a segment are no longer an art; they are something which specialists are assumed to be able to do with well established expertise.

To be seen as a source of comparative advantage, marketing,

both functionally and conceptually, must move from market and customer investigation to capability appraisal: it must busy itself increasingly with the other side of the assets and markets equation. The suggestion is that marketing should undertake, with all its managerial relationships problems, a quality-control (or quality-assurance to shareholders) function, with undertones of value assurance.

There has always been, in the best firms, a general management activity which constantly reviews company capability in relation to market and customer requirements, and to competitors. It is suggested that the marketing function should take over this critical appraisal function.

Marketing must not only study customers and markets, but also assess whether current capability can fully exploit such customers. It should make recommendations on all product and company features which are deficient in the compatibility equation, and monitor the execution of any changes made on the basis of these recommendations. Furthermore it must be an integral part of that future planning which evolves products but also prepares organizations which are the best suited to market requirements.

This would be a logical and organic development of the specialist sub-division of the general management function, but in an area of considerable managerial sensitivity. The critical aspect of the marketing function would move from product research (which was indirectly associated with design management) and sales-promotion methodology to the organizational features of the business unit itself; such features might be functional but they would also have personal implications.

Emphasis on delivery by a customer may highlight production planning and control defects. This may be due to a total lack of such a function, its inadequate practice, or its lack of organizational authority or status; but it could also result from personal managerial shortcomings. Even the causes which are not directly personal in nature often become so when the implications are seen; the elevation of production planning and control affects the standing of its executives in relation to other departmental heads. In the past such changes have tended to take place, often belatedly, through general management observation and action; it is suggested that this should become increasingly a marketing function aimed at the maintenance of optimum compatibility of assets and customers and consequently the improvement of the enterprise's position in the market.

This projected programme for marketing activity is in line with the movement of the source of comparative advantage from product to company; from material- to human-based activities such as delivery, quality assurance, after-sales services, technical co-operation. The incursion of the multiple store order has in many cases transformed the patronage sources for consumer goods, and this will continue. Consensus goods are known to be wanted; orders are then placed for them with manufacturers who possess the necessary company support services. The product is increasingly neutral, and to that extent choice is a function of company capability. In the industrial field this has been evident for some time. Everybody knows boiler-makers make boilers; it is how they respond to technical challenge, maintain quality standards, uphold delivery promises, and sustain high levels of technical co-operation which determines their relative strengths and weaknesses in a market. The marketing function must take over the objective appraisal of external credibility from general management.

Unfortunately, as stated earlier, the development of marketing towards a quality-control and value-assurance function has serious managerial implications. It would involve an appraisal of functional and personal performance, and, to be worthwhile, would mean communicating such an appraisal to top line management for their decisions and actions. The conclusion is marketing's; the decision is general management's. In any case the source of recommendation is obvious. Is there any alternative? Unfortunately, no.

If an enterprise wishes to stay profitably in business, and certainly if it wishes to optimize its prosperity, then it must extend its quality-control and appraisal function to those areas which are a source of such profits; and this control function must be outside line management in the same way as good quality control of workmanship is outside production. This movement of the marketing function is part of an organic response which must be made by an enterprise if it wishes to maintain or improve its comparative position. There is perhaps greater urgency in this change in the functional emphasis of marketing than is immediately apparent.

As buying becomes more professional, either in the basic industrial sense or in the highly rational activity of bulk retail orders, then motivation will become more overt and thus easier to respond to by suppliers. The consequence of this could well be an increasing state of market inertia as the buyer and supplier build up an intimate organic relationship with each other.

Such a situation will be hastened, to the advantage of the existing supplier, by the introduction of a formalized marketing function aimed at optimum reconciliation of the company and the dominant customer or customers. Marketing would thus diagnose motivation profiles, mainly economic, and recommend organizational and managerial changes in addition to any product variation in order to create a greater organic depth of relationship between customer and supplier. The consequences could be a state of total inertia – particularly with the professionalism existing on both sides, and the buyer's fear of the unknown as against the proven supplier.

To the unproven company outside the inert crystallized situation, the position could be serious and may well involve a much longer wait for the opportunity to enter than exists currently. The waiting period has always been dependent largely on the capability of the existing supplier; the future may make this capability more certain because of professional consolidation of the situation through the marketing function perpetually appraising and prescribing the methods of maintaining the optimum supplier–customer compatibility. Increasingly oligopsonistic markets, those with a few dominating buyers, lend themselves to this analysis and to the further suggestion that the achievement of a supplier situation is due to professional failure by competitors rather than a positive advantage claimed. Sales opportunity may become more dependent on a competitor's comparative disadvantage (proven) than on the new supplier's comparative advantage. The urgency is in achieving the necessary degree of market penetration, often through few and larger accounts, before the inert situation has been reached; and then to maintain this inertia through an extension to the marketing function. To wait will be to allow others to make *their* entry and to consolidate *their* position.

The emphasis in profit maximization will move from identification of market opportunity to its exploitation. Identification of market potential will be needed, but too often it will be obvious; the information is universal, and frequently transferable and 'copiable'. The capability to exploit the opportunity is a corporate one, requiring managerial and organizational efficiency to be superimposed on market identification.

The emphasis within the marketing function will require to move from the quantitative assessment of market potential and product identification into the area of total company appraisal which will enable sales potential to be fully and most profitably exploited. It will move from the supply of simple customer-motivation intelligence to examining the continuing capability of an enterprise to match the major desires and fears of consumers.

Perhaps more important will be its increasing subscription to forward planning through a continuous analysis of the real comparative standing of a company in a market and its recommendations on present and future actions and policy based on this analysis. Marketing should study the dynamics of comparative advantage enjoyed by companies within the competitive situation: the sources of such advantages and the extent to which they are entrenched within companies or their products; it will then discover the strength of competition both current and future. Some comparative advantages may be seen to be short-lived, e.g. those based on non-patentable product or process idiosyncrasies; others may have a long life potential, e.g. those which have arisen from total company proven capability. The strength of images in such conditions must also be assessed. Marketing must establish a hierarchy of the transferability or perishability of the company's current capabilities or assets. Such an exercise obviously involves a study of the customer's motivation priorities and also the comparative ability of competitors to meet these.

The type of analysis suggested could be the basis of company strategy, resource allocation, corporate planning, and, more immediately, changes in current company behaviour. It has normally been limited to the advantages or otherwise enjoyed by the product: this must be extended to non-product causes of advantages and disadvantages.

The function termed 'marketing' was always carried out by the entrepreneurial heads of successful business units; it is now necessary to allow this aspect of enterprise survival to be handed over to functional specialists. The flow of information is too big for conventional general-management or board consumption, analysis and prescription. Marketing is basically the entrepreneurial aspect of business; it seems logical that it should see its future in total entrepreneurial advice.

It has often been concluded fallaciously that marketing, as an information function leading to market identification and customer orientation, was *per se* the cause of business success for those firms which practised it, whereas, in fact, the real cause of success was the comparative advantage achieved by practising those techniques which were defined as marketing. Once all in a competitive market have achieved the same transferable competence then they are all equal again but on a higher plateau of common segments and consensus models. Competitive intensity is increased.

It is at this point that the true nature of marketing manifests itself in that it must still provide the entrepreneur with a further comparative advantage.

Suggestions for Further Reading

IN the past decade, the literature available to students and practitioners of marketing has changed beyond belief. This has occurred in two ways.

Firstly there has been a spate of textbooks enough to make up for the scarcity which previously existed. Secondly, and perhaps more important, is the continuous flow of highly informed comment on current marketing problems which is to be found in professional journals, some not wholly concerned with marketing, and the 'quality' newspapers. Research into the subject is increasing and is being reported in great detail, and the coverage given to marketing matters in such newspapers as the *Financial Times*, *The Times*, *Guardian*, *Telegraph*, and *Sunday Times* and *Observer* is up to the minute and often very intimate. It is in such reports that the student and practitioner will see the 'principles' being worked out against a real-life background. They provide a way of achieving experience 'by proxy'; a substitute, but a good one because of the standard of reporting achieved in these journals and newspapers. In addition, there are the more obvious journals and periodicals listed below. The selection cannot claim to be exhaustive and in fact special marketing may demand special references, e.g. the industrial marketeer may study journals dealing with industrial purchasing; the *Board of Trade Journal* should be a standard work for current reference in all market intelligence departments. Journals and press coverage give substance and meaning to the contents of books and provide a constant companion for the practising marketeer. Their importance cannot be over-emphasized in the dynamic conditions of today.

JOURNALS AND PERIODICALS

European Journal of Marketing
Journal of Marketing

Journal of Management Studies
Harvard Business Review
Journal of Marketing Research
Journal of Advertising Research
Commentary – Market Research Society
Advertising Quarterly
Journal of Business – University of Chicago
Management Decision
Marketing – Institute of Marketing and Sales Management.

For more general reading of particular importance to an understanding of the social, economic and political environment of marketing:
Economist
Journal of Industrial Economics
Journal of Economic Studies
Economica
Journal of Political Economy

Journals on management studies should also receive the attention of the marketeer who wishes to understand completely his function and its relationship to others.
Management Today
Business Management
The Director
Management International

BOOKS

Abundance for What? – and other essays, Riesman, D. (Chatto)
Stages of Economic Growth, Rostow, W. W. (Cambridge University Press)
The Affluent Society, Galbraith, J. K. (Pelican)
The Waste Makers, Packard, V. (Pelican)
Modern Marketing Thought, Westing and Albaum (Macmillan, New York)
Theory in Marketing, Cox, R., Alderson, W., and Shapiro, S. (Irwin)

The Meaning and Sources of Marketing Theory, Halbert, M. H. (McGraw-Hill)

Science in Marketing, Schwartz, G. (Wiley)

Leisure Spending Behaviour, Fisk, G. (University of Philadelphia Press)

Human Behaviour in Marketing, Douglas, J., Field, G. A., and Tarpy, L. X. (Charles E. Merrill)

Marketing and the Behavioural Sciences – Selected Readings, ed. Bliss, P. (Allyn & Bacon)

Consumer Behaviour and the Behavioural Sciences: Theories and Applications, ed. Britt, S. H. (Wiley)

The Environment of Marketing Behaviour: Selections from the Literature, Holloway and Hancock (Wiley)

Lectures in Market Research – Adler, M., ed. Marrian, J. (Crosby-Lockwood)

Marketing Research and Management, Irvine (Macdonald & Evans)

Marketing Research, Crisp (McGraw-Hill)

Marketing Research, Ferber, R., Blankertz, D. F., and Hollander, S. L. (Ronald Press)

Perspectives in Management, Marketing and Research, Henry, H. (Crosby-Lockwood)

Motivation and Market Behaviour, Ferber and Wales (Irwin)

Strategy of Desire, Dichter, E. (Boardman)

Why People Buy, Cheskin, L. (Business Publications)

Basis for Marketing Decision: Through Controlled Motivation Research, Cheskin, L. (Business Publications)

Product Strategy and Management, Berg, T. L., and Schuchman, A. (Holt, Rinehart & Winston)

New Product Decisions, Pessemier, E. A. (McGraw-Hill)

Management of New Products (Booz, Allen & Hamilton)

Innovation in Marketing: New Perspectives for Profit and Growth, Levitt, T. (McGraw-Hill)

Marketing Management and Administrative Action, Britt, S. H., and Boyd, H. W. (McGraw-Hill)

Marketing Management Analysis, Planning and Control, Kotler, P. (Prentice-Hall)

Marketing, Beckman and Davidson (Ronald Press)

Marketing, McIver, C. (Business Publications)

Elements of Marketing, Converse, P. D., Huegy, H. W., and Mitchell, R. V. (Pitman)

Marketing: An Introductory Analysis, Matthews, J. B., Buzzell, R. D., Levitt, T., and Frank, R. E. (McGraw-Hill)

Marketing for Profit, Hardy (Longmans)

Marketing Systems: An Introductory Analysis, Fisk, G. (Harper International)

Marketing in a Competitive Economy, Rodger, L. (Hutchinson)

Marketing Strategy and Functions, Kelley, E. J. (Prentice-Hall)

Modern Marketing Dynamics and Management, Hepner (McGraw-Hill)

Marketing Management: Analysis and Planning, Howard, J. A. (Irwin)

Industrial Management Methods, Hurst, R. (Hutchinson)

New Products and Diversification, Kraushar, P. M. (Business Books)

The Marketing Mode, Levitt, T. (McGraw-Hill)

Industrial Marketing Management and Controls, Williams, L. A. (Longmans)

Industrial Buying and Creative Marketing, Robinson and Faris (Allyn & Bacon)

Marketing Insights, Anderson and Cateora (Appleton-Century Crofts)

Application of Management Sciences in Marketing, Montgomery and Urban (Prentice-Hall)

Exploration in Marketing, Wills, G. (Bradford–Crosby-Lockwood)

Theory of the Firm – Resource Allocation in a Market Economy, Cohen, K. J., and Cyert, R. M. (Prentice-Hall)

Modern Marketing Strategy, Bursk, E. C., and Chapman, J. F. (Harvard University Press)

Product Analysis Pricing, Brown, W., and Jaques, E. (Heinemann)

Techniques of Persuasion: from Propaganda to Brainwashing, Brown, J. A. C. (Pelican)

Sales Promotion: Its Place in Marketing Strategy, Spillard, P. (Business Publications)

The Management of Promotion, Brink and Kelley (Prentice-Hall)

Promotional Decision Making: Practice and Theory, Robinson, P. J., and Luck, D. J. (McGraw-Hill)

Advertising and Competition, Telser, L. G. (Institute of Economic Affairs)

Growth, Advertising and the Consumer, Harris, R. (Institute of Economic Affairs)

Advertising in Action, Harris, R., and Seldon, A. (Institute of Economic Affairs–Hutchinson)

Advertising, Wright and Warner (McGraw-Hill)

Advertising and the Public, Harris, R., and Seldon, A. (Institute of Economic Affairs)

Management and Advertising Problems (Booz, Allen & Hamilton)

Advertising – A New Approach, Taplin, W. (Hutchinson)

Creative Communications with Consumers, Hepner (McGraw-Hill)

Measuring Advertising Effectiveness, Lucas and Britt (McGraw-Hill)

Competition for Consumers, Fulop, C. (Institute of Economic Affairs–Deutsch)

Studies in Retailing, McClelland, W. G. (Blackwell)

The Changing Pattern of Distribution, Stacey, N. A. H., and Wilson, A. (Pergamon)

Resale Price Maintenance and Shoppers' Choice, Yamey, B. S. (Institute of Economic Affairs)

Hire Purchase in a Free Society, Harris, R., Seldon, A., and Naylor, M. (Institute of Economic Affairs)

Fundamentals of Packaging (Institute of Packaging)

Control of the Field Sales Force, Smallbone, D. W. (Staples Press)

Industrial Marketing Research, Stacey, N. A. H., and Wilson, A. (Hutchinson)

The Marketing of Industrial Products, Wilson, A. (Hutchinson)

Industrial Advertising, Messner, F. (McGraw-Hill)

How British Industry Buys, Buckner, H. (Hutchinson)

Industrial Purchasing Behaviour: A Study of Communication Effects, Levitt, T. (Harvard School of Business)

Industrial Marketing, Alexander, R. S., Cross, J. S., and Cunningham, R. N. (Irwin)

Financial Management of the Marketing Function, Schiff and Mellman (Financial Executives Research Foundation, New York)

Cost Problems in Modern Marketing, Kjaer-Hansen, M. (North Holland)

Mathematical Models and Methods in Marketing, Bass, F. M., and others (Irwin)

New Decision Making Tools for Managers, Bursk, E. C., and Chapman, J. F. (New English Library)

Quantitative Techniques in Marketing Analysis, Frank, R. E., Kuehn, A. A., and Massy, W. F. (Irwin)

Models Measurement and Marketing, Langhoff, P. (Prentice-Hall)

Marketing and the Computer, Alderson, Roe and Shapiro (Prentice-Hall)

Index

More About Penguins and Pelicans

Penguinews, which appears every month, contains details of all the new books issued by Penguins as they are published. From time to time it is supplemented by *Penguins in Print*, which is a complete list of all available books published by Penguins. (There are well over three thousand of these.)

A specimen copy of *Penguinews* will be sent to you free on request, and you can become a subscriber for the price of the postage. For a year's issues (including the complete lists), please send 30p if you live in the United Kingdom, or 60p if you live elsewhere. Just write to Dept EP, Penguin Books Ltd, Harmondsworth, Middlesex, enclosing a cheque or postal order, and your name will be added to the mailing list.

Note: *Penguinews* and *Penguins in Print* are not available in the U.S.A. or Canada

PELICAN LIBRARY OF BUSINESS
AND MANAGEMENT

Management Decisions and the Role of Forecasting

James Morrell

Forecasting in business, though notably more sophisticated than crystal-gazing, is still an art rather than a science because of the imperfection of past statistics and our continuing ignorance of the future. The business wizard of today is the man who can, as scientifically as possible, lessen the uncertainties of the future and pinpoint the risks, whether at company or national level.

This Pelican is a guide, prepared by a specialist of more than twenty years' experience, to business forecasting in all its aspects and the role it fulfils for management. A team of economists engaged on the production of *Framework Forecasts* contribute articles on the national economy, the balance of payments and future government policy, trends in major industries, public spending and interest rates and, at the more workaday level of the individual company, show how forecasts are made of costs, prices, sales and profits.

With the aid of forty charts the book explains the different techniques for forecasting, the basic information required, and the ways in which findings can be interpreted.

The
Mystery
and Magic of
Trees and Flowers